STUDY GUIDE

FUNDAMENTALS OF MANAGERIAL ECONOMICS
Third Edition

STUDY GUIDE

Mark Hirschey
University of Kansas

FUNDAMENTALS OF MANAGERIAL ECONOMICS

Third Edition

James L. Pappas
University of South Florida

Mark Hirschey
University of Kansas

THE DRYDEN PRESS
Chicago New York San Francisco
Philadelphia Montreal Toronto
London Sydney Tokyo

ISBN 0-03-012358-5
Printed in the United States of America
 90-018-98765432

Address orders:
6277 Sea Harbor Drive
Orlando, Florida 32821

Address editorial correspondence:
908 N. Elm
Hinsdale, IL 60521

The Dryden Press
Holt, Rinehart and Winston
Saunders College Publishing

PREFACE

This *STUDY GUIDE* has been prepared to accompany *FUNDAMENTALS OF MANAGERIAL ECONOMICS,* Third Edition. It is designed as a supplement to the text, and will not substitute for it. Its use can, however, substantially enhance one's comprehension of the material presented in *FUNDAMENTALS OF MANAGERIAL ECONOMICS,* Third Edition and ease the process of gaining facility in the use of the tools and techniques of economic analysis.

Although there are numerous ways in which to incorporate the use of a study guide in a managerial economics course, many students have found the following four-step approach to be especially beneficial.

1. Read the chapter theme and outline in the *STUDY GUIDE* to obtain a quick preview of the material to be presented. This introduction to the chapter alerts the reader to key concepts being developed.

2. Read the chapter in *FUNDAMENTALS OF MANAGERIAL ECONOMICS,* Third Edition. Many students find that a rapid pass through the chapter, followed by a careful study of the material, leads to greater comprehension and understanding.

3. Work through the problems in the *STUDY GUIDE* and check your solutions with those provided. While obtaining the correct solution is unquestionably important at this stage, real facility in the use of the tools and techniques of economic analysis will come only with an understanding of why the problems were set up and solved as indicated in the *STUDY GUIDE* solution. It is crucial for students to gain an ability to interpret the economics of results obtained. A mastery of these aspects of the problems and solutions will enable students to transfer their skills to other managerial decision problems.

4. Work through the end-of-chapter problems in the textbook. Again, an analysis of why the problem is set up and solved in a particular fashion, as well as an interpretation of the results, will enhance comprehension and one's ability to use the concepts developed.

The use of this *STUDY GUIDE* in a comprehensive study of managerial economics is aimed at easing the student's burden in learning what for many is a difficult subject. The materials have proven helpful to students and the extensive feedback they have provided has substantially improved this *STUDY GUIDE*. Of course, comments from professors and students alike are both welcomed and encouraged.

And finally, sincere thanks go to Ms. Suzana G. Ramos for her highly capable typing assistance.

Mark Hirschey
October, 1988

TABLE OF CONTENTS

CHAPTER ONE: INTRODUCTION TO
MANAGERIAL ECONOMICS

Theme

The nature and scope of managerial economics is laid out in this chapter. A primary emphasis of managerial economics is the application of economic theory and methodology to the practice of business decision making. Since managers of not-for-profit and government agencies, for example, must also efficiently employ scarce resources, managerial economics is an important tool for them as well. An important secondary emphasis in managerial economics is the study of how managerial decisions are affected by the economic environment as described by competition, regulation and antitrust policy. Managerial economics, therefore, is applied economics. Generally speaking, the text is devoted to explaining how economic tools can be applied to achieve business goals, and how those goals relate to larger social objectives. As a starting point, we show how managerial economics incorporates material from the fields of economics, decision sciences and business administration. The basic valuation model of the firm is also presented in some detail. Despite obvious limitations, and the insights offered by various alternative theories of the firm, we firmly believe that sufficient analytical and empirical evidence is present to argue that wealth or value maximization is the primary objective of business. And finally, a discussion of the nature of profits and the role of business in society is provided.

Outline

I.   The Field of Managerial Economics

A.   Scope: Managerial economics is the use of economic analysis in the solution of managerial problems.

B.   Relation of managerial economics to other fields:

1.   Economics: Managerial economics makes heavy use of microeconomic theory in the analysis of output production and demand relations. Macro-economics is also studied since much of the success firms can achieve depends upon a successful understanding of the broader economic environment.

2.   Decision Sciences: Managerial economics draws heavily on such tools and techniques of analysis as:

a.   Mathematical programming for optimization analysis.

b. Probability concepts for decision making under conditions of risk.

c. Statistical estimation for empirical analysis of stochastic relations.

d. Forecasting methodology.

3. Business Administration: Managerial economics provides the tools necessary to solve specific managerial problems as well as a forum where integration of all functional areas of the firm is possible.

4. Public Policy: Managerial economics can help clarify the vital role business firms play in society and point out ways of improving their operations for society's benefit.

II. Theory of the Firm

A. Optimization: Microeconomic theory is based on an assumption that managers attempt to maximize the value of their firms, subject to constraints imposed by consumer preferences, technology, resource limitations, and society. While somewhat of an oversimplification, the resulting theory of firm behavior provides a useful foundation for the analysis of managerial decision making.

B. Definition of Value: The value of an economic enterprise is determined by the discounted present value of future net cash flows:

$$\text{Value} = \sum_{t=1}^{N} \frac{\text{Sales Revenues}_t - \text{Costs}_t}{(1 + \text{Discount rate})^t}$$

According to this model, managerial decisions reflect not only a consideration of the magnitude of output, costs and revenues, but their timing as well.

C. The Role of Constraints: Managers must consider both short- and long-run implications of their decisions, as well as the effects of various external restrictions, including:

1. Resource constraints.

2. Output quantity or quality constraints.

2

3.   Legal constraints.

Thus, in the real world, firms and other organizations optimize their objective function subject to constraints. This process is called constrained optimization.

D.   Motivation: According to the traditional viewpoint, value maximization is a competitive necessity. Should managers not maximize value, three outcomes are envisioned:

    1.   Bankruptcy: More efficient competitors will drive the less efficient nonvalue maximizers out of business.

    2.   Stockholder Revolt: Stockholders will replace managers who don't pursue stockholder interests.

    3.   Unfriendly Takeover: Inefficient management will be replaced by new owners who seek value maximization.

E.   Limitations: By its very nature, however, the value maximization theory of the firm is a simplified model of managerial objectives. Like any simple model that is meant to explain behavior in general, it will fail to explain the types of behavior observed in some isolated or anomalous instances. Some common criticisms of value maximization theory include:

    1.   Narrowness: Firms, like people, have many objectives which cannot be usefully summarized by any single money-oriented objective.

    2.   Difficulty: Optimization is too difficult to achieve, and is actually precluded due to imperfect information being available in the real world.

    3.   Unnecessary: Many firms face only imperfect competition and have complacent stockholders. Therefore, value maximization isn't necessary for managerial survival.

F.   Alternate Theories: In response to the limitations of the value maximization model, alternate theories of firm behavior have evolved including:

    1.   Growth Maximization: Some suggest that managers tend to pursue size (sales) rather than profitability

(value) in order to achieve the prestige and other benefits of running a large organization.

2. Utility Maximization: Managers may seek to maximize their own as opposed to their stockholders' wellbeing. As a result, managers may maximize their own utility which is determined not only by firm profitability, but also by such factors as firm size, executive salaries, product quality, etc.

3. Satisficing: Managers may not maximize anything. Instead, managers may function by choosing satisfactory over less desirable alternatives.

4. Adaptive: Firms (and their managers) survive and prosper not because of superior operating efficiency, but only if they can readily adapt to a changing environment. In fact, luck may play a big part in firm success.

G. Verdict: Despite its limitations, the value maximization model of managerial objectives has proven highly descriptive and relevant (see chapter references), thereby providing an attractive basis for our analysis of managerial decision making.

III. Profit

A. Business Profits: The term business profit is typically used to denote the entire return to the owners (equity position) of the firm, i.e., total net income.

B. Economic Profits: More narrow than business profits, economic profits refer to the difference between business profits and a "normal" or "required" return on capital. Various theories have been proposed to explain the origin of economic profits.

1. Frictional Theory: Economic profits or losses can result from sudden unanticipated changes in demand or supply conditions. Such profits are often characterized as "excess" because they can often be due to luck rather than superior efficiency, managerial talent, etc.

2. Monopoly Theory: Economic profits are commonly enjoyed by firms with dominant market positions. What is unclear, however, is whether

4

such profits have collusion-based or efficiency-based sources. The resolution of this issue is currently an important concern in managerial economics research.

3. Innovation Theory: Economic profits can follow successful invention or innovation. Such rewards measure, though imperfectly, social benefits due to technical change.

4. Compensatory Theory: Economic profits can constitute a reward for entrepreneurial talent and risk taking. Of course, while successful entrepreneurs earn positive returns, mistakes will result in losses.

C. The Role of Profits: In many instances, the explanation of economic profits requires consideration of simultaneous influences related to several theories of profits. Moreover, while from a social perspective normal profits constitute a just return on capital investment, economic or excess profits can serve a valuable social purpose in signalling needed changes in the allocation and/or use of scarce productive resources. Of course, competition has the important role of speeding this adjustment process so as to minimize the magnitude of economic profits.

IV. Role of Business in Society

A. Firm Existence: Firms exist because they are useful in the process of producing and distributing goods and services.

B. The Firm's Mandate: Firms learn what consumers desire by analyzing consumer purchase decisions, and then bid among themselves for the resources necessary to produce output to meet those desires.

C. Social Control: While unregulated market activity often leads to the efficient production of both the quantity and quality of output demanded by consumers, society sometimes regulates firms in order to minimize problems associated with economic power, worker exploitation and externalities (pollution, etc.).

D. Business Policy: Because business is such an important element in our economic system, business must participate actively in the process which defines public policy towards business.

V. Structure of this Text

A. Objectives

1. To present those aspects of economics and the decision sciences that are most relevant in managerial decision making.

2. To provide a framework to help the student understand the nature of the firm as an integrated whole.

3. To demonstrate the interrelation between the firm and society.

CHAPTER TWO: BASIC ECONOMIC RELATIONS

Theme

A basic objective of managerial economics is to provide a systematic framework for problem analysis so that optimal decisions can be made. Here, optimal decisions are defined as the choice of those alternative courses of action that further overall firm goals most effectively. This managerial decision-making process can be facilitated if the various alternate courses of action can be expressed in a basic common denominator. In managerial economics, we strive to quantify in dollar terms the pluses and minuses (revenues and costs) of alternate decisions. No decision is considered in isolation. Rather, each is evaluated in light of all available alternatives. In this chapter, we learn that the value of a function is at a maximum or minimum, when the marginal value equals zero. For example, total profits are maximized when marginal profit equals zero. Since marginal profit is the difference between marginal revenue and marginal cost, marginal revenue equals marginal cost at the profit maximizing activity level. For this reason, it is the marginal costs and marginal revenues corresponding to a given decision that are most important for decision making purposes.

Outline

I. Maximizing the Value of the Firm

A. Definition: Optimization is the process of determining the best possible solution to a given problem. Therefore, value maximization is the process of determining which managerial decisions or investment projects will yield the largest net benefit to shareholders. Revenues, costs and the relevant discount (interest) rate are all important components of this analysis.

B. Types of Optimization:

1. Total (or global): Total optimization is the analysis of all known alternatives for each aspect of the firm's operation. High costs of information gathering, however, usually restrict total optimization analyses to a limited number of fundamental business decisions.

2. Partial (or local): Partial optimization is a subpart of the total optimization process. In partial optimization, various alternatives are evaluated on the basis of their effects on specific departments, production centers, marketing campaigns, etc. Because partial optimization is quite localized in its focus, it can isolate superior alternatives

much more inexpensively than can total optimization analyses.

II. Methods of Expressing Economic Relations

A. Functional Relations: Equations: Algebraic methods often constitute the most useful method of expressing economic relations. Here, data is characterized by specific functional relations or equations. An important advantage to this approach is that it allows significant amounts of information to be expressed quite simply.

1. Tables: The most basic way of expressing economic relations is through simple tabular presentation. Through this method, otherwise unsuspected relations often become evident.

2. Graphs: A second common way of expressing economic relations is through graphic presentation. This method builds on the tabular approach by explicitly investigating relations among various economic variables.

3. Solution procedure: Both algebraic and graphic techniques can be used to arrive at optimal decisions once all available information has been expressed analytically. While graphic techniques can be usefully applied in many instances, algebraic methods are most appropriate for solving complex problems.

B. Functional Relations: Tables and Graphs: Tables and Graphs are often used to express economic relations.

1. Analytic expression: The optimization process requires that a given managerial problem, including perceived alternatives, be expressed analytically. Two aspects are involved. First, the costs and revenues of each alternative must be expressed in a common denominator (usually dollars) for comparison purposes. And second, any functional relations must be correctly specified.

III. Total, Average and Marginal Relations

A. Totals and Marginals: The total is always equal to the sum of the marginals up to that point. This implies that the total is increasing when the marginals are positive, and decreasing when the marginals are negative. Hence, the maximum of any total function occurs at that point where the marginal changes from positive to negative, i.e., where it is zero.

8

B. Averages and marginals: Since the marginal represents the change in the total, when the marginal is greater (less) than the average, the average must be increasing (decreasing). When the marginal and average values are equal, the average is at a maximum or minimum.

C. Graphical Relations

1. Totals and marginals: The slope of a total function is equal to the marginal of the function at that point.

2. Totals and averages: The slope of a ray from the origin to any point on a total curve is equal to the average of the function at that point.

IV. Marginal Analysis in Decision Making

A. Identify Maximum and/or Minimum: When the marginal, or slope, of a function is set equal to zero, a maximum or minimum point is identified. If the marginal is diminishing (increasing), then the value of the function is maximized (minimized).

B. Use of Marginals to Maximize the Difference Between Two Functions: The difference between two functions will be maximized when the slopes of the two individual functions are equal. The difference between total revenue and total cost is maximized where marginal revenue equals marginal cost. Thus, profit maximization requires:

$$M\pi = MR - MC = 0$$

or

$$MR = MC$$

V. The Incremental Concept in Economic Analysis

A. Incremental Analysis: The process of examining the impact of alternate decisions on revenue, cost or profit.

B. Relation to Marginal Concept: The concept of a marginal relates to a single unit of output. The incremental concept relates to a given managerial decision. For example, marginal revenue is the change in revenue following a one unit increase in sales. Incremental revenue is the change in revenue following a decision to add, say, a new product line involving several units in sales.

9

PROBLEMS AND SOLUTIONS

2.1

a. Given the price (P) and output (Q) data in the following table, calculate the related total revenue (TR), marginal revenue (MR), and average revenue (AR) figures:

Q	P	TR (Q×P)	MR ($TR_2 - TR_1$)	AR TR/Q
0	$80	$0	--	--
1	75	75	75	75
2	70	140	65	70
3	65	195	55	65
4	60	240	45	60
5	55	275	35	55
6	50	300	25	50
7	45	315	15	45
8	40	320	5	40
9	35	315	-5	35
10	30	300	-15	30

b. At what output level is revenue maximized?

Q=8

2.1 SOLUTION

a.

Q	P	TR	MR	AR
0	$80	$0	--	--
1	75	75	$75	$75
2	70	140	65	70
3	65	195	55	65
4	60	240	45	60
5	55	275	35	55
6	50	300	25	50
7	45	315	15	45
8	40	320	5	40
9	35	315	-5	35
10	30	300	-15	30

b. Revenue is maximized at Q = 8 and TR = $320.

2.2

a. Fill in the missing data for price (P), total revenue (TR), marginal revenue (MR), total cost (TC), marginal cost (MC), profit (π), and marginal profit (Mπ) in the following table:

Q	P	TR	MR	TC	MC	AC $\frac{TC}{Q}$	π	Mπ
0	$75	$0	--	$25 FC	--	--	-$25	--
1	70	70	$70	44	$19	$44	26	$51
2	68	136	66	68	24	34	68	42
3	66	198	62	93	25	31	105	37
4	64	256	58 54	120 160	27 40	30	136 150	14 31
5	62	310	54	160	40	32	150	14
6	57	342	32	204	44	34	138	-12
7	53	371	29	252	48	36	119	-19
8	46	368	-3	304	52	38	64	-55
9	40	360	-8	360	56	40	0	-64
10	35	350	-10	420	60	60	-70	-70

(TR/Q) (Q×P) (TR₂-TR₁) (TC₁-TC₂) (MR-MC)

b. At what output (Q) level is average cost minimized?
   Q= 4

c. At what output (Q) level is profit maximized?
   Q=5

d. At what output (Q) level is zero profit earned?
   Q=9

11

2.2 SOLUTION

a.

Q	P	TR	MR	TC	MC	AC	π	Mπ
0	$75	$0	--	$25	--	--	-$25	--
1	70	70	$70	44	$19	$44	26	$51
2	68	136	66	68	24	34	68	42
3	66	198	62	93	25	31	105	37
4	64	256	58	120	27	30	136	31
5	62	310	54	160	40	32	150	14
6	57	342	32	204	44	34	138	-12
7	53	371	29	252	48	36	119	-19
8	46	368	-3	304	52	38	64	-55
9	40	360	-8	360	54 56	40	0	-64
10	35	350	-10	420	60	60	-70	-70

b. Average cost is minimized at Q = 4 and AC = $30. Note that average cost is falling when MC < AC over the range $0 < Q \leq 4$, but that average cost is rising when MC > AC over the range $4 < Q \leq 10$.

c. Profit is maximized at Q = 5 and π = $150. Note that profit is rising when MR > MC and Mπ > 0 over the range $0 < Q \leq 5$, but that profit is falling when MR < MC and Mπ < 0 over the range $5 < Q \leq 10$.

d. Zero profits are earned when TR = TC at Q = 9, the breakeven level of output.

2.3

Jessica Hauschel is a student at Midwest State University. She is preparing for final exams and has decided to devote five hours to the study of managerial economics and management. Hauschel's goal is to maximize the average grade earned in the two courses, and she must decide how much time to spend on each exam. Hauschel realizes that maximizing the average grade in the two courses is equivalent to maximizing the sum of the grades. According to her best estimates, Hauschel's grades will vary according to the schedules shown below.

Managerial Economics		Management	
Hours of Study	Grade	Hours of Study	Grade
0	25	0	50
1	45	1	62
2	65	2	72
3	75	3	81
4	83	4	88
5	90	5	93

a. Describe the manner in which Hauschel could make use of the marginal-total relation she has studied in managerial economics to assist in determining the optimal allocation of five hours between the two courses.

b. How much time should Hauschel spend studying each subject?

c. In addition to managerial economics and management, Hauschel is also taking a business law course. She estimates that each hour spent studying business law will result in an eight point increase on the business law examination score. She has tentatively decided to spend three hours preparing for the business law exam. Will Hauschel maximize her average grade in all three courses with three hours devoted to business law and five hours devoted to managerial economics and management (allocated as in part b)? Why?

2.3 SOLUTION

a. An optimal allocation of study time is one which will permit Hauschel to maximize the average grade earned in her managerial economics and management courses. This maximization will occur when Hauschel allocates each hour of study time to that course where the marginal grade value of study time is greatest.

b. In order to determine how much time Hauschel should spend studying each subject a table illustrating the marginal grade value of each hour of study time must be constructed. This table reads as follows:

Managerial Economics			Management		
Hours of Study	Grade	Marginal Grade Value	Hours of Study	Grade	Marginal Grade Value
0	25	--	0	50	--
1	45	20	1	62	12
2	65	20	2	72	10
3	75	10	3	81	9
4	83	8	4	88	7
5	90	7	5	93	5

With only five hours to study, Hauschel should spend three hours on managerial economics and two hours on management.

c. No. Hauschel's decision to spend three hours studying for her business law exam is incorrect if her objective is to maximize the average grade received in managerial economics, management and business law. Only two hours should be allocated to studying business law since an additional hour spent on management would increase her total grade by nine points; one point more than the eight point gain associated with the third hour spent preparing for the business law exam, and will lead to a maximum average grade.

2.4

John Elwell is a regional media consultant for Creative Images, Inc., a Boston-area marketing firm. Elwell has gathered the following data on weekly advertising media expenditures and gross sales for a major client, Danish Design, Ltd.

Media Expenditure	Gross Sales Following Promotion in:					
	Newspaper	MS	Radio	MS	Television	MS
$ 0	$10,000	–	$10,000	–	$10,000	–
100	12,000	2000	14,000	4000	13,000	3000
200	13,800	1800	17,600	3600	15,600	2600
300	15,400	1600	20,200	2600	18,000	2400
400	16,600	1200	22,000	1800	18,600	600
500	17,200	600	22,400	400	18,800	200

a. Construct a table showing marginal sales following promotion in each media. (Assume here and throughout there are no synergistic effects across medias.)

b.   If Danish Design has an advertising budget of $500 per week, how should it be spent? Why?

c.   Calculate the profit maximizing advertising budget and media allocation assuming Danish Design enjoys an average profit contribution before media expenditures of 6 percent on store-wide sales. How much are maximum weekly profits (before taxes)?

2.4 SOLUTION

a.

Media Expenditures	Marginal Sales Following Promotion By:		
	Newspaper	Radio	Television
$ 0	--	--	--
100	$2,000	$4,000	$3,000
200	1,800	3,600	2,600
300	1,600	2,600	2,400
400	1,200	1,800	600
500	600	400	200

b.   Using the data in part a, and given a $500 advertising budget, gross sales and profit contribution will be maximized by allocating $300 to radio and $200 to television advertising. Therefore, irrespective of whether Danish Design seeks to maximize revenues or profit, this expenditure allocation is optimal.

c.   Given an average profit contribution before media expenditures of 6 percent on store-wide sales, an additional dollar of advertising will be profitable so long as it returns more than $16.67 in additional revenues. That is, the profit contribution on additional revenues of $16.67 will be just sufficient to cover media costs of $1 ($= \$16.67 \times 0.06$). Therefore, the profit maximizing advertising budget is $900 per week allocated as: $200 on newspaper, $400 on radio, and $300 on television.

15

Maximum weekly profits can be calculated as:

Base sales	$10,000
+ Newspaper sales	3,800
+ Radio sales	12,000
+ Television sales	8,000
	$33,800
× Gross margin	0.06
Gross profit	2,028
- Media costs	900
Net profit (before tax)	$ 1,128

2.5

Assume that Lowell Electronics, Inc., operates with the total revenue (TR) and total cost (TC) functions:

<u>Revenue</u>   <u>Cost</u>

$$TR = \$100Q - \$0.5Q^2 \quad TC = \$1,500 - \$10Q + \$0.5Q^2$$

$$MR = \$100 - Q \qquad MC = -\$10 + Q$$

<u>Profit</u>

$$\pi = TR - TC$$

$$= \$100Q - \$0.5Q^2 - \$1,500 + \$10Q - \$0.5Q^2$$

$$= -\$1,500 + \$110Q - Q^2$$

$$M\pi = \$110 - \$2Q$$

where Q represents the quantity of output produced and sold.

a.   Calculate the profit maximizing output and profit levels for Lowell using its marginal profit function.

b.   Show that marginal revenue equals marginal cost at this profit maximizing output level.

2.5   SOLUTION

a.   Set $M\pi = 0$ to maximize profits, where:

$$M\pi = \$110 - \$2Q = 0$$

16

1.) $2Q = 110$

$\qquad Q = \underline{\underline{55}}$

$\qquad \pi = -\$1,500 + \$110Q - Q^2$

$\qquad = 1,500 + 110(55) - 55^2$

$\qquad = \underline{\underline{\$3,975}}$

(Note: profit is falling for Q > 55.)

b. At Q = 55, we note:

$MR = \$100 - Q = 100 - 55 = \underline{\underline{\$45}}$

$MC = -\$10 + Q = -10 + 55 = \underline{\underline{\$45}}$

This numerical finding illustrates the general result that if $M\pi$ = MR - MC = 0, then MR = MC will always be true.

2.6

Revenue, cost, and profit curves for Quick Alert Alarm Systems, Inc., are given by the equations:

Revenue	Cost
$TR = \$56Q - \$2Q^2$	$TC = \$50 + \$2Q + \$0.25Q^2$
$MR = \$56 - \$4Q$	$MC = \$2 + \$0.5Q$

Profit

$\qquad \pi = TR - TC$

$\qquad = \$56Q - \$2Q^2 - \$50 - \$2Q - \$0.25Q^2$

$\qquad = -\$50 - \$54Q - \$2.25Q^2$

$\qquad M\pi = -\$54 - \$4.5Q$

a. Calculate the revenue maximizing price/output combination.

b. Calculate the profit maximizing price/output combination.

c.   Calculate that output level at which average costs are minimized.

d.   Discuss any differences between your answers to parts a and b above.

e.   Discuss any differences between your answers to parts b and c above.

2.6   SOLUTION

a.   Set MR = 0 to find revenue maximizing output level:

$$MR = \$56 - \$4Q = 0$$

$$4Q = 56$$

$$Q = \underline{\underline{14}}$$

$$P = \$56 - \$2Q$$

$$= 56 - 2(14)$$

$$= \$\underline{\underline{28}}$$

(Note: revenue is falling for Q > 14.)

b.   Set Mπ = 0 to find profit maximizing output level:

$$M\pi = \$54 - \$4.5Q = 0$$

$$4.5Q = 54$$

$$Q = \underline{\underline{12}}$$

$$P = \$56 - \$2Q$$

$$= 56 - 2(12)$$

$$= \$\underline{\underline{32}}$$

(Note: profit is falling for Q > 12.)

c.   Set AC = MC to find the output level at which average costs are minimized:

18

$$AC = \frac{TC}{Q} = MC$$

$$\frac{(\$50 + \$2Q + \$0.25Q^2)}{Q} = \$2 + \$0.5Q$$

$$\frac{50}{Q} + 2 + 0.25Q = 2 + 0.5Q$$

$$\frac{50}{Q} = 0.25Q$$

$$\frac{50}{Q^2} = 0.25$$

$$\frac{Q^2}{50} = \frac{1}{0.25}$$

$$Q^2 = 200$$

$$Q = \underline{\underline{14.14}}$$

(Note: average cost is rising for Q > 14.14)

d.   In part a, we found that revenues are maximized at Q = 14 and P = $28. By definition, this is the point where MR = 0. In part b, we found that profits are maximized at Q = 12 and P = $32. By definition, this is the point where MR = MC. Since demand curves always slope downward, revenue maximizing prices will typically be lower, and output levels will typically be greater, than in the case of profit maximization. Only in the unlikely event that MC = 0 will revenue and profit maximizing price and output levels be identical.

e.   In part b, we found that profits are maximized when Q = 12. In part c, we found that average costs are minimized when Q = 14.14. These output levels often differ because the underlying objective functions being considered are different. Importantly, the output where average costs are minimized is not typically the point where profits are maximized.

2.7

Kwik-Clean, Inc. has a number of outlets in the Detroit, Michigan area that feature laundry and drycleaning services at popular prices. Recent data suggest that the weekly revenue for mens' dress shirt laundry service, a very popular item, is described by the relation:

$$TR = \$160Q - \$0.02Q^2$$

$$MR = \$160 - \$0.04Q$$

where Q is the number of shirts laundered and P is price in cents.

a.   Calculate the revenue maximizing price/output combination.

b.   Assume laundry costs are stable at 40¢ per shirt. Calculate the profit maximizing price/output combination.

c.   Are the differences in your answers to parts a and b typical or atypical? Explain.

2.7   SOLUTION

a.   Set MR = 0 to maximize revenue:

$$MR = \$160 - \$0.04Q = 0$$

$$0.04Q = 160$$

$$Q = \underline{\underline{4,000}}$$

$$P = \$160 - \$0.02(4,000)$$

$$= \underline{\underline{80¢}}$$

(Note: revenue is falling for Q > 4,000.)

b.   To find the profit maximizing activity level, set MR = MC. Since unit costs are stable at 40¢, AC = MC and,

$$MR = MC$$

$$\$160 - \$0.04Q = \$40$$

$$0.04Q = 120$$

$$Q = 3,000$$

$$P = \$160 - \$0.02(3,000) = \underline{\underline{100¢}} \text{ or } \$1$$

c.   <u>Typical</u>. Revenue maximization will result in greater optimal output (here, 4,000 versus 3,000) and lower prices (here, 80¢ versus $1) than is true with profit maximization.

CHAPTER THREE: DEMAND AND SUPPLY

Theme

This chapter provides a basic introduction to demand and supply concepts, and provides a framework for our more detailed study of these subjects in later chapters. Demand is the quantity of a good or service that customers are willing and able to buy during a given period. This includes direct demand for consumption products, as well as demand for inputs used in production. Whereas consumer demand is based on the utility gained through consumption, derived demand is based on the profits that can be earned through production. A demand function shows the relation between the quantity demanded and all factors affecting this quantity. When all nonprice variables are fixed at a given level during a given period, the price-quantity relation can be plotted out as a demand curve. Supply is the quantity of a good or service that producers are willing and able to offer for sale during a given period. As in the case of demand, supply functions and supply curves are developed to analyze the effects of all factors influencing supply (supply functions), as well as to focus on the important price-quantity supplied relations (supply curves). And finally, our study of demand and supply is integrated in comparative statics analysis where the effects of changing demand and supply conditions are investigated. The effect of a change in price is referred to as a change in the quantity demanded or supplied, whereas the effects of changes in any nonprice variable are referred to as shifts in demand or supply.

Outline

I. Demand and Supply

A. Demand: The amount of a product that people are willing and able to buy under a given set of market conditions is called demand.

B. Supply: The amount of a product that firms make available for sale under a given set of market conditions is called supply.

    1. Importance: The successful operation of any organization fundamentally depends on its understanding of the demand and supply conditions for goods and services provided to customers.

II. The Basis for Demand

A. Origin: Demand is created when customers perceive value (desire) and have the capability to make purchase decisions.

1. Direct Demand: Demand for personal goods and services based on the utility gained through consumption.

    a. Consumers demand products that yield satisfaction.

2. Derived Demand: Demand for inputs that can be used in production is derived from the demand for consumer goods and services.

    a. Firms demand inputs that can be profitably employed.

III. The Market Demand Function

A. Demand Function: A demand function shows the relation between the quantity demanded and all factors that affect it. Factors included are: price, price of other goods, income, advertising, and so on.

B. Industry Demand versus Firm Demand: Demand functions can be specified for an entire industry or individual firm.

1. Industry Demand: Overall industry demand is subject to general economic influences (population, GNP, interest rates, and so on).

2. Firm Demand: Firm demand is affected by general economic influences and competitor decisions (prices, advertising, and so on).

IV. The Demand Curve

A. Demand Curve: A demand curve shows the price-quantity relation, holding constant the effects of all other demand-determining influences.

B. Relation Between Demand Curve and Demand Function: A demand curve can be plotted when all variables other than price and quantity in a given demand function are fixed at specific levels.

1. A change in the quantity demanded reflects a movement along a given demand curve following a price change.

2. A shift in demand occurs when change in a nonprice variable leads to a shift from one demand curve to another.

V. The Basis for Supply

A. Origin: Supply is offered when producers are able to at least cover the marginal cost of production.

   1. Determinants: Factors influencing supply include: price, price of other products, technology, input prices, and so on.

VI. The Market Supply Function

A. Supply Function: A supply function describes the relation between the quantity supplied and all factors that affect it.

B. Industry versus Firm Supply: Supply functions can be specified for an entire industry or individual firm.

   1. Industry Supply: Overall industry supply is subject to general economic influences (GNP, tax rates, weather).

   2. Firm Supply: Firm supply is affected by general economic influences and competitor decisions (prices, wage rates, interest rates, and so on).

VII. The Supply Curve

A. Supply Curve: A supply curve shows the price-quantity relation, holding constant the effects of all other supply-determining influences.

B. Relation Between Supply Curve and Supply Function: A supply curve can be plotted when all variables other than price and quantity in a given supply function are fixed at specific levels.

   1. A change in the quantity supplied reflects a movement along a given supply curve following a price change.

   2. A shift in supply occurs when change in a nonprice variable leads to a shift from one supply curve to another.

VIII. Market Equilibrium

A. Definition: Market Equilibrium is perfect balance in demand and supply under a given set of market conditions.

B. Surplus and Shortage: Both of these conditions reflect disequilibrium in the marketplace.

   1. Surplus is excess supply.

2. Shortage is excess demand.

C. Comparative Statics: Comparative statics analysis is the study of the effect of changing demand and supply conditions.

PROBLEMS AND SOLUTIONS

3.1

The following relations describe monthly demand and supply conditions in the market for No. 1 grade cotton blue denim:

$$Q_D = 100,000 - 40,000P \qquad \text{(Demand)}$$

$$Q_S = -5,000 + 30,000P \qquad \text{(Supply)}$$

where Q is quantity measured in thousands of square yards and P is price per square yard in dollars.

a. Complete the following table:

Price (1)	Quantity Supplied (2)	Quantity Demanded (3)	Surplus (+) or Shortage (-) (4) = (2) - (3)
$2.00	55,000	20,000	+35,000
1.75	47,500	30,000	+ 17,500
1.50	40,000	40,000	-0-
1.25	32,500	50,000	-17,500
1.00	25,000	60,000	-35,000

3.1 SOLUTION

a.

Price (1)	Quantity Supplied (2)	Quantity Demanded (3)	Surplus (+) or Shortage (-) (4) = (2) - (3)
$2.00	55,000	20,000	35,000
1.75	47,500	30,000	17,500
1.50	40,000	40,000	0
1.25	32,500	50,000	-17,500
1.00	25,000	60,000	-35,000

3.2

The market for oil is highly price sensitive. Indicate the effects of each of the following influences on demand and/or supply conditions:

a. A major oil discovery. increase supply

b. A $5 per barrel tax on oil. decrease supply

25

c. An improvement in oil recovery technology. *incr. supply*

d. An unusually hot summer causing an increase in the demand for air conditioning. *incr. demand*

e. An increase in energy conservation. *decr. demand*

3.2 SOLUTION

a. <u>Increase supply/rightward shift in supply curve</u>. A major oil discovery will increase the quantity supplied at every price level.

b. <u>Decrease supply/leftward shift in supply curve</u>. A $5 per barrel tax on oil will reduce the share of total oil-related expenditures going to producers, and thus reduce the quantity supplied at every price level.

c. <u>Increase supply/rightward shift in supply curve</u>. An improvement in technology will make it possible to supply more oil at every price level.

d. <u>Increase demand/rightward shift in demand curve</u>. With an increase in air conditioning demand, electricity usage will rise, as will the demand for oil at every price level.

e. <u>Decrease demand/leftward shift in demand curve</u>. Increased energy conservation will cut oil usage at every price level.

3.3

Describe the effects of each of the following influences on demand and/or supply conditions in the market for MBAs.

a. An economic recession (fall in national income). *↓D ↑S*

b. An increase in MBA graduate salaries. *↓D ↑S*

c. An increase in the availability of low-cost student loans. *↑S*

d. A rise in tuition costs. *↓S*

e. A rise in relative productivity of MBA versus BA/BS job candidates. *↑D*

3.3 SOLUTION

a. <u>Decrease demand/leftward shift in demand curve</u> and <u>Increase supply/rightward shift in supply curve</u>. With a fall in national income, the profitability of added employment will fall, thereby

26

causing a decline in the demand for labor. A recession can also reduce job opportunities for BAs and BSs, thereby reducing the income loss incurred while in graduate school, and thus can actually increase the supply of MBAs. Despite this often observed counter-cyclical relation between enrollment and economic activity, recessions can also limit the return to an MBA and thereby limit MBA supply. Thus, the *net* effect on supply can be uncertain.

b. <u>Decrease in the quantity demanded/upward movement along demand curve</u> and <u>Increase the quantity supplied/upward movement along supply curve</u>. Rising prices cut the quantity demanded while increasing the quantity supplied.

c. <u>Increase supply/rightward shift in supply curve</u>. An increase in student loan availability will cut the cost of an MBA education, and increase the expected net return, and increase supply at every expected wage level.

d. <u>Decrease supply/leftward shift in supply curve</u>. A rise in tuition costs increases the cost of an MBA education, cuts the expected net return, and will decrease supply at each expected wage level.

e. <u>Increase demand/rightward shift in demand</u>. An increase in the relative productivity of MBAs will increase demand for MBAs at every price level.

3.4

Kurt Stillwell is a product manager at E-6, Inc., a nation-wide supplier of tools and accessories to independent electricians and plumbers. A study of annual demand in several regional markets suggests the following demand function for a popular socket wrench set:

$$Q = -500 - 10P + 0.001Pop + 0.05I + 20A$$

where Q is quantity, P is price ($), Pop is population, I is disposable income per person ($), and A is advertising measured in terms of personal selling days per year by E-6's sales staff.

a. Determine the demand curve faced by E-6 in a typical market where P = $250, Pop = 1,000,000, I = $10,000, and A = 200 days.

$Q = 2500$

b. Calculate the quantity demanded at prices of $250, $275, and $300.

$Q = 2250$

$Q = 2000$

c. Calculate the prices necessary to sell 2,000, 3,000, and 4,000 units.

$Q = 5000 - 10P$

$P = \dfrac{5000 - Q}{10}$ or $(500 - .1Q)$

3.4 SOLUTION

a.   The demand curve can be calculated by substituting each
     respective variable into the firm's demand function:

$$Q = -500 - 10P + 0.001Pop + 0.05I + 20A$$

$$= -500 - 10P + 0.001(1,000,000) + 0.05(10,000) + 20(200)$$

$$Q = 5,000 - 10P$$

Then, price as a function of quantity can be written:

$$Q = 5,000 - 10P$$

$$5,000 - Q = 10P$$

$$Q = \$500 - \$0.1Q$$

b.   At,

$$P = \$250: Q = 5,000 - 10(250) = \underline{2,500}$$
$$P = \$275: Q = 5,000 - 10(275) = \underline{2,250}$$
$$P = \$300: Q = 5,000 - 10(300) = \underline{2,000}$$

c.   At,

$$Q = 2,000: P = \$500 - \$0.1(2,000) = \underline{\$300}$$
$$Q = 3,000: P = \$500 - \$0.1(3,000) = \underline{\$200}$$
$$Q = 4,000: P = \$500 - \$0.1(4,000) = \underline{\$100}$$

3.5

Tex-Mex Restaurants, Ltd., is a rapidly growing chain offering high
quality Mexican food at popular prices. An analysis of monthly
customer traffic at its restaurants revealed the following:

$$Q = 200 - 500P + 450P_F + 0.02Pop + 2,000S$$

where Q is quantity measured by the number of customers served per
month, P is the average meal price per customer (\$), P_F is the average
meal price at fast-food restaurants, Pop is the population of the
restaurant market area, and S, a binary or dummy variable, equals 1 in
summer months and zero otherwise.

a. Determine the demand curve facing the company during the month of December if P = \$8, P_F = \$4, Pop = 300,000, and S = 0.

Q= 8000 - 500P + 2000   P= $\frac{8000 - Q}{500}$ = (16 - .002Q)

b. Calculate the quantity demanded and total revenues during the summer month of August if all demand-related variables are specified above.

Q= 10000 - 500 (8) =
10,000 - 4000 = 6000

TR= PQ
= (8) 6000
= 48,000.

3.5 SOLUTION

a. With quantity expressed as a function of price, the firm demand curve can be calculated by substituting the value for each respective variable into the demand function:

$$Q = 200 - 500P + 450P_F + 0.02Pop + 2,000S$$

$$Q = 200 - 500P + 450(4) + 0.02(300,000) + 2,000(0)$$

$$Q = 8,000 - 500P$$

Then, with price as a function of quantity, the firm's demand curve is:

$$Q = 8,000 - 500P$$

$$500P = 8,000 - Q$$

$$P = \$16 - \$0.002Q$$

b. The total quantity demanded is found from the demand function:

$$Q = 200 - 500P + 450P_F + 0.02Pop + 2,000S$$

$$= 200 - 500(8) + 450(4) + 0.02(300,000) + 2,000(1)$$

$$= \underline{6,000}$$

Thus, total revenue is:

$$TR = PQ$$

$$= \$8(6,000)$$

$$= \$480,000$$ *NO!*

$48,000

29

3.6

A review of industry-wide data for residential construction industry suggests the following industry supply function:

$$Q = 1,000,000 + 10,000P - 7,000P_L - 30,000P_K$$

where Q is housing starts per year, P is the average price of new homes (in $ thousands), P_L is the average price paid for skilled labor ($), and P_K is the average price of capital (in percent).

a. Determine the industry supply curve for a recent year when P = $100(000), P_L = $20, and P_K = 12 percent, show the industry supply curve with quantity expressed as a function of price, and price expressed as a function of quantity.

b. Calculate the quantity supplied by the industry at new home prices of $50(000), $75(000), and $100(000).

c. Calculate the prices necessary to generate a supply of 1 million, 1.5 million, and 2 million new homes.

3.6 SOLUTION

a. With quantity expressed as a function of price, the industry supply curve can be written:

$$Q = 1,000,000 + 10,000P - 7,000P_L - 30,000P_K$$

$$= 1,000,000 + 10,000P - 7,000(20) - 30,000(12)$$

$$Q = 500,000 + 10,000P$$

With price expressed as a function of quantity, the industry supply curve can be written:

$$Q = 500,000 + 10,000P$$

$$10,000P = -500,000 + Q$$

$$P = -\$50 + \$0.0001Q$$

b. Industry supply at each respective price (in thousands) is:

P = $50(000): Q = 500,000 + 10,000(50) = 1,000,000

P = $15(000): Q = 500,000 + 10,000(75) = 1,250,000

30

$$P = \$100(000): Q = 500,000 + 10,000(100) = \underline{\underline{1,500,000}}$$

c.   The price necessary to generate each level of supply is:

$$Q = 1,000,000: P = -\$50 + \$0.0001(1,000,000) = \underline{\underline{\$50(000)}}$$

$$Q = 1,500,000: P = -\$50 + \$0.0001(1,500,000) = \underline{\underline{\$100(000)}}$$

$$Q = 2,000,000: P = -\$50 + \$0.0001(2,000,000) = \underline{\underline{\$150(000)}}$$

3.7

Uniform Supply Services, Inc. is a local supplier of uniform rental services. The company has estimated the following relation between its marginal cost per unit and weekly output:

$$MC = \$3 + \$0.001Q$$

a.   Calculate marginal costs per unit for 1,000, 2,000, and 3,000 uniform rentals per week.

b.   Express output as a function of marginal cost. Calculate the level of output when MC = $5, $7.50, and $10.

c.   Calculate the profit maximizing level of output if prices are stable in the industry at $7.50 per unit and, therefore, P = MR = $7.50.

d.   Again assuming prices are stable in the industry, derive USS's supply curve. Express price as a function of quantity *and* quantity as a function of price.

3.7 SOLUTION

a.   Marginal production costs at each level of output are:

$$Q = 1,000: MC = \$3 + \$0.001(1,000) = \underline{\underline{\$4}}$$

$$Q = 2,000: MC = \$3 + \$0.001(2,000) = \underline{\underline{\$5}}$$

$$Q = 2,000: MC = \$3 + \$0.001(3,000) = \underline{\underline{\$6}}$$

b.   When output is expressed as a function of marginal cost, we find:

$$MC = \$3 + \$0.001Q$$

$$0.001Q = -3 + MC$$

31

$$Q = -3{,}000 + 1{,}000MC$$

The level of output at each respective level of marginal cost is:

$$MC = \$5 : Q = -3{,}000 + 1{,}000(5) = \underline{\underline{2{,}000}}$$

$$MC = \$7.50 : Q = -3{,}000 + 1{,}000(7.5) = \underline{\underline{4{,}500}}$$

$$MC = \$10.00 : Q = -3{,}000 + 1{,}000(10) = \underline{\underline{7{,}000}}$$

c. We note from part b that MC = $7.50 when Q = 4,500. Therefore, when MR = $7.50, Q = 4,500 will be the profit maximizing level of output. More formally:

$$MR = MC$$

$$\$7.50 = \$3 + \$0.001Q$$

$$0.001Q = 4.50$$

$$Q = \underline{\underline{4{,}500}}$$

d. Since prices are stable in the industry, P = MR. This means that USS will supply chips at the level of output where:

$$MR = MC$$

and, therefore, that:

$$P = \$3 + \$0.001Q$$

This is the supply curve for USS service, where price is expressed as a function of quantity. When quantity is expressed as a function of price, we find:

$$P = \$3 + \$0.001Q$$

$$0.001Q = -3 + P$$

$$Q = -3{,}000 + 1{,}000$$

3.8

Silicon Valley, Inc. and Nehkdi Trading, Ltd. supply 1MB-DRAM chips to the computer industry. Confidential cost and output information for each company reveal the following relations between marginal cost and output:

$$MC_S = \$10 + \$0.0004Q_S \qquad \text{(Silicon)}$$

$$MC_N = \$2.50 + \$0.0001Q_N \qquad \text{(Nehkdi)}$$

The wholesale market for these chips is vigorously price-competitive, and neither firm is able to charge a premium for its products. Thus, P = MR in this market.

a.   Determine the supply curve for each firm. Express price as a function of quantity *and* quantity as a function of price.

b.   Calculate the quantity supplied by each firm at prices of $5, $10, and $15. What is the minimum price necessary for each individual firm to supply output?

c.   Determine the industry supply curve when P < $10.

d.   Determine the industry supply curve when P > $10. To check your answer, calculate quantity at an industry price of $15 and compare your answer with part b.

3.8   SOLUTION

a.   Each company will supply output to the point where MR = MC. Since P = MR in this market, the supply curve for each firm can be written with price as a function of quantity as:

Silicon	Nehkdi
$MR_S = MC_S$	$MR_N = MC_N$
$P = \$10 + \$0.0004Q_S$	$P = \$2.50 + \$0.0001Q_N$

When quantity is expressed as a function of price, we find:

Silicon   Nehkdi

$$P = \$10 + \$0.0004Q_S \qquad P = \$2.50 + \$0.0001Q_N$$

$$0.0004Q_S = -10 + P \qquad 0.0001Q_N = -2.50 + P$$

$$Q_S = -25,000 + 2,500 \qquad Q_P = -25,000 + 10,000P$$

b.   The quantity supplied at each respective price is:

Silicon

$$P = \$5: Q_S = -25{,}000 + 2{,}500(5) = -12{,}500 \Rightarrow \underline{\underline{0}}$$
$$\text{(since } Q < 0 \text{ is impossible)}$$

$$P = \$10: Q_S = -25{,}000 + 2{,}500(10) = \underline{\underline{0}}$$

$$P = \$15: Q_S = -25{,}000 + 2{,}500(15) = \underline{\underline{12{,}500}}$$

Nehkdi

$$P = \$5: Q_N = -25{,}000 + 10{,}000(5) = \underline{\underline{50{,}000}}$$

$$P = \$10: Q_N = -25{,}000 + 10{,}00010) = \underline{\underline{75{,}000}}$$

$$P = \$15: Q_N = -25{,}000 + 10{,}000(15) = \underline{\underline{125{,}000}}$$

For Silicon, MC = \$10 when $Q_S = 0$. Since marginal cost rises with output, Silicon will never supply a positive level of output unless a price in excess of \$10 per unit can be obtained. Negative output is not feasible. Thus, Silicon will simply fail to supply output when P < \$10. Similarly, $MC_N = \$2.50$ when $Q_N = 0$. Thus, Nehkdi will never supply output unless a price in excess of \$2.50 per unit can be obtained.

c. When P < \$10, only Nehkdi can profitably supply output. The Nehkdi supply curve will be the industry curve when P < \$10:

$$P \ = \$2.50 + \$0.0001Q$$

or

$$Q \ = -25{,}000 + 10{,}000P$$

d. When P > \$10, both companies can profitably supply output. To derive the industry supply curve in this circumstance, we simply sum the quantities supplied by each firm:

$$Q \ = Q_S + Q_N$$

$$= -25{,}000 + 2{,}500P + (-25{,}000 + 10{,}000P)$$

$$= -50{,}000 + 12{,}500P$$

To check, at P = \$15:

34

$$Q = -50,000 + 12,500(15)$$

$$= 137,500$$

which is supported by the answer to part b, since $Q_S + Q_N = 12,500 + 125,000 = 137,500$.

(Note: Some students mistakenly add prices rather than quantities in attempting to derive the industry supply curve. To avoid this problem, it is important to remember that industry supply curves are found through adding up output (horizontal summation), not by adding up prices (vertical summation)).

3.9

The Hari-Kari is a subcompact sport vehicle exported to the U.S. by a leading Japanese automobile manufacturer. Demand and supply conditions for the vehicle are as follows:

$$Q_D = 75,000 - 4P \qquad \text{(Demand)}$$

$$Q_S = 6P \qquad \text{(Supply)}$$

where P is average price per unit ($).

a. Calculate the Hari-Kari surplus or shortage when P = $6,000, $7,000, and $8,000.

b. Calculate the market equilibrium price/output combination.

3.9 SOLUTION

a. The surplus or shortage can be calculated at each price level:

Price (1)	Quantity Supplied (2)	Quantity Demanded (3)	Surplus (+) or Shortage (-) (4) = (2) - (3)
$6,000	$Q_S = 6(6,000)$ = 36,000	$Q_D = 75,000 - 4(6,000)$ = 51,000	-15,000
7,000	$Q_S = 6(7,000)$ = 42,000	$Q_D = 75,000 - 4(7,000)$ = 47,000	-5,000
8,000	$Q_S = 6(8,000)$ = 48,000	$Q_D = 75,000 - 4(8,000)$ = 43,000	+5,000

b. The equilibrium price is found by setting the quantity demanded equal to the quantity supplied and solving for P:

35

$$Q_D \ = \ Q_S$$

$$75{,}000 - 4P \ = \ 6P$$

$$75{,}000 \ = \ 10P$$

$$P \ = \ \$\underline{7{,}500}$$

To solve for Q, set:

Demand: $Q_D = 75{,}000 - 4(7{,}500) = \underline{45{,}000}$

Supply: $Q_S = 6(7{,}500) = \underline{45{,}000}$

In equilibrium, $Q_D = Q_S = 45{,}000$.

CHAPTER FOUR: DEMAND ANALYSIS

Theme

Demand analysis is an important part of the firm's overall operations since it forms the basis for refinements in production and marketing strategies for current products, as well as points the way for new product development. Demand analysis considers those factors that influence customer buying decisions under a given set of circumstances. Final or direct demand is demand by customers for products or services that they themselves wish to use and enjoy (e.g., car buyers and cars). Derived demand is demand by customers for intermediate products or services that are used to create other consumer goods (e.g., car companies purchasing steel and tires). In both instances, demand analysis involves considering endogenous factors within the control of the firm such as firm advertising, as well as exogenous factors beyond the control of the firm such as weather. Demand curve analysis is an important aspect of demand analysis. Here, the effect of product price on quantity sold is considered holding constant all other factors influencing demand. The responsiveness of demand in demand analysis, and quantity demanded in demand curve analysis, is often quantified in terms of percentage change measures or elasticity. Demand elasticities are simply the percentage change in sales relative to a one percent change in some factor embodied in the demand relation. Because of its direct relevance for product development and promotion, demand elasticity analysis constitutes a key aspect of managerial economics.

Outline

I.   The Basis for Demand

A.   Definition of Demand: Demand refers to the number of units of a particular good or service that customers are willing to purchase during a specific period and under a given set of conditions. Two models of demand are analyzed, including:

1.   Final Demand: Final demand is demand by customers for goods or services which they themselves wish to use and enjoy. Utility theory is used to explain the nature and scope of final demand.

2.   Derived Demand: Derived demand is demand by customers for goods or service inputs which will be used to produce output. The profit motive provides the rationale for derived demand.

B.   Utility Functions: A utility function is a descriptive statement that relates total satisfaction or well-being (utility) to consumption.

C.   Marginal Utility: The additional satisfaction derived from increased consumption is called marginal utility.

D.   The Law of Diminishing Marginal Utility: The marginal utility derived from consumption tends to fall as consumption increases.

II. Consumer Choice

A.   Indifference Curves: An indifference curve represents all market bookets that provide a given consumer with the same level of satisfaction.

B.   Marginal Rate of Substitution: The amount of one product that must be substituted for another if utility is to remain unchanged is called the marginal rate of substitution.

C.   Budget Lines: All combinations of goods and services that can be purchased for a fixed dollar amount constitute a budget line.

D.   Income and Substitution Effects: The effects of price changes are described in terms of income and substitution effects.

1.   A income effect describes the higher (lower) level of overall consumption made possible following a price decrease (increase).

2.   The substitution effect describes the substitution of cheaper products for more expensive ones following a price change.

III. Optimal Consumption

A.   Utility Maximization: Utility will be maximized when products are purchased at levels such that relative prices equal the relative marginal utility derived from consumption:

$$\frac{MU_X}{MU_Y} = \frac{P_X}{P_Y}$$

IV. Demand Sensitivity Analysis: Elasticity

A.   Definition: Elasticity measures the percentage change in one variable associated with a one percent change in some other factor. In demand analysis, we consider the percentage change in quantity sold due to a one percent change in some demand related factor X.

$$\text{Elasticity} = \frac{\%\Delta Q}{\%\Delta X} = \frac{\Delta Q/Q}{\Delta X/X} = \frac{\Delta Q}{\Delta X} \times \frac{X}{Q}$$

where Δ designates change.

B.   Point elasticity: A measure of elasticity at a given point along a demand function:

$$\varepsilon = \frac{\Delta Q}{Q} \div \frac{\Delta X}{X} = \frac{\Delta Q}{\Delta X} \times \frac{X}{Q}$$

Point elasticities are useful in predicting the sales effect of "small" changes in X (i.e., $\Delta X/X \leqq 5\%$).

C.   Arc elasticity: A measure of average elasticity over some range of the demand function is the arc elasticity:

$$E = \frac{Q_2 - Q_1}{(Q_2 + Q_1)/2} \div \frac{X_2 - X_1}{(X_1 + X_2)/2} = \frac{Q_2 - Q_1}{X_2 - X_1} \times \frac{X_2 + X_1}{Q_2 + Q_1}$$

Arc elasticities are useful in predicting the sales effect of "substantial" changes in X (i.e., $\Delta X/X > 5\%$).

V.   Price Elasticity of Demand

A.   Definition: The price elasticity of demand, or "own" price elasticity, measures the responsiveness of the quantity demanded to changes in the price of a product, holding constant the values of all other variables in the demand function. Since demand curves slope downward, price increases cause quantity demanded to fall, and price decreases cause quantity demanded to rise. It follows that own price elasticities will always have a negative sign.

B.   Relation between Price Elasticity and Revenue: Depending upon the degree of price elasticity, a given change in price will result in an increase, decrease, or no change in total revenue.

1.   Total revenue is unaffected by changes in price if elasticity is unitary:

39

$$|\varepsilon_p| = 1$$

2. Total revenue declines with price increases and rises with price decreases if demand is elastic:

$$|\varepsilon_p| > 1$$

3. Total revenue rises with price increases and declines with price decreases if demand is inelastic:

$$|\varepsilon_p| < 1$$

4. The limiting cases:

    a. Perfectly Inelastic Demand: If $|\varepsilon_p| = 0$, a firm could charge any price and sell the same number of units, i.e., its demand curve is vertical.

    b. Perfectly Elastic Demand: If $|\varepsilon_p| = \infty$, a firm could sell an unlimited amount at the market price, but sell nothing if it raises its price at all, i.e., its demand curve is horizontal.

(Note: Since the negative sign on own price elasticities is obvious, it is often ignored for convenience.)

C. Varying Elasticity at Different Points on a Demand Curve: The price elasticity of demand will vary at different points along a given demand curve. As price increases, the price elasticity of demand will also increase. As price decreases, the price elasticity of demand will also decrease.

D. Price Elasticity and Revenue:

1. In the elastic portion of the demand curve when $|\varepsilon_p| > 1$, marginal revenue is greater than zero, and total revenue increases with reductions in price since this leads to a greater than proportional increase in quantity sold.

2. When $|\varepsilon_p| = 1$, marginal revenue equals 0, and total revenue is maximized.

3.   In the inelastic range of the demand curve when $|\varepsilon_p| < 1$, marginal revenue is negative, implying that when price is reduced, the quantity sold increases but revenue declines.

E.   Price Elasticity and Optimal Pricing Policy:

1.   Relation Between Marginal Revenue, Price and Price Elasticity: There is a simple direct relation between marginal revenue, price and price elasticity, where:

$$MR = P(1 + \frac{1}{\varepsilon_p})$$

2.   Optimal Price Formula: Since profits are maximized when MC = MR, the optimal price formula can be written:

$$P = \frac{MC}{(1 + \frac{1}{\varepsilon_p})}$$

Therefore, optimal prices can be easily calculated solely on the basis of marginal cost and point price elasticity of demand information.

F.   Determinants of Price Elasticity: Price elasticity is affected by:

1.   The extent to which a good is considered to be a necessity.

2.   The availability of substitutes.

3.   The proportion of income spent on the product.

G.   Uses of Price Elasticity: Price elasticity of demand information can be used for:

1.   Inventory control.

2.   Production planning.

3.   Optimal pricing.

VI. Cross-Price Elasticity of Demand

A.   Definition: The responsiveness of demand for one product to changes in the price of some other product, holding all other variables constant is given by the cross-price elasticity of demand:

41

$$\varepsilon_{PX} = \frac{\Delta Q_Y}{Q_Y} \div \frac{\Delta P_X}{P_X} = \frac{\Delta Q_Y}{\Delta P_X} \times \frac{P_X}{Q_Y}$$

1. If $\varepsilon_{PX} > 0$, products are substitutes and the price of one product and the demand for the other move in the same direction.

2. If $\varepsilon_{PX} < 0$, products are complements and the price of one product and the demand of the other move in opposite directions.

3. If $\varepsilon_{PX} = 0$, the demand for two products are unrelated.

4. Usefulness of cross-price elasticity:

    a. The formulation of a firm's pricing strategy is dependent on how demand for its products are affected by changes in the prices of other goods.

    b. Cross-price elasticity is used in industry studies to measure interrelations among products and, therefore, to define markets.

VII. Income Elasticity of Demand

A. Definition: Income elasticity measures the responsiveness of demand to changes in income, holding all other variables constant:

$$\varepsilon_I = \frac{\Delta Q}{Q} \div \frac{\Delta I}{I} = \frac{\Delta Q}{\Delta I} \times \frac{I}{Q}$$

1. Normal Goods: If $\varepsilon_I > 0$, products are normal or superior goods, and sales will rise with rising personal income and, in general, with economic growth.

    a. Noncyclical: If $\varepsilon_I < 1$ for a particular good, producers of that good will not share proportionally in increases in income.

b.   Cyclical: If $\varepsilon_I > 1$, the industry will gain (lose) more than a proportionate share of increases (decreases) in income.

VIII. Other Demand Elasticities

A.   Examples: Demand elasticities can be calculated for any endogenous or exogenous factors influencing demand, including: firm advertising, competitor advertising, weather, interest rates, and so on.

IX. Time Impact on Elasticity

A.   The Time Factor: Generally speaking, demand relations tend to be more highly elastic in the long-run rather than the short-run. Improved information and a reduced importance of fixed costs are often cited as reasons underlying this phenomenon.

PROBLEMS AND SOLUTIONS

4.1

The Lilly Pad, Inc., has estimated the following demand and marginal revenue curves for its deluxe model waterbed in the Seattle area:

$$P = \$500 - \$0.25Q$$

$$MR = \$500 - \$0.50Q$$

where P is price and Q is quantity (in units).

a. Plot the demand, marginal, and total revenue curves.

b. At what price would the Lilly Pad fail to sell any waterbeds?

c. What is the maximum quantity that the Lilly Pad could give away?

d. What is the maximum revenue that the firm could receive?

e. For a given percentage change in price, what would be the percentage change in quantity demanded at the output level Q = 600?

f. What is the arc price elasticity of demand for the quantity range of 600-700 units?

4.1 SOLUTION

a. Here we note that:

Demand Curve = $P = \$500 - \$0.25Q$

Total Revenue Curve = $TR = PQ = \$500Q - \$0.25Q^2$

Marginal Revenue Curve = $MR = \Delta TR/\Delta Q = \$500 - \$0.5Q$

Q	×	P	=	Total Revenue
0		$500		$ 0
400		400		160,000
800		300		240,000
1,000		250		250,000
1,200		200		240,000
1,600		100		160,000
2,000		0		0

44

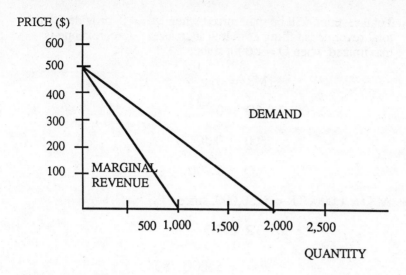

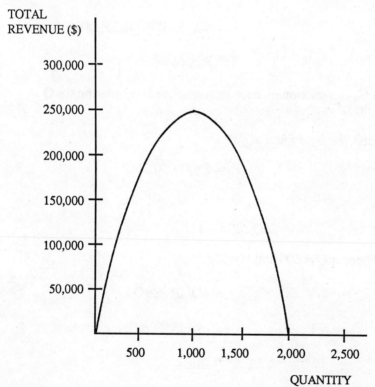

b. At P = $\underline{\underline{\$500}}$, Q = 0 since P = 500 - 0.25(0) = $500.

c. At a price of $0, Q = 2,000 - 4Q = 2,000 - 4(0) = $\underline{\underline{2,000}}$ units.

45

d.   Total revenue will be maximized when MR = 0, provided that total revenue is falling as output increases. Here, revenue is maximized when Q = 1,000, since:

$$MR = 0$$

$$\$500 - \$0.5Q = 0$$

$$500 = 0.5Q$$

$$Q = 1,000$$

At Q = 1,000, TR = $250,000, since:

$$TR = PQ$$

$$= \$500Q - \$0.25Q^2$$

$$= 500(1,000) - 0.25(1,000)^2$$

$$= \underline{\underline{\$250,000}}$$

(This is a maximum since total revenue is decreasing for Q > 1,000).

e.   First, we determine $\Delta Q/\Delta P$ as:

$$P = \$500 - \$0.25Q$$

$$Q = 2,000 - 4P$$

$$\Delta Q/\Delta P = -4$$

Then, at Q = 600 and P = 350:

$$\varepsilon_p = \Delta Q/\Delta P \times P/Q$$

$$= -4 \times (\$350/600)$$

$$= \underline{\underline{-2.33}}$$

The percentage change in quantity demanded would be -2.33 times the percentage change in price. That is, the point price elasticity is -2.33.

f.   Since P = $500 - $0.25Q,

46

At Q = 600: P = \$500 - \$0.25(600) = \$350

At Q = 700: P = \$500 - \$0.25(700) = \$325

Therefore:

$$\text{Arc Price Elasticity} = \frac{Q_2 - Q_1}{P_2 - P_1} \times \frac{P_2 + P_1}{Q_2 + Q_1}$$

$$= \frac{700 - 600}{\$325 - \$350} \times \frac{\$325 + \$350}{700 + 600}$$

$$= \underline{\underline{-2.1}}$$

As is typical, the price elasticity of demand is decreasing in absolute terms, here from $\varepsilon_P = -2.33$ to $\varepsilon_P = -2.1$, as price decreases.

4.2

Security Systems, Inc., markets electronic surveillance equipment used to control inventory "shrinkage" (shoplifting, employee theft) at retail clothing stores.

The demand function for a new portable tag sensor is:

$$Q = 100 - 20P + 0.4A + 0.05I$$

where Q = quantity demanded, P = price, A = advertising expenditures, and I = disposable income per family.

a. Assuming P = \$150, A = \$6,000, and I = \$30,000, what is the demand curve for the tag sensor?

b. What is the price elasticity of demand, and the income elasticity of demand under the assumptions of part a?

4.2 SOLUTION

a. The demand curve for the tag sensor is simply:

$$Q = 100 - 20P + 0.4A + 0.05I$$

$$= 100 - 20P + 0.4(6,000) + 0.05(30,000)$$

$$= 4,000 - 20P$$

47

or

$$P = \$200 - \$0.05Q$$

b.   We note that:

$$Q = 100 - 20P + 0.4A + 0.05I$$

$$= 100 - 20(150) + 0.4(6,000) + 0.05(30,000)$$

$$= 1,000$$

Thus, the own price elasticity is:

$$\varepsilon_P = \Delta Q/\Delta P \times P/Q$$

$$= -20 \times (\$150/1,000)$$

$$= \underline{\underline{-3}}$$

The income elasticity of demand is:

$$\varepsilon_I = \Delta Q/\Delta I \times I/Q$$

$$= 0.05 \times (\$30,000/1,000)$$

$$= \underline{\underline{1.5}}$$

Since $\varepsilon_I = 1.5 > 0$, the tag sensor is a cyclical normal good.

4.3

A recent study of the Fargo, North Dakota market by Chemyard, Inc. found that the local demand for weed control and fertilizer services is described by the following elasticities: price elasticity = -1.5, cross-price elasticity with department store fertilizer = 2, income elasticity = 5, TV advertising elasticity = 3. Indicate whether each of the following statements is true or false, and explain your answer.

a.   A price reduction for Chemyard services will increase both the number of units demanded and Chemyard revenues.

b.   A 15 percent reduction in Chemyard prices would lead to a 10 percent increase in unit sales.

48

c. The cross-price elasticity indicates that a 10 percent increase in Chemyard prices would lead to a 20 percent increase in department store fertilizer demand.

d. The demand for Chemyard services is price elastic and typical of noncyclical normal goods.

e. A 4 percent increase in TV advertising would be necessary to overcome the negative effect on Chemyard sales caused by a 6 percent decrease in department store fertilizer prices.

4.3 SOLUTION

a. <u>True</u>. Quantity demanded will always rise following a price reduction. In the case of elastic demand (here $|\varepsilon_p| = 1.5 > 1$), the percentage increase in quantity will be greater than the percentage decrease in price, and total revenue will rise.

b. <u>False</u>. Given $\varepsilon_p = -1.5$, a 15 percent reduction in Chemyard prices would lead to a 22.5 percent increase in unit sales.

c. <u>False</u>. The $\varepsilon_{PX} = 2$ indicates that a 10 percent reduction in department store fertilizer prices would lead to a 20 percent reduction in the demand for Chemyard services.

d. <u>False</u>. The demand for Chemyard services is price elastic, but $\varepsilon_I = 5 > 1$ indicates that service demand is cyclical.

e. <u>True</u>. A 4 percent increase in TV advertising would increase service demand by 12 percent. Conversely, a 6 percent decrease in department store prices would decrease service demand by 12 percent. Therefore, these changes would be mutually offsetting.

4.4

The demand for automobile tires is characterized by the following elasticities: price elasticity = -3.5, cross-price elasticity with automobiles = -2.5, income elasticity = 2. Indicate whether each of the following statements is true or false and why.

a. The demand curve for tires is downward sloping.

b. A price increase for tires will reduce the number of units demanded, and increase the total revenue received by sellers.

c. The price elasticity indicates that a 2 percent reduction in tire prices will lead to a 7 percent increase in tire revenues.

d. A 10 percent increase in automobile prices will lead to a 25 percent decline in tire demand.

e. Tires and automobiles are complementary goods, and tires are inferior goods.

4.4 SOLUTION

a. <u>True</u>. A price elasticity of -3.5 indicates a one percent increase (decrease) in price will cause a 3.5 percent decrease (increase) in quantity demanded. With a negative price elasticity, price and quantity will always move in opposite directions, thereby indicating a downward sloping demand curve.

b. <u>False</u>. Price increases always reduce the quantity demanded, given a downward sloping demand curve. However, given elastic tire demand, we know $\%\Delta Q > \%\Delta P$ and revenues will fall following a price increase.

c. <u>False</u>. The price elasticity of -3.5 indicates a 2 percent reduction in price will lead to a 7 percent increase in units (tires) sold. Revenues will increase by a somewhat smaller amount.

d. <u>True</u>. The cross-price elasticity of -2.5 indicates a 10 percent increase in automobile prices will lead to a 25 percent decline in tire demand.

e. <u>False</u>. A negative cross-price elasticity between tires and automobiles indicates they are complements, but $\varepsilon_I = 2 > 0$ indicates tires are cyclical normal goods.

4.5

During September, in an effort to reduce end-of-the-model-year inventory, Newark Mercedes-Benz offered a $6,000 discount from the $60,000 sticker price on the Mercedes 500 SEL model. Due to the success of the promotion, monthly sales rose from 15 to 23 units.

a. Calculate the arc price elasticity for the 500 SEL model.

b. Calculate the sticker price reduction necessary to eliminate Newark's remaining inventory of 27 units during the month of October.

4.5 SOLUTION

a. $E_P = \dfrac{\Delta Q}{\Delta P} \times \dfrac{P_2 + P_1}{Q_2 + Q_1}$

$\qquad = \dfrac{23 - 15}{\$54,000 - \$60,000} \times \dfrac{\$54,000 + \$60,000}{23 + 15}$

$\qquad = \underline{\underline{-4}}$

b. The new price, P_2, required to sell 27 units during October, can be calculated from the arc price elasticity formula:

$$E_P = \dfrac{\Delta Q}{\Delta P} \times \dfrac{P_2 + P_1}{Q_2 + Q_1}$$

$$-4 = \dfrac{27 - 15}{P_2 - \$60,000} \times \dfrac{P_2 + \$60,000}{27 + 15}$$

$$-4 = \dfrac{12(P_2 + 60,000)}{42(P_2 - 60,000)}$$

$$-168P_2 + 10,080,000 = 12P_2 + 720,000$$

$$180P_2 = 9,360,000$$

$$P_2 = \$52,000$$

A new $P_2 = \$52,000$ implies a sticker price reduction of $8,000 since:

$$\Delta P = P_2 - P_1$$

$$= \$52,000 - \$60,000$$

$$= \underline{\underline{-\$8,000}}$$

4.6

The Adirondack Paper Company conducted a research study to determine how the demand for high strength paper boxes, product X, is affected by price changes of paper towels, product Y. The research staff estimated that the following function expressed the relation between sales of X and the price of Y, holding other things constant: $Q_Y = 1,000 - 0.6P_X$.

a. How would you classify the relation between X and Y: substitute, complement, or independent?

b. Determine the quantities demanded of Y for the following prices of X: $P_X = \$100, \$80, \$60, \$40$.

c. Determine the point cross-price elasticity of demand at $P_X = \$80$ and at $P_X = \$40$.

d. Determine the arc cross-price elasticity for these price ranges: $P_X = \$100$ to $\$80$; $\$60$ to $\$40$.

e. Now, reconsider your answer to part a. Can the word close be added to describe the observed relation?

f. Can you visualize the cross-price elasticity concept being used in antitrust cases to help define markets?

4.6 SOLUTION

a. X and Y are complement products. A rise in P_X causes a decrease in the demand for Y. Apparently, Adirondack's customers are more likely to buy its paper boxes if they are already a paper towel customer.

b. Given the functional relation $Q_Y = 1,000 - 0.6P_X$:

P_X	Y(units)
$100	940
80	952
60	964
40	976

c. At $P_X = 80$,

$$\varepsilon_{PX} = \Delta Q_Y / \Delta P_X \times P_X / Q_Y$$

$$= -0.6 \times (\$80/952)$$

$$= \underline{-0.05}$$

At $P_X = 40$,

$$\varepsilon_{PX} = -0.6 \times (\$40/976)$$

$$= \underline{\underline{-0.02}}$$

d.   For the range \$100 to \$80:

$$E_{PX} = \frac{Y_2 - Y_1}{P_{X2} - P_{X1}} \times \frac{P_{X2} + P_{X1}}{Y_2 + Y_1}$$

$$= \frac{952 - 940}{\$80 - \$100} \times \frac{\$80 + \$100}{952 + 940}$$

$$= \underline{\underline{-0.06}}$$

For the range \$60 to \$40:

$$E_{PX} = \frac{964 - 976}{\$60 - \$40} \times \frac{\$60 + \$40}{964 + 976}$$

$$= \underline{\underline{-0.03}}$$

e.   Over the range of prices considered, the cross-price elasticities are quite low--the maximum elasticity is only -0.06. Accordingly, a given percentage change in P will have only a slight effect on Q, so the relation cannot be called close. Products X and Y are weak complements.

f.   In defining markets for antitrust purposes, one must take account of substitutes, and since cross-price elasticities indicate the degree of substitutability, the concept is useful in antitrust work. This point is discussed in more detail in Chapter 12.

4.7

Laguna Sporting Goods sells Roller-Ball roller skates for \$60 per pair. During 1985, its sales volume was 10,000 pairs. In January 1986, a competitor, Oceanside Sports, cut the price of Roller-Ball skates from \$65 to \$55 per pair. As a result, Laguna sold only 8,000 pairs of skates during 1986.

a.   Determine the arc cross-price elasticity of demand between Laguna's and Oceanside's roller skates. (Assume that Laguna's price is held constant).

b.   Assume that the arc price elasticity for Laguna's skates is $\varepsilon_p =$

53

-2. Assume also that Oceanside keeps the price of its skates at $55. What price cut must be made by Laguna in order to increase its annual sales volume back to 10,000 pairs?

4.7 SOLUTION

a. Using the arc cross-price elasticity formula:

$$E_{PX} = \frac{Q_2 - Q_1}{P_{X2} - P_{X1}} \times \frac{P_{X2} + P_{X1}}{Q_2 + Q_1}$$

$$= \frac{8,000 - 10,000}{\$55 - \$65} \times \frac{\$55 + \$65}{8,000 + 10,000}$$

$$= \underline{\underline{1.33}}$$

Thus, since $E_{PX} > 0$, a substitute good relation exists between Laguna and Oceanside roller skates (as expected).

b. Using the formula for arc price elasticity of demand:

$$E_P = \frac{Q_2 - Q_1}{P_2 - P_1} \times \frac{P_2 - P_1}{Q_2 + Q_1}$$

$$-2 = \frac{10,000 - 8,000}{P_2 - \$60} \times \frac{P_2 + \$60}{10,000 + 8,000}$$

$$-2 = \frac{2,000}{18,000} \times \frac{P_2 + 60}{P_2 - 60}$$

$$-18 = \frac{P_2 + 60}{P_2 - 60}$$

$$1,080 - 18P_2 = P_2 + 60$$

$$19P_2 = 1,020$$

$$P_2 = \underline{\underline{\$53.68}}$$

Thus, $53.68 is the price required to again sell 10,000 pairs. This involves a $6.32 price reduction since,

$$\Delta P = P_2 - P_1$$

$$= \$53.68 - \$60$$

$$= \underline{-\$6.32}$$

4.8

The Video Station sells video recordings of recent movies and blank video cassettes for home recording use. During recent years, the Video Station has run a Christmas special on its products, reducing average prices of video recordings from \$29.99 to \$24.97, and blank cassette prices from \$19.99 to \$14.97. Galien Hite, manager of a new Video Station outlet, questions the wisdom of this pricing policy in light of a recent trade association study which found point price elasticity estimates of $\varepsilon_P = -1.5$ for video recordings, and $\varepsilon_P = -4$ for blank cassettes.

a. Is a price reduction likely to increase unit sales of video recordings and blank cassettes?

b. What is the likely impact on total revenues of the Christmas price reductions?

c. Determine optimal average prices if video recordings cost the Video Station \$10 and blank video cassettes cost \$8?

d. Is the Christmas special pricing policy desirable?

4.8 SOLUTION

a. <u>Yes</u>. Price reductions will always increase unit sales.

b. Given $|\varepsilon_P| > 1$ for both video recordings and blank cassettes, demand is elastic and price reductions will increase not only units sold but also total revenues.

c. Profit maximizing prices will be obtained when MR = MC. To determine optimal prices here, we must remember:

$$MR = P(1 + \frac{1}{\varepsilon_P})$$

Since MC = MR at the profit maximizing level of output, the optimal pricing formula is:

$$P = \frac{MC}{(1 + \frac{1}{\varepsilon_P})}$$

<u>Video Recordings</u>

$$P = \frac{MC}{(1 + \frac{1}{\varepsilon_P})}$$

$$\$24.97 \overset{?}{=} \frac{\$10}{(1 + \frac{1}{-1.5})}$$

$$\$24.97 \neq \underline{\underline{\$30}}$$

<u>Blank Cassettes</u>

$$P = \frac{MC}{(1 + \frac{1}{\varepsilon_P})}$$

$$\$14.97 \overset{?}{=} \frac{\$8}{(1 + \frac{1}{-4})}$$

$$\$14.97 \neq \underline{\underline{\$10.67}}$$

d. <u>No</u>. Given the data at our disposal, Hite seems correct in questioning the Christmas special pricing policy. At P = $24.97, the MR < MC for video recordings. Prices for video recordings should be set at P = $30. On the other hand, the prices for blank video cassettes are still too high since profits will be maximized when P = $10.67 for blank cassettes. Some adjustments to the Video Station's pricing policies seems in order.

4.9

B.B. Lean's summer catalog of outdoor sporting specialities featured $1 off the regular $36 price on Walk-'n-Sport casual shoes. Customer response was enthusiastic, with sales rising from 9,000 to 11,000 units.

a. Using the regular $36 price as a base, calculate the point price elasticity for Walk-'n-Sport shoes.

b. B.B. Lean's buys the shoes from a distributor for $28, and incurs $3.50 in marginal selling costs per unit. On the basis of these data and the price elasticity information from part a, is the regular $36 price optimal in the sense of maximizing profits on the shoes?

4.9 SOLUTION

a. $\varepsilon_P = \Delta Q/\Delta P \times P/Q$

$$= \frac{11{,}000 - 9{,}000}{\$35 - \$36} \times \frac{36}{9{,}000}$$

$$= \underline{\underline{-8}}$$

b. <u>Yes</u>. We use the optimal pricing formula to check if the regular $36 price will result in maximum profits:

$$P = \frac{MC}{(1 + \frac{1}{\varepsilon_P})}$$

$$\$36 \overset{?}{=} \frac{\$28 + \$3.50}{(1 + \frac{1}{-8})}$$

$$\$36 \overset{\surd}{=} \$36$$

Therefore, the regular $36 price is optimal, and the pricing promotion should be discontinued.

4.10

Kitchen Art, Ltd., sells its basic food processor model for $150. The company's experience indicates that sales volume is affected by changes in consumers' income as well as by the price of the product. Specifically, the market research department estimates that the arc price elasticity of demand is -9, whereas the arc income elasticity is 4. These relations are expected to remain stable in the near future over the contemplated range of price and incomes.

Last year, sales volume for the food processor was 100,000 units, and total personal income was $750 billion. Estimated personal income for this year is $850 billion.

a. Using the arc elasticity of demand formula, calculate the income effect on sales.

b. Using the arc price elasticity of demand formula, and holding all else equal, calculate the price effect of a $25 price reduction during 1987.

c. Based on your answers to parts a and b, calculate the total effect on sales of a $750 billion to $850 billion increase in income and a $25 price reduction.

4.10 SOLUTION

a. Using the arc income elasticity of demand formula to find Q:

$$E_I = \frac{Q_2 - Q_1}{I_2 - I_1} \times \frac{I_2 + I_1}{Q_2 + Q_1}$$

$$4 = \frac{Q_2 - 100,000}{\$850 - \$750} \times \frac{\$850 + \$750}{Q_2 + 100,000}$$

$$4 = \frac{Q_2 - 100,000}{Q_2 + 100,000} \times \frac{1,600}{100}$$

$$4Q_2 + 400,000 = 16Q_2 - 1,600,000$$

$$12Q_2 = 2,000,000$$

$$Q_2 = \underline{166,667} \text{ units}$$

b. Using the arc price elasticity of demand formula to find Q:

$$E_P = \frac{Q_2 - Q_1}{P_2 - P_1} \times \frac{P_2 + P_1}{Q_2 + Q_1}$$

$$-9 = \frac{Q_2 - 100,000}{\$125 - \$150} \times \frac{\$125 + \$150}{Q_2 + 100,000}$$

58

$$-9 = \frac{Q_2 - 100{,}000}{Q_2 + 100{,}000} \times \frac{275}{(-25)}$$

$$-9Q_2 - 900{,}000 = -11Q_2 + 1{,}100{,}000$$

$$2Q_2 = 2{,}000{,}000$$

$$Q_2 = \underline{1{,}000{,}000} \text{ units}$$

c.   To estimate sales when income rises from $750 billion to $850 billion and price falls from $150 to $125, we simply calculate the price effect from the Q = 166,667 base, or the income effect from the Q = 1,000,000 base.

Using the first approach:

$$E_P = \frac{Q_2 - Q_1}{P_2 - P_1} \times \frac{P_2 + P_1}{Q_2 + Q_1}$$

$$-9 = \frac{Q_2 - 166{,}667}{\$125 - \$150} \times \frac{\$125 + \$150}{Q_2 + 166{,}667}$$

$$-9 = \frac{Q_2 - 166{,}667}{Q_2 + 166{,}667} \times \frac{275}{(-25)}$$

$$-9Q_2 - 1{,}500{,}000 = -11Q_2 + 1{,}833{,}337$$

$$2Q_2 = 3{,}333{,}337$$

$$Q_2 = \underline{1{,}666{,}667} \text{ units}$$

Using the second approach:

$$E_I = \frac{Q_2 - Q_1}{I_2 - I_1} \times \frac{I_2 + I_1}{Q_2 + Q_1}$$

$$4 = \frac{Q_2 - 1{,}000{,}000}{\$850 - \$750} \times \frac{\$850 + \$750}{Q_2 + 1{,}000{,}000}$$

$$4Q_2 + 4{,}000{,}000 = 16Q_2 - 16{,}000{,}000$$

$$12Q_2 = 20,000,000$$

$$Q_2 = \underline{\underline{1,666,667}} \text{ units}$$

CHAPTER FOUR APPENDIX: DEMAND ESTIMATION

Theme

The empirical estimation of demand relations is an important function of the managerial economist. In this appendix, three approaches to demand estimation are explored. They are: consumer interviews, market experiments, and regression analysis. Best results using the consumer interview or survey technique are most often obtained when skilled interviewers deal with carefully selected samples. Experiments in actual or controlled market settings can also be conducted in order to gain important insight regarding consumer attitudes and preferences. An advantage of both the market survey and experiment techniques is that meaningful information can often be gained from only limited data. An important drawback of each technique is that they simulate actual customer decisions only imperfectly. The third common approach to demand estimation, regression analysis, also has important advantages and drawbacks. Given adequate market transaction data and skilled personnel, least squares regression analysis allows one to analyze in depth the demand function for a good or service. While statistical estimates of demand parameter values and reliability are highly useful, expenses involved in data collection can tend to offset these advantages. Since each technique of demand estimation has important pluses and minuses, managerial economists must make their choice of demand estimation method, or an appropriate combination of methods, on the basis of individual estimation problem characteristics.

Outline

I.   The Identification Problem

A.   Definition: The problem of estimating one function when simultaneous relations exist is known as the identification problem.

B.   Treatment: When the identification problem is serious, consumer interviews and market experiments can sometimes be used to gain important demand function information. When the identification problem does not appear to be serious, statistical estimation of simple econometric models can be conducted.

II. Consumer Interviews

A.   Method: Consumers are questioned about their probable response to a change in price (or other variable under consideration). By aggregating the data obtained, the firm can develop a better understanding of key factors in its demand function.

B.   Advantages: In short-term demand or sales forecasting, subjective information about consumer attitudes and expectations, obtainable only through interview methods, frequently makes the difference between an accurate estimate and one that misses by a wide margin.

    C.   Limitations: Consumers are often unable, and sometimes unwilling, to provide accurate answers to hypothetical questions about how they would react to changes in key demand variables.

III. Market Studies and Experimentation

    A.   Studies in Actual Markets: A firm locates one or more markets with specific characteristics, then varies prices, advertising, and other controllable variables in the demand function, with the variations occurring either over time or between markets.

        1.   Advantages: Because important variables in the demand function such as price and advertising are controlled by the experimenter, some insight regarding the short-run effects of wide swings in important demand-related factors can be gained.

        2.   Limitations:

            a.   Experiments are expensive and, therefore, usually undertaken on a scale too small to allow high levels of confidence in the results.

            b.   Experiments are seldom run for sufficiently long periods to indicate long-run effects. The experimenter is thus forced to examine short-run data and must attempt to extend it to a longer period.

            c.   Uncontrollable changes in economic conditions or competitor behavior during the experiment can invalidate the results.

    B.   Controlled Laboratory Experiments: In an experiment, consumers are given "funds" with which to "shop" in a simulated store.

        1.   Advantages: The cost involved is typically lower than that of field experiments, and the experimenter has a greater control over extraneous factors.

        2.   Limitations: Subjects invariably know that they are part of an experiment, and this knowledge may distort their shopping habits.

    C.   Demand for Oranges: An Illustrative Market Experiment

IV. Regression Analysis

A. Basic Requirements: Regression analysis is a common statistical technique for demand estimation. Accurate demand estimation requires a successful specification, estimation and interpretation of the demand function relation. Important aspects of each of these crucial steps are outlined below.

B. Specifying the Variables: Accurate specification of the demand relation is an important first step in the statistical estimation process. Two types of specification problems are often encountered and are sometimes responsible for what is known as misspecification bias.

1. Omitted Variables Problem: All relevant variables must be included if the analysis is to be fully descriptive of the demand relation. Omitted variables will tend to be a more serious problem the lower is the overall explanatory power (R^2) of the regression.

2. Functional Form Problem: Fully descriptive analyses also require that the form of the relation (linear, log-linear, etc.) between the dependent and independent variables be correctly specified. As above, where the form of the demand relation is incorrectly specified, the overall explanatory power of the regression analysis will tend to be low.

C. Obtaining Data on the Variables: Publications by trade groups and associations, government documents and the firm's own proprietary data are all valuable sources of information.

D. Specifying the Regression Equation: Ordinary least squares regression is by far the most common method of statistical demand estimation. In this method, the relation between a dependent variable (e.g., sales) and independent variable (e.g., advertising) is characterized by that line which minimizes the sum of squared vertical deviations from all independent variable observations. The two most common regression models are:

1. Linear functions: A simple linear form can be written:

$$S_t = a + b_1 P_t + b_2 A_t + b_3 I_t + u_t$$

where S is sales, P is price, A is advertising and I is income--all during period t. Here, u_t is a disturbance term reflecting estimation error. Beyond the advantage of its obvious ease in application, the linear approach is often an

63

accurate approximation over the narrow range for which data are typically encountered.

2. Power functions: A second highly popular method of demand estimation is through use of log-linear models which reflect multiplicative relations. If the above relation were multiplicative rather than additive, then:

$$S_t = aP_t^{b_1} \cdot A_t^{b_2} \cdot I_t^{b_3} \cdot u_t$$

and

$$\log S_t = \log a + b_1 \log P_t + b_2 \log A_t$$
$$+ b_3 \log I_t + \log u_t$$

In this approach, the effect of advertising on sales $(\Delta S_t / \Delta A_t)$, for example, would depend upon price and income levels. Often, such an approach is more realistic than simple linear models. As an aside, it is interesting to note that b_1, b_2, and b_3 are demand elasticity estimates for price, advertising and income, respectively.

3. Choosing the form of the equation: The choice of an appropriate form for estimation is made on the basis of underlying theory.

E. Estimating the Regression Parameters: Estimation is usually accomplished using "canned" computer programs employing the least squares technique.

F. Interpretation: Substantial skill is involved in interpreting the reliability of individual statistical demand analyses. This interpretation must be based on an understanding of the specific variable and overall explanatory power of the analysis.

1. Specific variable explanation: This is judged based on the estimates and standard errors of individual coefficients.

a. The intercept term, a, generally has no economic meaning since it typically lies far outside the range of observed data. This is not always the case, however, and the intercept term will sometimes provide economically meaningful information.

b. The slope coefficient, b, provides an estimate of the change in the dependent variable associated with a one-unit change in the independent variable. In multiple regression, any slope coefficient represents the expected change in the dependent variable related to a one-unit change in the independent variable under consideration; holding constant all other independent variables.

c. The standard error of individual coefficients is used to judge the accuracy with which parameters, or population characteristics, have been estimated.

2. Coefficient of Determination: R^2 represents the portion of total variation in the dependent variable that is explained by the full set of independent variables included in the model.

a. As $R^2 \to 1.0$, the model approaches full descriptive capability.

b. As $R^2 \to 0.0$, the model approaches zero descriptive capability.

3. Standard Error of the Estimate: S.E.E. is used to determine a range within which we can predict the value of the dependent variable with varying degrees of statistical confidence.

a. By definition,

$$Q = \hat{Q} \pm (t_{n-k, \alpha = 0.05})(\text{S.E.E.}) \text{ with 95}$$
percent confidence.

$$Q = \hat{Q} \pm (t_{n-k, \alpha = 0.01})(\text{S.E.E.}) \text{ with 99}$$
percent confidence.

4. T-statistic: The t-statistic provides a measure of the confidence we can place in the strength of the relation between the dependent variable Y and a given independent variable X.

a.   By definition, $t_{n-k} = \dfrac{b - b^*}{\sigma_b}$ where b is an estimated coefficient, and σ_b is the standard error of difference b.

V.   Frozen Fruit Pie Demand: An Illustrative Regression Analysis Problem

PROBLEMS AND SOLUTIONS

4A.1

The Getaway Travel Company has hired a management consulting firm to analyze demand in 26 regional markets for one of its major products. A preliminary report from the consultant contained the following regression results:

$$Q = 1,572 + 2A + 10I + 3P_X - 4P$$
$$\quad\;\; (2,050)\;(0.4)\;(3.5)\;(0.9)\;(1.2)$$

$$R^2 = 0.86$$

Standard Error of the Estimate = 27

Here, Q is the annual demand for the tour in question, P is the price charged by Getaway in dollars, A is thousands of dollars of advertising expenditures, P_X is the average price of another product (unidentified), also measured in dollars, and I is thousands of dollars of per family income in the market area. The terms in parentheses are standard errors of the coefficients.

a. Interpret the demand equation and explain the use of the regression statistics provided.

b. Assuming that the current price is $400, advertising expenditures are $20,000, P_X is $500, and average family income is $15,000, what is the point price elasticity of demand? Would a reduction in price result in an increase in total revenues? Why?

c. Given the data in part c, what is the point cross-price elasticity between the tour and Product X?

d. If Getaway wished to use this equation for forecasting purposes, what is the size of the 99 percent confidence interval for predicting Q?

4A.1   SOLUTION

a. The regression equation relates the number of tours sold annually to the value of four variables: advertising expenditures, A, per family income, I, the average price of the unidentified product, P_X, and the price charged by Getaway, P. More specifically, the expected sales quantity for any year is equal to 1,572 plus 2 times the advertising expenditures (measured in thousands of dollars), plus 10 times the per family income in the market area (in thousands of dollars), plus 3 times the average price of another unidentified product (in dollars), minus 4 times the price charged by Getaway (also measured in dollars).

The individual coefficients of the equation provide estimates of the marginal relations between the annual number of tours sold and each of the independent variables in the model. All of the other information provided relates to the accuracy of the empirical estimation of the demand equation. $R^2 = 0.86$ is the coefficient of determination. It measures the proportion of the total variation in the annual number of tours sold that has been explained by the regression model as a whole. That is, it measures the percentage of total variation in Q that has been accounted for by variation in A, I, P_X and P taken together.

The standard error of the estimate provides information about the level of accuracy one can expect when using the equation for forecasting purposes. The standard error of the estimate corresponds to the standard deviation of a probability distribution and thus can be used to develop a confidence interval for sales predictions.

Letting $\hat{Q}_t$ represent the sales forecast for a given set of values for A, I, P_X and P, there is approximately a 95 percent probability that actual sales, Q_t, will fall in the range $Q_t = \hat{Q}_t \pm 2.08$ standard errors (where $t^*_{26-5=21, \alpha=0.05} = 2.08$), and a 99 percent probability that $Q_t = \hat{Q}_t \pm 2.831$ standard errors of the estimate (where $t^*_{26-5=21, \alpha=0.01} = 2.831$). For simplicity, these critical t values are often rounded off to $t = 2$ (for 95 percent confidence), and $t = 3$ (for 99 percent confidence).

The standard errors of the coefficient estimate provide information about the level of accuracy with which the individual relations between the independent variables and sales of the tour have been estimated. The standard errors of the coefficients can be used to estimate confidence intervals within which the true parameter relating each independent variable to sales will lie with varying degrees of probability. For example, there is a 95 percent probability that the true parameter relating price to quantity sold lies in the interval -1.5 (= - 4 + 2(1.22)) to -6.5 (= -4 - 2(1.22)) which is the estimated parameter -4 ± 2 times the coefficient standard error of 1.22. Thus, the smaller the relative size of a coefficient's standard error, the greater the level of accuracy we can ascribe to the parameter estimation.

b. To calculate the point price elasticity, we must first substitute the values of the independent variables into the demand model to obtain $\hat{Q}$.

$$\hat{Q} = 1{,}572 + 2A + 10I + 3P_X - 4P$$

$$= 1{,}572 + 2(20) + 10(15) + 3(500)$$

$$- 4(400)$$

$$= 1{,}662$$

Therefore,

$$\varepsilon_P = \Delta Q / \Delta P \times P/Q$$

$$= -4 \times (\$400/1{,}662)$$

$$= \underline{\underline{-0.96}}$$

A price reduction would lead to a decrease in total revenue since demand is inelastic ($|\varepsilon_P| < 1$).

c. Using the point cross-price elasticity formula, we find:

$$\varepsilon_{PX} = \Delta Q_Y / \partial P_X \times P_X / Q_Y$$

$$= 3 \times (\$500/1{,}662)$$

$$= \underline{\underline{0.90}}$$

Since $\varepsilon_{PX} = 0.9 > 0$, a substitute good relation exists between X and tours. This is consistent with the individual coefficient analysis of part b.

d. The 99 percent confidence interval for Q is $\hat{Q} \pm 3$ times the standard error of the estimate. Given the current values for A, I, P_X and P, the 99 percent confidence interval would be Q = 1,662 ± 3(27) = 1,662 ± 81.

4A.2

The Washington Life Insurance Company offers a wide variety of insurance products, including whole-life and term policies. The company has compiled the following data concerning policy sales during recent years:

Year	Whole-life		Term	
	Price*	Quantity	Price*	Quantity
1985	$2.00	240,000	$1.50	100,000
1986	2.00	200,000	1.45	130,000
1987	1.90	230,000	1.45	150,000
1988	1.80	280,000	1.40	200,000
1989	1.80	238,000	1.33	270,000

*Price is quoted in terms of cost per $1,000 of coverage.

a. What is the point price elasticity of demand for whole-life insurance?

b. What is the point price elasticity of demand for term insurance?

c. Evaluate the percentage change in whole-life demand given a one percent change in the price of term insurance. Is term insurance a substitute for whole-life?

4A.2   SOLUTION

a. In order to evaluate the point price elasticity of demand for whole-life insurance, we must only consider years when the price of whole-life changed but the price of term remained constant. Therefore, only the 1986-1987 period is relevant.

$$\varepsilon_P = \Delta Q/\Delta P \times P/Q$$

$$= \frac{230,000 - 200,000}{\$1.90 - \$2} \times \frac{\$2}{200,000}$$

$$= -\underline{3} \text{ (Elastic)}$$

b. In order to evaluate the point price elasticity of demand for term insurance, we must only consider years when the price of term changed, but the price of whole-life remained constant. Therefore, only the 1985-1986 and 1988-1989 periods are relevant.

1985-1986

$$\varepsilon_P = \Delta Q/\Delta P \times P/Q$$

70

$$= \frac{130,000 - 100,000}{\$1.45 - \$1.50} \times \frac{\$1.50}{100,000}$$

$$= \underline{\underline{-9}}$$

1988-1989

$$\varepsilon_P = \Delta Q / \Delta P \times P/Q$$

$$= \frac{270,000 - 200,000}{\$1.33 - \$1.40} \times \frac{\$1.40}{200,000}$$

$$= \underline{\underline{-7}}$$

Average: $\varepsilon_P = (-9 + -7)/2 = \underline{\underline{-8}}$ (Highly elastic)

c.   In order to evaluate the relevant cross-price elasticity of demand, we must consider periods when only the price of term insurance changed.

Thus, only the 1985-1986 and 1988-1989 periods are relevant.

1985-1986

$$\varepsilon_{PX} = \Delta Q_Y / \Delta P_X \times P/Q$$

$$= \frac{200,000 - 240,000}{\$1.45 - \$1.50} \times \frac{\$1.50}{240,000}$$

$$= \underline{\underline{5}}$$

1988-1989

$$\varepsilon_{PX} = \Delta Q_Y / \Delta P_X \times P/Q$$

$$= \frac{238,000 - 280,000}{\$1.33 - \$1.40} \times \frac{\$1.40}{280,000}$$

$$= \underline{\underline{3}}$$

Average: $\varepsilon_{PX} = (5 + 3)/2 = \underline{\underline{4}}$ (Substitutes)

Yes, term insurance appears to be a substitute for whole-life insurance.

4A.3

Body Fit, Inc. runs a California-based chain of health clubs featuring aerobic exercise, racket sports, swimming and weight training facilities. An in-house study of monthly sales by 9 outlets during the past year (a total of 108 observations) revealed the following (standard errors in parentheses):

$$Q_Y = 410 - 4P_Y + 2P_X + 8A + 50T - 5W$$
$$ (250)\ (1.5)\ \ (1.2)\ \ (3.5)\ (10)\ (2.8)$$

$$R^2 = 0.96$$

Standard Error of the Estimate = 10

Here, Q_Y = membership sales (in units), P_Y = average membership price (in dollars), P_X = average membership price charged by competitors (in dollars), A = advertising expenditures (in thousands of dollars), T = time (in months of continuous operation), W = weather (in average monthly temperature).

a. What share of overall variation in membership sales is explained by the regression equation? What share is left unexplained?

b. Using a 95 percent confidence level criterion, which independent factors have an influence on membership sales?

c. During a recent month, the San Diego outlet's average price was $750, the average competitor price was $600, advertising was $67,500, the outlet had been in operation for 3 years, and the average monthly temperature was 70°. Assuming this was a typical observation included in the study, derive the relevant demand curve for Body Fit memberships.

d. Assume the model and data given above are relevant for the coming period. Calculate the range within which you would expect to find actual monthly sales revenue with 95 percent confidence.

4A.3   SOLUTION

a. $R^2 = 0.96$ means that 96 percent of the total variation in demand is explained by the regression model. This implies that 4 percent of demand variation remains unexplained.

b. Roughly speaking, a coefficient estimate more than twice as large as the coefficient's standard deviation, or a t-statistic of more than two, is necessary before we can conclude that a given independent variable influences Q at the 95 percent confidence level. Therefore, from the regression equation:

	Variable	Influence

Price: $\quad t = \dfrac{b_{P_Y}}{\sigma_{P_Y}} = \dfrac{4}{1.5} = 2.67 > 2$ Yes.

Competitor Price: $\quad t = \dfrac{b_{P_X}}{\sigma_{P_X}} = \dfrac{2}{1.2} = 1.67 < 2$ No.

Advertising: $\quad t = \dfrac{b_A}{\sigma_A} = \dfrac{8}{3.5} = 2.29 > 2$ Yes.

Time: $\quad t = \dfrac{b_T}{\sigma_T} = \dfrac{50}{10} = 5.00 > 2$ Yes.

Weather: $\quad t = \dfrac{b_W}{\sigma_W} = \dfrac{5}{2.8} = 1.79 < 2$ No.

c. The demand curve for Body Fit memberships is given by the expression:

$$Q_Y = 410 - 4P_Y + 2P_X + 8A + 50T - 5W$$

$$= 410 - 4P_Y + 2(600) + 8(67.5) + 50(36) - 5(70)$$

$$= 3{,}600 - 4P_Y$$

d. Given a membership price $P_Y = \$750$, the estimated value for membership demand (in units) is:

$$\hat{Q} = 3{,}600 - 4(750)$$

$$= \underline{\underline{600}}$$

Therefore, using the standard error of the estimate S.E.E. = 10, the 95 percent confidence region for membership sales (in units) is:

$$Q_Y = \hat{Q} \pm 2 \times \text{S.E.E. (with 95 percent confidence)}$$

$$= 600 \pm 2(10)$$

$$= 600 \pm 20$$

or

580 to 620

And finally, given a membership price $P_Y = \$750$, the 95 percent confidence region for monthly sales revenue is:

$$580 \times \$750 \text{ to } 620 \times \$750$$

or

$$\$\underline{\underline{435,000}} \text{ to } \$\underline{\underline{465,000}}$$

CHAPTER FIVE: FORECASTING

Theme

This chapter investigates important questions concerning how economic variables are forecast. As a first step in the analysis, three broad approaches to forecasting are analyzed, including: qualitative analyses, time series analysis and projection, and econometric models. All these approaches make use of historical data with important differences in the amount of allowance made for current market conditions. Forecasting via trend projection is often labeled "naive" since the method is a simple extrapolation of past experience into future time periods with no allowance for current market conditions being made. At the other end of the spectrum, qualitative analyses are heavily employed when historical data are thought to provide little insight regarding future trends. By understanding both the strengths and weaknesses of multiple forecasting methodologies, managers can select an appropriate combination of methods to generate a range of forecast values involving optimistic to pessimistic assumptions. An important benefit to such an approach is that it forces the manager to critically analyze his or her assumptions and their underlying rationale, and can also suggest possible improvements in forecasting techniques.

Outline

I.   **Forecasting Methodologies**

    A.   Techniques: Multiple forecasting techniques are available and must be understood if accurate managerial forecasts are to be obtained. Common methods of forecasting include:

        1.   Qualitative analyses.

        2.   Time series analysis and projection.

        3.   Econometric models.

    B.   Forecasting Problems: A number of factors influence the level of accuracy obtained. Especially relevant are:

        1.   The distance into the future that one must forecast.

        2.   The lead time available for making decisions.

        3.   The level of accuracy required.

        4.   The quality of data available for analysis.

5. The nature of the relations included in the forecasting problem.

6. The costs and benefits associated with the forecasting problem.

C. Consistency: The ultimate test of a particular forecast's reliability is how well actual data were predicted. Important insight regarding this reliability can be gained beforehand if one considers:

1. Historical success: Has the economic relationship in question been successfully forecast earlier, or are the underlying data so unstable as to preclude successful forecasting?

2. Cross validity checks: Important insight regarding forecast validity can be gained if consistent results are obtained through multiple forecasting methodologies.

II. Qualitative Analyses

A. Expert Opinion: When quantitative information is unavailable, qualitative analysis must be relied upon to prepare required forecasts. Prevalent types of qualitative analyses include:

1. Personal insight.

2. Panel consensus.

3. The Delphi method.

B. Survey Techniques: Accurate forecasting using survey techniques requires the careful selection of a sample which is fully representative of the entire population, as well as a skillful interpretation of sample results. Samples may be drawn in a random fashion, or stratified in an explicit attempt to match overall population characteristics.

1. Advantages: Surveys based on mailed questionnaires or individual interviews can be a low cost way of adding valuable background and depth to the sometimes superficial data available for statistical analyses.

2. Limitations: Unlike "hard" market transactions data, survey data can be "soft" as many consumers are unwilling or incapable of revealing true preferences prior to actual purchase decisions.

III. Time-Series Analysis and Projection

A. Time-Series Methods: In trend projection, past economic relations are projected to continue into the future with little concern for the importance of exogenous "shocks" to the system. Trend projection assumes that historical relations will be essentially maintained subject to historical patterns of variability. Among those causes of historical variability are:

    i. Secular trends: long-run growth or decline.

    ii. Cyclic fluctuations: rhythmic variations from boom to recession.

    iii. Seasonal variations: variations caused by weather or custom.

    iv. Irregular or random influences: unpredictable variations.

1. Advantages: Forecasting through extrapolation is often straightforward when graphic analysis or regression techniques are used. Furthermore, quite accurate forecasts can sometimes be achieved since many economic variables grow at roughly consistent rates per year due to technology, population growth or other such "real" factors.

2. Limitations: The most severe limitation to trend projection is that exogenous shocks to the economic system (such as oil embargoes) can have major unanticipated consequences. Similarly, structural changes in the economic environment can reduce the accuracy of forecasts based on extending past historical data.

B. Trend Analysis: Regression analysis is a powerful tool that can be used to analyze trends in sales and other important variables over time.

C. Seasonal and Cyclical Variations: Many economic data have regular patterns following the effects of seasonal variations due to weather or custom, or due to the effects of the overall business cycle (boom and recession).

D. Barometric Methods: Barometric, or leading indicator, forecasting is based on the observation that there are leading or lagged relations between many economic time series. The method simply requires isolating an economic time series that consistently leads the series being forecast, and tracking movements in this "leading indicator."

    1.   Advantages: Economic analysis has isolated leading indicators which forecast quite accurately 80 to 90 percent of the time many important economic variables (e.g., building permits and housing starts). Such forecasting accuracy can be highly useful to business and other planners.

    2.   Limitations: No series accurately indicates changes in another economic variable all the time. Thus, over reliance on any single leading indicator can lead to costly errors. To illustrate, and despite its success as a leading indicator, one wag has suggested that stock prices have accurately predicted 10 out of the last 6 recessions.

IV. Econometric Models

    A.   Method: Forecasting with econometric models involves using theoretically derived models of economic relations as the basis for statistical forecasts of economic variables. In some instances, multiequation methods are used to identify complex "systems" of economic relations.

        1.   Advantages: Among the advantages of using econometric models in forecasting are: causal relations are analyzed on the basis of theoretical propositions, forecast error information can be used to improve subsequent forecasts, and not only directions of change but also magnitudes of change are estimated.

        2.   Limitations: Despite its advantages, forecasting with econometric models is still in its infancy. Because too much is still unknown about economic relations, disconcertingly large levels of forecast error are commonly encountered when econometric models are employed.

    B.   Single Equation Models: Simple equations can be used for simple forecasting problems.

    C.   Multiple Equation Systems: A more complex method of forecasting whereby important interrelations among important variables are explicitly recognized in multiple equation systems.

V. Input-Output Analysis

    A.   Input-Output Tables: The input-output approach to forecasting uses historical tabular data on intersectoral output and material flows to predict demand and supply changes for individual industries. This method depends heavily on data provided by the Commerce Department's Office of Business Economics.

1. Advantages: An important advantage of the approach is that it explicitly recognizes the complex nature of demand and supply interrelations in the economy. Thus, short- and long-run multiplier ("ripple") effects can be accounted for.

2. Limitations: The most basic limitation to the input-output approach is cost. Development of accurate supplements to Commerce Department data is prohibitively expensive except for the largest companies. In addition, input-output analysis is a linear method of forecasting and thereby fails to incorporate important non-linear relations.

B. Forecasting with Input-Output Tables: Large data requirements and high computing costs often limit the usefulness of detailed input-output analysis.

VI. Judging Forecast Reliability

A. Correlation Analysis: The simple correlation between actual and forecast values provides an attractive index of forecast accuracy where:

$$r = \frac{\sigma_{fx}}{\sigma_f \sigma_x}$$

and r is the simple correlation coefficient, σ_{fx} is the covariance between the forecast and actual series, and σ_f and σ_x are the standard deviations of the forecast and actual series, respectively.

1. Generally speaking, when $r \geq 0.95$ or 0.99 (95 or 99 percent), a high level of forecast accuracy has been achieved in terms of predicting variation in an important series.

B. Mean Forecast Error Analysis: This index of forecast reliability, denoted by U, provides valuable insight regarding the absolute level of forecast accuracy where

$$U = \sqrt{\frac{1}{n} \sum_{i=1}^{n} (f_i - x_i)^2}$$

where n is the number of sample observations, f_i is a forecast value, and x_i is the corresponding actual value.

1. Generally speaking, when the mean or average forecast error is a small fraction, 0.05 or 0.01 (5 or 1 percent), of actual values, a high level of absolute forecast accuracy has been achieved.

PROBLEMS AND SOLUTIONS

5.1

The following figures constitute annual sales for Ray's Restaurant for the 1979-89 period.

t	Year	Sales	
0	1979	$284,000	— BASE YEAR
1	1980	266,000	
2	1981	287,000	$S_t = S_0(1+g)^t$
3	1982	315,000	
4	1983	353,000	$568 = 284(1+g)^{10}$
5	1984	384,000	
6	1985	427,000	$568/284 = (1+g)^{10}$
7	1986	462,000	
8	1987	520,000	$2.0 = (1+g)^{10}$
9	1988	575,000	
10	1989	568,000	

a. Calculate the rate of growth in sales for 1979-89 using the constant rate of change model with annual compounding. (Note: $t = 0$ in 1979).

b. Provide both 5-year and 10-year sales forecasts

5.1 SOLUTION

a.
$$S_t = S_0(1 + g)^t$$

$$\$568,000 = \$284,000(1 + g)^{10}$$

$$568,000/284,000 = (1 + g)^{10}$$

$$2 = (1 + g)^{10}$$

$$\ln 2 = 10 \cdot \ln(1 + g)$$

$$0.693/10 = \ln(1 + g)$$

$$e^{0.0693} = 1 + g$$

$$g = \underline{\underline{0.0718}} + \mu \text{ or } 7.18 + \mu \text{ percent}$$

b. <u>5-year Forecast</u>

$$S_t = S_0(1 + g)^t$$

$$= \$284{,}000(1 + 0.0718)^{15}$$

$$= 284{,}000(2.829)$$

$$= \underline{\underline{\$803{,}436}} + \mu$$

<u>10-year Forecast</u>

$$S_t = S_0(1 + g)^t$$

$$= \$284{,}000(1 + 0.0718)^{20}$$

$$= 284{,}000(4.002)$$

$$= \underline{\underline{\$1{,}136{,}568}} + \mu$$

5.2

The quantity demanded of Product A in any given week is inversely proportional to the sales of Product B in the previous week. That is, if sales of B rose by X percent last week, sales of A can be expected to fall by X percent this week.

a. Write the equation for next week's sales of A, using the symbols A = sales of Product A, B = sales of Product B, and t = time. Assume there will be no shortages of either product.

b. Two weeks ago, 200 units of Product A and 150 units of Product B were sold. Last week, 160 units of A and 180 units of B were sold. What would you predict sales of A to be this week?

c. What is the significance of the error term? What property must the error term have to allow use of regression results in forecasting?

5.2 SOLUTION

a. An equation for next week's sales of A is:

$$A_t = A_{t-1} + \Delta A_{t-1} + u$$

$$= A_{t-1} - \left(\frac{B_{t-1}}{B_{t-2}} - 1\right)A_{t-1} + u$$

b.   For A_t we find:

$$A_t = A_{t-1} - \left(\frac{B_{t-1}}{B_{t-2}} - 1\right)A_{t-1} + u$$

$$= 160 - \left(\frac{180}{150} - 1\right)160 + u$$

$$= \underline{\underline{128}} + u \text{ units}$$

c.   The error term represents the "margin of error" in forecasting. For forecasting to be viable, the average value of the error term must be zero or $E(u) = 0$.

5.3

The manager of Nick's Grocery has noticed over the past several months that sales of Toasties breakfast cereal have typically been close to 40 cases per week. Recently, however, sales declined to 20 cases per week. During this period, the store was running a special on Oaties which had reduced the box price from $2.50 to $2.

a.   What is the arc cross-price elasticity between Toasties and Oaties?

b.   What level of Toasties sales would you forecast if the regular price on Oaties were raised from $2.50 to $2.90?

5.3 SOLUTION

a. $E_{PX} = \dfrac{\Delta Q}{\Delta P_X} \times \dfrac{P_{X2} + P_{X1}}{Q_2 + Q_1} = \dfrac{(20 - 40)}{(2 - 2.50)} \times \dfrac{(2 + 2.50)}{(20 + 40)} = \underline{\underline{3}}$

b.

$$E_{PX} = \frac{\Delta Q}{\Delta P_X} \times \frac{P_{X2} + P_{X1}}{Q_2 + Q_1}$$

$$3 = \frac{Q_2 - 40}{(2.90 - 2.50)} \times \frac{2.90 + 2.50}{(Q_2 + 40)}$$

$$3(Q_2 + 40) = 13.5(Q_2 - 40)$$

83

$$3Q_2 + 120 = 13.5Q_2 - 540$$

$$10.5Q_2 = 660$$

$$Q_2 = \underline{\underline{62.9}} \text{ units}$$

(Note: The arc cross-price elasticity formula is used in this problem given the large percentage changes in price being considered).

5.4

To convince potential investors of the viability of your new store, Nite Life Fashions, Ltd., you would like to generate a sales forecast. Based on your assumption that next-period sales are a function of current-period local disposable income, own advertising, and advertising by a competing retailer:

a.   Specify a demand equation.

b.   Write an equation for predicting sales if you assume that the percentage growth (or decline) in sales is twice as large as the sum of the current period's percentage changes in local disposable income and own advertising, plus one-half of the current period's percentage change in competitor advertising.

c.   Forecast sales if during the current period sales total $300,000, local disposable income is $204 million, own advertising is $24,000, and competitor advertising is $66,000. Previous period levels were $200 million for disposable income, $30,000 for own advertising, and $60,000 for competitor advertising.

5.4 SOLUTION

a.   A demand equation can be written:

$$S_{t+1} = b_0 + b_1 Y_t + b_2 A_t - b_3 A_{Xt} + u$$

b. $S_{t+1} = S_t + \Delta S + u$

$$= S_t + 2\left(\frac{Y_t}{Y_{t-1}} - 1\right)S_t + 2\left(\frac{A_t}{A_{t-1}} - 1\right)S_t$$

$$- \frac{1}{2}\left(\frac{A_{Xt}}{A_{Xt-1}}\right)S_t + u$$

84

$$= S_t + 2S_t \left(\frac{Y_t}{Y_{t-1}}\right) - 2S_t + 2S_t \left(\frac{A_t}{A_{t-1}}\right) - 2S_t$$

$$-\frac{1}{2} S_t \left(\frac{A_{Xt}}{A_{Xt-1}}\right) + \frac{1}{2} S_t + u$$

$$= 2S_t \left(\frac{Y_t}{Y_{t-1}}\right) + 2S_t \left(\frac{A_t}{A_{t-1}}\right) - \frac{1}{2} \left(\frac{A_{Xt}}{A_{Xt-1}}\right)$$

$$- 2.5 S_t + u$$

c. Forecast sales are:

$$S_{t+1} = 2(\$300{,}000)(1.02) + 2(\$300{,}000)(0.80)$$

$$- \frac{1}{2} (\$300{,}000)(1.10) - 2.5(\$300{,}000) + u$$

$$= \underline{\underline{\$177{,}000}} + u$$

5.5
$S_{t+1} = S_t$

Joe Braun, operations manager at Armstrong & Boulger, Inc., believes that sales in the coming year are related to family disposable income during this year.

a. Write an equation for next year's sales, using the symbols S = sales, Y = income, t = time, a_0 = constant term, a_1 = regression slope coefficient, and u = random disturbance term.

b. Now assume that sales in the coming year increase by the same percentage as income increased during the past year. Write an equation for predicting next year's sales.

c. This year, sales totaled $500,000, while family disposable income increased from $25,000 to $26,500. Forecast next year's sales using your forecast equation from part b.

5.5 SOLUTION

a. A forecast equation for next year's sales is:

$$S_{t+1} = a_0 + a_1 Y_t + u$$

b. A forecast equation relating percent changes in sales and income is:

$$S_{t+1} = S_t + \Delta S + u$$

$$= S_t + \left(\frac{Y_t}{Y_{t-1}}\right)S_t + u$$

$$= \left(\frac{Y_t}{Y_{t-1}}\right)S_t + u$$

c.   Next year's sales are:

$$S_{t+1} = (\$26{,}500/\$25{,}000)\$500{,}000 + u$$

$$= \underline{\underline{\$530{,}000}} + u$$

5.6

Logican, Inc. is a regional provider of software and technical services to state governments and government contractors. The company has found that state-wide demand for its services tends to be closely related to levels of both state government spending and regional economic activity.

The company has collected the following data in order to forecast economic activity in an important northeastern market:

Last Year's Total Profits
(state corporations), P_{t-1} = $300

This Year's State Plus
Federal Government
Expenditures, G   = $500

Annual Consumption
Expenditures, C   = $60 + 0.7Y + u

Annual Investment
Expenditures, I   = $4 + 0.85$P_{t-1}$ + u

Annual state plus federal
Tax Receipts, T   = 0.25 SGNP

State Income, Y   = SGNP - T

State GNP, SGNP   = C + I + G

Assuming that all random disturbances average out to zero, forecast each of the above variables through the simultaneous relations

86

expressed in the multiple equation system. All dollar values are in millions of dollars.

5.6 SOLUTION

Investment

$$I = 4 + 0.85P_{t-1}$$
$$= 4 + 0.85(300)$$
$$= \underline{\$259} + u \text{ million}$$

State Gross National Product

$$SGNP = C + I + G$$
$$SGNP = 60 + 0.7(SGNP - T) + 259 + 500$$
$$SGNP = 60 + 0.7(SGNP - (0.25 \, SGNP)) + 259 + 500$$
$$SGNP = 60 + 0.525 \, SGNP + 259 + 500$$
$$0.475 \, SGNP = 819$$
$$SGNP = \underline{\$1,724} + u \text{ million}$$

Consumption

$$C = 60 + 0.7Y$$
$$= 60 + 0.7(SGNP-T)$$
$$= 60 + 0.7(SGNP - 0.25GNP)$$
$$= 60 + 0.525SGNP$$
$$= 60 + 0.525(1,724)$$
$$= \underline{\$965} + u \text{ million}$$

Taxes

$$T = 0.25SGNP$$
$$= 0.25(1,724)$$

$$= \underline{\underline{\$431}} + u \text{ million}$$

State Income

$$Y = GNP - T$$
$$= 1,724 - 431$$
$$= \underline{\underline{\$1,293}} + u \text{ million}$$

CHAPTER SIX: PRODUCTION

Theme

In Chapter Six, we return to the "supply side" of the firm's value maximization problem. Production theory is a necessary first step in this analysis because it considers important aspects of the relation between inputs and outputs. As such, it deals with two important and related concepts. First, production theory considers the returns to a factor. This is simply the output effect of small increases in a single input, holding all other inputs constant. And secondly, production theory considers returns to scale, which is the output effect of a small increase in all inputs. While returns to a factor diminish quite quickly in every known production system, returns to scale vary widely ranging from diminishing to constant to increasing. As will be seen in Chapters 9 and 10, the nature of returns to scale in an industry can have important implications for competition. And finally, since production inputs must be bought in generally competitive input markets, optimal input use requires that firms not only consider the physical productivity of inputs, but input and output prices as well. Profit maximization requires optimal input usage, and involves equating the marginal revenue product (marginal revenue) and input price (marginal cost) for each and every input employed by the firm.

Outline

I. Production Function

    A.   Definition: A production function specifies the maximum possible output that can be produced using a given combination of inputs; or alternatively, the minimum quantity of inputs necessary to produce a specified level of output. Production functions are determined by the technology and equipment available to firms, and the prices of resources employed.

    B.   Returns to Scale: The magnitude of a percentage change in output following a given percentage change in all inputs identifies returns to scale.

    C.   Returns to a Factor: The magnitude of a percentage change in output following a given percentage change in a single input identifies returns to that factor.

II. Total, Marginal and Average Product

    A.   Total Product: Total product is the quantity of output or product which results from employing a specific level of resources in a production system.

B. Marginal Product: Marginal product is the change in output caused by a unit change in a given input, holding all else constant:

$$MP_X = \frac{\Delta Q}{\Delta X} = \frac{\Delta Q}{\Delta X}$$

1. Relation to total product: MP_X is the slope of the total product curve. Total product will rise when $MP_X > 0$, and fall when $MP_X < 0$. When $MP_X = 0$, total product will be maximized.

2. Relation to average product: Average product will rise when $MP_X > AP_X$, and fall when $MP_X < AP_X$. When $MP_X = AP_X$, average product will be maximized.

C. Average Product: Average product is simply total product divided by the amount of input employed:

$$AP_X = \frac{Q}{X}$$

D. The Law of Diminishing Returns to a Factor: If a given variable factor input is increased while all other inputs are held constant, the marginal product of that factor (MP_X) will eventually diminish. This law is useful in defining rational and irrational stages of production.

III. Input Combination Choice

A. Production Isoquants: An isoquant is a curve that shows all possible input combinations which, when used efficiently, produce a specified constant quantity of output.

B. Substituting Input Factors: The shape of an isoquant indicates the degree of substitutability among input factors.

1. A straight line isoquant implies perfect substitutability.

2. Isoquants which are made up of two straight lines perpendicular to each other (L-shaped) imply complete non-substitutability.

3. C-shaped or curved isoquants imply that while substitutability is possible, it is limited.

C. Marginal Rate of Technical Substitution: The marginal rate of technical substitution ($MRTS_{XY}$) of factor inputs measures the amount of one input factor X which must be substituted for some other input factor Y in order to hold output constant.

1. Graphic Interpretation: $MRTS_{XY}$ is simply -1 times the slope of an isoquant drawn on a graph where X is on the horizontal axis and Y is on the vertical axis.

2. Algebraic Interpretation: The $MRTS_{XY}$ can be thought of as the marginal productivity of X relative to the marginal productivity of Y:

$$MRTS_{XY} = -\frac{MP_X}{MP_Y}$$

By substitution, we find that this ratio is equal to the slope of the production isoquant since:

$$MRTS_{XY} = -\frac{MP_X}{MP_Y}$$

$$= -\frac{\Delta Q/\Delta X}{\Delta Q/\Delta Y}$$

$$= -\frac{1/\Delta X}{1/\Delta Y}$$

$$= -\frac{\Delta Y}{\Delta X}$$

3. Ridge Lines: Ridge lines are constructed by connecting the points of tangency between isoquants and a set of lines drawn perpendicular to the X and Y axes. Interpretation: Limits to the range of substitutability for X and Y (or Y for X) are indicated by the tangencies between the isoquants and a set of lines drawn perpendicular to the Y axis (or X axis). By connecting these points, we construct ridge lines indicating the boundary for a rational firm's behavior. Outside the ridge lines, output can be increased by reducing the amount of the relatively more abundant factor employed (i.e., the marginal product of the relatively more abundant factor is negative). Hence, such input combinations should never be employed.

IV. The Role of Revenue and Cost in Production

A. Importance: Since inputs must be purchased in generally competitive input markets, determination of optimal input proportions requires a combination of information about production processes, input cost and output revenue data.

B. Marginal Revenue Product: Marginal Revenue Product (MRP) is the value of a marginal unit of a particular input factor when used in the production of a specific product.

1. In dollar terms: MRP_X is the amount by which firm revenues increase when X usage rises by one unit. Algebraically,

$$MRP_X = MP_X \times MR_Q$$

$$= \frac{\Delta Q}{\Delta X} \times \frac{\Delta TR}{\Delta Q}$$

$$= \frac{\Delta TR}{\Delta X}$$

where X is any single input and Q is output.

C. Optimal Level of a Single Input: The profit maximizing level of usage will be at the point where the marginal revenue product of the last input unit employed is equal to the input price. Algebraically,

$$\begin{matrix} \text{Marginal} \\ \text{Input Revenue} \end{matrix} = \begin{matrix} \text{Marginal} \\ \text{Input Cost} \end{matrix}$$

$$\frac{\Delta TR}{\Delta X} = \frac{\Delta TC}{\Delta X}$$

$$MRP_X = P_X$$

D. Optimal Combination of Multiple Inputs

1. Graphic solution: An isocost line, representing the various combinations of inputs that can be purchased for a given expenditure, is combined with the set of production isoquants to find an optimal employment level. The optimal solution occurs at the point of tangency between

the isocost line and a production isoquant. No other combination of inputs that can be purchased for a given expenditure will produce as much output.

2.   Algebraic solution: The above result can be demonstrated by algebraically equating the slopes of the isocost and isoquant curves. This reflects the economic principle that the least cost combination of inputs requires that the marginal product to price ratios be equal for all inputs, or:

$$\frac{MP_X}{P_X} = \frac{MP_Y}{P_Y}$$

D.   Optimal Levels of Multiple Inputs: Profits will be maximized when each input's price equals its marginal revenue product:

$$P_X = MP_X \times MR_Q = MRP_X$$

and

$$P_Y = MP_Y \times MR_Q = MRP_Y$$

V. Returns to Scale

A.   Definition: The returns to scale of a production system describes the increase in output resulting from a proportionate increase in all inputs.

B.   Possibilities:

1.   Increasing returns to scale: If the percentage increase in output is greater than the percentage increase in inputs, then increasing returns prevail.

2.   Constant returns to scale: If the percentage increase in output is precisely equal to the percentage increase in inputs, then constant returns prevail.

3.   Decreasing returns to scale: If the percentage increase in output is less than the percentage increase in inputs, then decreasing returns prevail.

C.   Graphic Interpretation: Returns to scale can be inferred from two input-one output graphs showing isoquants for various levels of input usage. If the distance between isoquants for successive output quantities is constant, then when output doubles input usage will also have doubled and constant returns to scale prevails. Similarly, if the distance between successive output

93

quantities diminishes (increases) then doubling output requires less (more) than a doubling of inputs, and increasing (diminishing) returns are indicated.

D. Output Elasticity and Returns to Scale: Output elasticity, ε_Q, is defined as the percentage change in output associated with a one percent increase in all inputs. As such, it is a useful approach to returns to scale estimation. By definition:

$$\varepsilon_Q = \frac{\Delta Q}{Q} \div \frac{\Delta X}{X} = \frac{\Delta Q}{\Delta X} \times \frac{X}{Q}$$

where $\underline{X}$ represents all inputs (capital, labor, etc.). Possibilities:

1. $\varepsilon_Q > 1$ implies increasing returns to scale.

2. $\varepsilon_Q = 1$ implies constant returns to scale.

3. $\varepsilon_Q < 1$ implies diminishing returns to scale.

VI. Empirical Production Functions

A. A cubic function is theoretically appealing for empirical estimation of production relations, since it can exhibit ranges of increasing, constant, and decreasing returns to scale.

B. Power Functions: The power function, while somewhat less general than the cubic, possesses a number of valuable characteristics for empirical production estimation and is probably the most popular structural form employed. Importantly, power functions permit the marginal productivity of individual inputs to vary depending upon the levels of other inputs used.

C. Selection of a Functional Form for Empirical Studies: As in demand estimation, estimation of production relations requires care so that misspecification bias can be minimized. This means that all relevant inputs and their interrelationships must be considered if accurate estimation is to be possible.

94

PROBLEMS AND SOLUTIONS

6.1

Determine whether the following production functions exhibit constant, increasing or decreasing returns to scale.

a. $Q = 0.6X + 20Y + 10Z$

b. $Q = 200 + 4L$

c. $Q = 20L + 16K + 10LK$

d. $Q = 2A^2 + 3AB + 5B^2$

e. $Q = 20L^{0.25} K^{0.70}$

f. $Q = \sqrt{3X^2 + 2Y^2 + 15Z^2}$

6.1 SOLUTION

a.   Returns to scale can be determined by evaluating the percentage increase in output which follows any given percentage increase in inputs. Answers to parts a, b and c reflect this approach. Alternatively, returns to scale can be evaluated using the more general algebraic approach of parts d, e and f. Both approaches work; use the one that is easiest for you.

If $X = Y = Z = 100$, then:

$$Q_1 = 0.6X + 20Y + 10Z$$

$$= 0.6(100) + 20(100) + 10(100)$$

$$= 3,060$$

Increasing each input by one percent yields:

$$Q_2 = 0.6(101) + 20(101) + 10(101)$$

$$= 3,090.6$$

which implies a one percent increase in output ($Q_2/Q_1 = 3,090.6/3,060 = 1.01$), and therefore, the function exhibits <u>constant</u> returns to scale.

b.   If L = 100, then:

$$Q_1 = 200 + 4L$$

$$= 200 + 4(100)$$

$$= 600$$

Increasing labor by two percent yields:

$$Q_2 = 200 + 4(102)$$

$$= 608$$

which implies a 1.3 percent increase in output (Q_2/Q_1 = 608/600 = 1.013, and therefore, the function exhibits <u>diminishing</u> returns to scale. (Note: Q = 200 even though L = 0 could be descriptive of an agricultural production function).

c.   If L = K = 100, then:

$$Q_1 = 20L + 16K + 10LK$$

$$= 20(100) + 16(100) + 10(100)(100)$$

$$= 103,600$$

Increasing each input by three percent yields:

$$Q_2 = 20(103) + 16(103) + 10(103)(103)$$

$$= 109,798$$

which implies a 5.98 percent increase in output (Q_2/Q_1 = 109,798/103,600 = 1.0598), and therefore, the function exhibits <u>increasing</u> returns to scale.

Alternatively, for a k proportionate increase in all inputs (where k > 1) we note:

$$Q = 20L + 16K + 10LK$$

$$hQ = 20(kL) + 16(kK) + 10(kL)(kK)$$

$$= k^1(20L + 16K + 10kLK)$$

$$= k^1(Q^*)$$

96

Here, returns to scale would be constant if $Q^* = Q$. However, since $k > 0$, we know that $Q^* > Q$. This implies that returns to scale for this production function are <u>increasing</u> (as before).

d. For a k proportionate increase in all inputs, we note:

$$Q = 2A^2 + 3AB + 5B^2$$

$$hQ = 2(kA)^2 + 3(kA)(kB) + 5(kB)^2$$

$$= k^2(2A^2 + 3AB + 5B^2)$$

$$= k^2Q$$

$$h = k^2$$

Therefore, $h > k$ and the production function demonstrates <u>increasing</u> returns to scale.

e. For a k proportionate increase in all inputs, we note:

$$Q = 20L^{0.25}K^{0.70}$$

$$hQ = 20(kL)^{0.25}(kK)^{0.70}$$

$$= k^{0.25 + 0.70}(20L^{0.25}K^{0.70})$$

$$= k^{0.95}Q$$

$$h = k^{0.95}$$

Since $h < k$, the production function exhibits <u>diminishing</u> returns to scale.

f. For a k proportionate increase in all inputs, we note:

$$Q = \sqrt{3X^2 + 2Y^2 + 15Z^2}$$

$$hQ = \sqrt{3(kX)^2 + 2(kY)^2 + 15(kZ)^2}$$

$$= \sqrt{k^2(3X^2 + 2Y^2 + 15Z^2)}$$

$$= k^1 \sqrt{3X^2 + 2Y^2 + 15Z^2}$$

$$= k^1 Q$$

$$h = k^1 1$$

Therefore, h = k and the production function demonstrates <u>constant</u> returns to scale.

6.2

Sigma Marketing's Order Processing Division has production and marginal product functions described by the relations:

$$Q = 0.4K^2 + 0.2KL + 0.3L^2$$

$$MP_K = 0.8K + 0.2L$$

$$MP_L = 0.2K + 0.6L$$

where Q is output in orders processed, K is capital in terms of the number of computer hours, and L is the number of labor hours employed.

Assume a weekly rate of use where K = 40 computer hours and L = 150 labor hours.

a.   What will be the total product per week?

b.   What will be the marginal products for computer hours and for labor hours when K = 40 and L = 150?

6.2 SOLUTION

a.
$$Q = 0.4K^2 + 0.2KL + 0.3L^2$$

$$= 0.4(40^2) + 0.2(40)(150) + 0.3(150^2)$$

$$= \underline{\underline{8,590}} \text{ orders processed}$$

b. $\dfrac{\text{Marginal product}}{\text{of computer time}} = MP_K = 0.8K + 0.2L$

$$= 0.8(40) + 0.2(150)$$

$$= \underline{\underline{62}} \text{ orders processed}$$

$$\text{Marginal product of labor} = MP_L = 0.2K + 0.6L$$

$$= 0.2(40) + 0.6(150)$$

$$= \underline{\underline{98}} \text{ orders processed}$$

6.3

Quickcuts, Inc. is a regional chain offering walk-in haircut services at popular prices. The company currently has two employee job classifications. Inexperienced haircutters (I) have six months or less job experience, and, on average, are able to cut a customer's hair in 20 minutes. Experienced haircutters (E), employees with more than six months experience, can provide one haircut in 15 minutes.

a. If inexperienced haircutters are readily available at a wage of $6 per hour, what is the maximum hourly wage that could be justified for experienced haircutters?

b. What would be your employment recommendation to the company if experienced haircutters can be readily employed at a wage of $7.50 per hour?

6.3 SOLUTION

a. The rule for optimal relative employment of inexperienced (I) and experienced (E) haircutters is:

$$\frac{MP_I}{P_I} = \frac{MP_E}{P_E} \text{ or } \frac{MP_I}{MP_E} = \frac{P_I}{P_E}$$

Since inexperienced haircutters can provide one haircut in 20 minutes, or 1/3 hour, their marginal product per hour is $MP_I = 3$. Similarly, since experienced haircutters can provide one haircut in 15 minutes, or 1/4 hour, their marginal product per hour is $MP_E = 4$. Therefore, given $P_I = \$6$ per hour, the maximum hourly wage that could be justified for experienced haircutters is:

$$\frac{MP_I}{P_I} = \frac{MP_E}{P_E}$$

$$\frac{3}{\$6} = \frac{4}{P_E}$$

$$P_E = \underline{\$8} \text{ per hour}$$

99

b. If experienced haircutters can be readily employed at a wage of $7.50 per hour, then relative to inexperienced haircutters, the experienced haircutters represent an employment bargain. Whereas the labor cost per haircut with inexperienced haircutters is $2(= P_I/MP_I)$, the labor cost per haircut with experienced haircutters is only $1.875(= P_E/MP_E)$. The superior productivity of experienced haircutters more than compensates for their higher wages. Quickcuts should employ relatively more experienced haircutters. Indeed, if the marginal productivity of each employment class is independent, experienced haircutters would be employed exclusively.

6.4

Staples Vegetable Farm is a moderate-sized Arizona carrot grower. Staples estimates that carrot output would increase by 600 bushels with an additional 1,000 gallons of water provided to its irrigation system. Alternatively, carrot output could be increased by 500 bushels with an additional 2 tons of lime fertilizer.

a. Estimate the marginal products of water and fertilizer.

b. What is the marginal rate of technical substitution between these inputs?

c. Assuming the cost of water is 6¢ per 1,000 gallons and the cost of fertilizer is $25 per ton, is Staples currently using an optimal combination of fertilizer and water?

6.4 SOLUTION

a.
$$\text{Marginal product of water} = MP_W = \frac{\Delta Q}{\Delta W}$$

$$= \frac{600}{1,000}$$

$$= \underline{\underline{0.6}} \text{ bushels per gallon}$$

$$\text{Marginal product of fertilizer} = MP_F = \frac{\Delta Q}{\Delta F}$$

$$= \frac{500}{2}$$

$$= \underline{\underline{250}} \text{ bushels per ton}$$

b. Marginal rate of technical substitution

$$\text{MRTS} = -\frac{MP_W}{MP_F} = -\frac{0.6}{250}$$

$$-\frac{\Delta Q/\Delta W}{\Delta Q/\Delta F} = -0.0024$$

$$-\frac{\Delta F}{\Delta W} = -0.0024$$

which implies:

$\Delta F = \underline{\underline{0.0024\ \Delta W}}$ or $\Delta W = \underline{\underline{416.6\ \Delta F}}$

c. <u>Yes</u>, Staples' current combination of water and fertilizer is optimal, since:

$$\frac{MP_W}{MP_F} = \frac{P_W}{P_F}$$

$$\frac{0.6}{250} \overset{?}{=} \frac{\$0.06}{\$25}$$

$$0.0024 \overset{\surd}{=} 0.0024$$

6.5

The production and marginal product function for the electronics assembly division of Omicron Electronics, Inc., can be written:

$$Q = L^{0.5}K^{0.5}$$

$$MP_L = 0.5L^{-0.5}K^{0.5}$$

$$MP_K = 0.5L^{0.5}K^{-0.5}$$

where Q is output, L is labor (in hours) and K is capital (in hours of equipment time).

a. Determine returns to scale for the above production function.

b. Determine returns to each factor.

6.5 SOLUTION

a. $$Q = L^{0.5}K^{0.5}$$

$$hQ = (kL)^{0.5}(kK)^{0.5}$$

$$= k^{0.5 + 0.5}(L^{0.75}K^{0.25})$$

$$= k^1Q$$

$$h = k^1$$

Therefore, $h = k$ and the above production function exhibits <u>constant</u> returns to scale.

b. Returns to each factor can be determined by looking at how each marginal product changes with increased input usage. For example, note the effect on each marginal product when usage rises from 100 to 144 units (a 44% increase):

<u>Returns to Labor:</u>

At $L = K = 100$: $MP_L = 0.5(100)^{-0.5}(100)^{0.5} = 0.50$

At $L = 144$, $K = 100$: $MP_L = 0.5(144)^{-0.5}(100)^{0.5} = 0.42$

Since $\Delta MP_L < 0$, <u>diminishing</u> returns to the labor factor is evident.

<u>Returns to Capital:</u>

At $L = K = 100$: $MP_K = 0.5(100)^{0.5}(100)^{-0.5} = 0.50$

At $L = 100$, $K = 144$: $MP_K = 0.5(144)^{0.5}(100)^{-0.5} = 0.42$

Since $\Delta MP_K < 0$, <u>diminishing</u> returns to the capital factor is evident. (Remember: $L^{-0.5} = 1/L^{0.5} = 1/\sqrt{L}$.)

6.6

Clini-Tec Laboratories offers a wide variety of clinical tests to private employers and government agencies. In order to better serve the rapidly growing demand for its testing services, a new lab technician was recently hired at a salary of $2,500 per month. This increased

Clini-Tec's monthly capacity from 60,000 to 62,000 tests. While Clini-Tec is pleased with this new employee's productivity, the company is reconsidering its employment policy in light of new testing equipment now available from a leading medical equipment manufacturer. The new C3PO-1 is capable of increasing current staff output by 4,000 tests per month, and can be obtained for a monthly lease rate of $5,000.

a. Does company usage reflect an optimal mix of labor technicians and capital equipment?

b. If each test provides a $1.50 net marginal revenue before labor and capital costs, would further expansion be advisable?

6.6 SOLUTION

a. The rule for an optimal mix of labor and capital is:

$$\frac{MP_L}{P_L} = \frac{MP_K}{P_K} \quad \text{or} \quad \frac{MP_L}{MP_K} = \frac{P_L}{P_K}$$

On a monthly basis, the relevant question is:

$$\frac{MP_L}{P_L} \overset{?}{=} \frac{MP_K}{P_K}$$

$$\frac{2,000}{\$2,500} \overset{?}{=} \frac{4,000}{\$5,000}$$

$$0.8 \overset{\surd}{=} 0.8$$

Therefore, the marginal effect on output of one dollar spent on either labor technicians or capital equipment is 0.8 tests. This indicates an optimal mix of labor and capital since output could not be increased by changing the relative usage of labor and capital.

b. Yes. Expansion would be profitable. The rule for an optimal level of input employment is:

$$MRP = MP \times MR_Q = \text{Input Price}$$

In this instance, for each input:

$$MRP_L = MP_L \times MR_Q \overset{?}{=} P_L \quad MRP_K = MP_K \times MR_Q \overset{?}{=} P_K$$

$$2,000 \times \$1.5 \overset{?}{=} \$2,500 \qquad 4,000 \times \$1.5 \overset{?}{=} \$5,000$$

$$\$3,000 > \$2,500 \qquad\qquad \$6,000 > \$5,000$$

In both cases, we see that inputs generate net marginal revenues in excess of marginal costs. As a result, expansion would be profitable.

6.7

The Big Northern Railway (BNR) is in the process of establishing a natural resources division to develop its vast coal holdings. A preliminary engineering analysis suggests the following production and marginal product functions:

$$Q = 300L^{0.5}K^{0.5}$$

$$MP_L = 150L^{-0.5}K^{0.5}$$

$$MP_K = 150L^{0.5}K^{-0.5}$$

where

Q = Coal output (in thousands of tons).

L = Labor (in hundreds of employees).

K = Capital (in hundreds of millions of dollars).

At peak production, the natural resources division is expected to employ 10,000 workers and require a $900 million capital investment. Coal output is to be sold in competitive markets at an expected price of $50 per ton.

a. Determine and interpret returns to scale.

b. What is the maximum annual salary the BNR would be willing to pay in order to attract a full labor force of 10,000 employees?

c. How many workers would the BNR willingly employ in light of union demands for a $25,000 annual salary?

(Note: Beware the units problem!)

6.7 SOLUTION

a. $Q = 300L^{0.5}K^{0.5}$

104

$$hQ = 300(kL)^{0.5}(kK)^{0.5}$$

$$= k^{0.5 + 0.5}(300L^{0.5}K^{0.5})$$

$$= k^1 Q$$

$$h = k^1$$

Therefore, $h = k$ and the above production exhibits <u>constant</u> returns to scale.

b. We consider the optimal employment rule, $P_i = MRP_i$, in order to determine the maximum annual salary the BNR would willingly pay 10,000 employees.

$$\frac{\text{Price}}{\text{of labor}} = \frac{\text{Marginal revenue}}{\text{product of labor}}$$

$$P_L = MP_L \times MR_Q$$

$$= (150L^{-0.5}K^{0.5})(\$50 \times 1,000)$$

$$= \frac{150K^{0.5}}{L^{0.5}} \times 50,000$$

$$= \frac{150(9^{0.5})}{100^{0.5}} \times 50,000$$

$$= \underline{\$2,250,000}\,\text{per hundred workers}$$
$$\text{or } \$22,500 \text{ per worker}$$

We must be careful that our numerical calculations reflect the fact that Q is in thousands of tons, L is in hundreds of employees, and K is in hundreds of millions of dollars of capital. For example, since coal sells for $50 per ton, the $MR_Q = \$50,000$ since Q is one thousand tons of coal. Similarly, the P_L derived above is for one hundred employees since the MP_L is also for one hundred employees. At first, making such unit adjustments may seem confusing. With practice, however, you will become able to deal with such difficulties and thereby be able to use studies compiled by subordinates, consultants, government agencies, etc.

c.   Again, we use the optimal employment rule:

$$\begin{matrix} \text{Price} \\ \text{of labor} \end{matrix} = \begin{matrix} \text{Marginal revenue} \\ \text{product of labor} \end{matrix}$$

$$P_L = MP_L \times MR_Q$$

$$\$25,000 \times 100 = (150L^{-0.5}K^{0.5})(\$50 \times 1,000)$$

$$2,500,000 = \frac{150K^{0.5}}{L^{0.5}} \times 50,000$$

$$2,500,000 = \frac{150(9^{0.5})}{L^{0.5}} \times 50,000$$

$$2,500,000 = \frac{22,500,000}{L^{0.5}}$$

$$L^{0.5} = \frac{22,500,000}{2,500,000}$$

$$L^{0.5} = 9$$

$$L = \underline{\underline{81}}(00) \text{ or } 8,100 \text{ workers}$$

Thus, at a wage of $25,000, the BNR would only be willing to employ 8,100 workers.

6.8

Data Analysis, Inc., has employed Cassi Hastings, a recent MBA graduate, to recommend a hiring policy for its soon to be opened office in West Lafayette, Indiana. Hastings has conducted a statistical study of operations at twelve similar-sized DAI offices in order to aid in her analysis. Her statistical study revealed (standard errors in parentheses):

$$\begin{aligned} \ln Q &= 0.50 \ln L + 0.25 \ln C + 0.25 \ln B \\ &\quad\ (0.13) \qquad (0.06) \qquad (0.11) \end{aligned}$$

$$R^2 = 0.87$$

Q = word processing output.

L = labor hours.

C = word processor time in hours.

B = office building space in hundreds of square feet.

These findings imply:

$$Q = L^{0.5}C^{0.25}B^{0.25}$$

$$MP_L = 0.5L^{-0.5}C^{0.25}B^{0.25}$$

$$MP_C = 0.25L^{0.5}C^{-0.75}B^{0.25}$$

$$MP_B = 0.25L^{0.5}C^{0.25}B^{-0.75}$$

a. Describe the economic logic underlying Hastings' choice of the above log-linear production relation as opposed to, say, a linear relation.

b. Determine the optimal relation between total expenditures for L and C.

c. Hastings projects computer costs of $60 per hour, and anticipates needing to pay $24,000 per year to attract and retain quality word processing personnel. If a total labor and computer time budget of $360,000 has been established for the West Lafayette office, and programmers work 2,000 hours per year, how many programmers should be hired and how much computer time should be purchased?

6.8 SOLUTION

a. Log-linear (and power) production relations deal effectively with cases where the marginal products of individual inputs depend upon the levels of other inputs employed. While many other functional forms (quadratic and cubic, for example) also enjoy this feature, log-linear forms are easy to estimate and results are easily interpreted.

b. The optimal combination rate for L and C is determined by the relation:

$$\frac{MP_L}{MP_C} = \frac{P_L}{P_C}$$

$$\frac{\partial Q/\partial L}{\partial Q/\partial C} = \frac{0.5L^{-0.5}C^{0.25}B^{0.25}}{0.25L^{0.5}C^{-0.75}B^{0.25}} = \frac{P_L}{P_C}$$

$$\frac{2C}{L} = \frac{P_L}{P_C}$$

which implies an optimal relation between total expenditures for L and C of:

$$2C \times P_C = P_L \times L$$

$$2 \times \frac{\text{Expenditures}}{\text{on computer}} = \frac{\text{Expenditures}}{\text{on labor}}$$

Thus, expenditures on labor will be twice the total level of expenditures on computer time. Alternatively, expenditures on computer time will be one-half expenditures on labor.

c. From part b, we know that:

$$\begin{array}{ccc} \text{Total} & \text{Labor} & \text{Computer} \\ \text{budget} = & \text{expenditures} + & \text{expenditures} \\ & \text{(two thirds)} & \text{(one third)} \end{array}$$

$$\$360,000 = \$240,000 + \$120,000$$

Given a salary of \$24,000 per employee and assuming 2,000 worker hours per year, a wage of \$24,000/2,000 = \$12 per hour is implied. We can determine the number of programmers to be hired as follows:

$$\text{Labor expenditures} = \$240,000$$

$$P_L \times L = 240,000$$

$$12 \times = 240,000$$

$$L = 20,000$$

If each programmer works 2,000 hours per year, then:

$$\frac{\text{New}}{\text{programmers}} = \frac{20,000}{2,000}$$

$$= \underline{\underline{10}} \text{ employees}$$

Similarly, the amount of computer time to be purchased is determined as:

$$\text{Computer time expenditures} = \$120,000$$

$$P_C \times C = 120,000$$

$$60 \times C = 120,000$$

$$C = \underline{\underline{2,000}} \text{ hours}$$

CHAPTER SEVEN: COST ANALYSIS

Theme

This chapter focuses on how costs and output are related on a theoretical level, as well as on the implications of these relations for managerial decisions. An important element in cost theory is the treatment of time. The short-run is an operating period during which at least one input (typically capital) is fixed in supply. On the other hand, the long-run is an operating period during which firms have complete input flexibility. It follows that day-to-day production and marketing decisions are made on the basis of short-run costs, while long-run costs form the basis for long-run planning decisions. Both short- and long-run cost relations can be understood more fully when integrated with revenue data in breakeven, degree of operating leverage, and cost-volume-profit analyses. In breakeven analysis, fixed and variable costs are compared with firm revenue data in order to identify the operating level(s) at which total costs are fully covered. Both degree of operating leverage and cost-volume-profit analyses provide important insight regarding the change in profits which can be expected following changes in sales or changes in other operating circumstances. Thus, an understanding of cost-output relations is essential in order for effective managerial decision making.

Outline

I. Relevant Cost Concept

    A. Definition: The cost figure that should be used in a specific application is defined as the relevant cost. Relevant costs are those which are affected by the decision. Costs which are invariant across the various decision alternatives are irrelevant and should not enter the analysis.

II. Opportunity Costs

    A. Definition: The current use of a given resource is usually only one of many possible uses. The foregone value of the best alternative use is called the opportunity cost of current resource employment.

III. Explicit and Implicit Costs

    A. Explicit Costs: Costs associated with cash outlays.

    B. Implicit Costs: Costs that do not involve cash outlays and arise from the alternative use or opportunity cost concept.

IV. Incremental and Sunk Costs in Decision Analysis

A. Incremental Costs: These are costs associated with any managerial decision. This concept is analogous to, but somewhat broader than, the marginal cost concept since multiple rather than unitary changes in output may be involved.

B. Sunk Costs: Sunk costs result from past rather than current managerial decisions. Sunk costs are unchanged by the current decision problem and, hence, are irrelevant for current decision making purposes.

V. Short-Run and Long-Run Costs

A. Cost Functions: A cost function is the functional relation between production costs and output. This relation is determined by:

1. Technology: the firm's production function.

2. Input Prices: where these prices are determined by market supply functions.

B. The Concept of Time: The short-run is the operating period during which at least one input (typically capital) is fixed in supply. The long-run is the operating period during which firms have complete input flexibility. Therefore, the degree of input flexibility determines whether specific costs are short- or long-run in nature.

C. Fixed and Variable Costs: The distinction between fixed and variable costs is very important in managerial economics:

1. Fixed Costs: Fixed costs are costs that don't vary with output. Since firms can liquidate in the long-run, there are no long-run fixed costs.

2. Variable Costs: Variable costs are costs that vary closely with output.

3. Semivariable Costs: Semivariable costs are costs that vary with output, but do so over ranges of output rather than with single units of output. Semivariable costs cover a substantial grey area between the fixed and variable cost categories.

VI. Short-Run Cost Curves

A. Total, Average, and Marginal Costs in the Short-Run:

1. Total Cost (TC) = Fixed Costs (TFC)
   + Total Variable Costs (TVC)

2. Average Fixed Cost (AFC) = TFC/Q

3. Average Variable Cost (AVC) = TVC/Q

4. Average Total Cost (ATC or AC) = TC/Q

5. Marginal Cost (MC) = $\Delta TC/\Delta Q$ = dTC/dQ

B. Important Short-Run Cost Relations:

1. The slope of the total cost curve is identical to the slope of the total variable cost curve. Fixed costs merely shift the total cost curve to a different level, which implies that marginal costs are independent of fixed costs.

2. Assuming constant input prices, the shape of the total variable cost curve is determined by the productivity of the variable input factors employed.

VII. Long-Run Cost Curves

A. Long-Run Total Costs: All long-run cost curves are based on the assumption that an optimal scale of plant is used to produce any given output level. If input prices are held constant, there is a direct relation between cost and production. That is, both long-run total cost functions and production functions provide identical information regarding returns to scale.

B. Returns to Scale: Returns to scale can be either increasing, constant or diminishing depending upon the relation between increases in long-run total costs and output. Though sometimes confusing, economists often use the term economies of scale as synonymous with increasing returns to scale.

C. Cost Elasticities and Returns to Scale: Cost elasticity, ε_C, measures the percentage change in total cost associated with a one percent change in output. By definition:

$$\varepsilon_C = \Delta C/C + \Delta Q/Q = \Delta C/\Delta Q \times Q/C$$

1. The relation between cost elasticity and returns to scale is straightforward:

112

If	Returns to scale are
$\varepsilon_C < 1$	Increasing
$\varepsilon_C = 1$	Constant
$\varepsilon_C > 1$	Decreasing

C.   Long-Run Average Costs: The long-run average cost curve is the envelope of the short-run average cost curves for various plant sizes. Given constant input prices and unchanging technology, there is a straightforward relation between long-run average costs and returns to scale.

If	Returns to scale are
LRAC are falling	Increasing
LRAC are constant	Constant
LRAC are rising	Decreasing

VIII. Minimum Efficient Scale

A.   Definition: The minimum efficient scale of plant is defined as that plant size at which long-run average costs are first minimized. MES is:

1.   The minimum point of a "U-shaped" LRAC curve.

2.   The "corner" point of an "L-shaped" LRAC curve.

B.   Transportation Costs and MES: When transportation costs are substantial, the productive efficiency of MES plant sizes can be overcome by the transport cost savings of regional, as opposed to centralized, production. In such instances, and when total production plus distribution costs are considered, firms of smaller than MES plant sizes can not only survive, but prosper.

IX. Firm Size and Plant Size

A.   Cost Relations: The cost function of a multiplant firm can be simply the sum of the cost functions of the individual plants, or it can exhibit economies or diseconomies of combined operation.

1.   Constant average costs for multiplant operations indicate that there are no economies or diseconomies in combining plants.

B. Plant Size and Flexibility: Plant size decisions are often made with an eye towards maintaining production flexibility over the course of the business cycle.

    2. If long-run average costs decline, multiplant firms are more efficient than single-plant operations.

    3. If average costs first decline and then rise, economies of scale for the multiplant firm dominate initially, but eventually diseconomies result.

B. Plant Size and Flexibility: In choosing a plant to produce a certain output, the firm should select the plant with the lowest expected average total cost over the range of possible output levels rather than the lowest potential average cost at one specific level of production.

X. Learning Curves

A. Definition: Learning curves illustrate the predictable decrease in average production costs which often accompanies greater learning or experience in production.

    1. Like any technical innovation, learning results in an inward (leftward) shift in the firm's LRAC curve.

B. Strategic Implications of the Learning Curve Concept: Early in the development of important industries featuring new products and/or new production techniques, learning curve advantages have allowed industry leaders to enhance their relative cost advantage over nonleading firms.

XI. Economies of Scope

A. Definition: Economies of scope exist when it is cheaper on a per unit basis to produce and/or deliver goods or services in tandem rather than individually.

    1. With scope economies, firms will sell multiple outputs (e.g., copier machines and service).

    2. Without scope economies, firms will specialize (e.g., gourmet ice cream shops).

XII. Cost-Volume-Profit Analysis

A. Definition: Cost-volume-profit (or breakeven) analysis is an analytic technique used to study the relations among costs, revenues, and profits. The object of the analysis is to discover the output quantity where total costs and various profit targets are fully realized.

B.   Linear Cost-Volume-Profit Analysis:

    1.   Construction of a linear cost-volume-profit chart: On a graph where the X axis represents the quantity of units sold and the Y axis is income and cost; fixed costs, total cost and total revenue are graphed. The point where total revenue equals total costs is the firm's breakeven output level.

C.   Algebraic Cost-Volume-Profit Analysis: The breakeven quantity is defined as:

$$Q = \frac{TFC}{P - AVC}$$

where TFC is total fixed costs, P is price per unit sold, and AVC is average variable costs.

D.   Cost-Volume-Profit Analysis and Operating Leverage: The degree of operating leverage is the percentage change in profit that results from a one percent change in units sold.

    1.   Degree of Operating Leverage: When price and variable costs per unit are constant, DOL can be calculated as:

$$DOL = \frac{Q(P - AVC)}{Q(P - AVC) - TFC}$$

where P, AVC and TFC are defined above.

    2.   Since profit contribution is defined as revenue minus total variable costs, DOL is the profit contribution to net profit ratio.

    3.   DOL can also be interpreted as the elasticity of profit with respect to output.

XIII. Limitations of Linear Cost-Volume-Profit Analysis:

A.   Linearity: Linear cost and revenue relations typically do not hold at all output levels.

B.   Narrowness: Since any given linear cost-volume-profit chart is based on a constant selling price, a whole series of charts is necessary in order to study profit possibilities under different prices.

C.   Usefulness: In the short-run, many of the firm's costs are fixed and, hence, invariant with respect to incremental sales and output decisions. Thus, cost-volume-profit analysis, a variant of the breakeven concept, provides a useful analytical tool.

PROBLEMS AND SOLUTIONS

7.1

Holding all else equal, describe the decline in average costs caused by each of the following as due to economies of scale, economies of scope, or learning curve advantages. Explain.

a. Increased worker specialization as output expands.

b. Growing levels of output per period.

c. Product line extension.

d. Better labor-management coordination over time.

e. Growing practical experience in production.

7.1 SOLUTION

a. <u>Economies of Scale</u>. Increased worker specialization as output expands is a prime cause of increasing returns to scale in production.

b. <u>Economies of Scale</u>. As output per period expands, increased worker specialization and other advantages of large size become operative. As in part a, this involves a downward movement along the average cost curve.

c. <u>Economies of Scope</u>. Product line extension allows a firm to extend to related products the special productive capabilities and marketing skills gained in the production and sale of a given product. The cost savings which result are due to economies of scope.

d. <u>Learning curve advantages</u>. Better labor-management coordination over time is an example of how greater experience in production can lead to substantial cost savings. Since such advantages are a function of time (cumulative output), they can be described as learning curve advantages.

e. <u>Learning curve advantages</u>. Growing practical experience in production is a prime source of learning curve advantages.

7.2

A year ago, your good friend, Paul Fox, quit a promising career in law in order to take over the daily operations of Foxy Printing, Inc. Fox purchased the assets of FPI for $80,000, and has devoted his full-time efforts toward turning the company around. FPI is no longer on the verge of bankruptcy (as it was a year ago), but appears to have reached its potential as a stable, though unspectacular, business.

Fox was a valued member of his law firm, and his former employer has been persistent in its efforts to get Fox to return. They have offered Fox a promotion from his old position to the rank of partner with a starting salary of $75,000 per year. Fox has asked your opinion as to whether or not it would be financially wise to do so, and has provided you with the following data on FPI.

Income Statement

Revenues		$235,000
Expenses:		
Materials	$80,000	
Labor	60,000	
Miscellaneous	10,000	150,000
		$ 85,000

Balance Sheet

Assets:		
Accounts Receivable	$20,000	
Net Plant & Equipment	62,000	
Land	20,000	$102,000
Liabilities:		
Accounts Payable	$10,000	
Note Payable	10,000	20,000
Net Book Value		$ 82,000

You make a few phone calls and find out that FPI's plant and equipment can be sold to a local printer for book value, while a local factor will purchase FPI's accounts receivable for 80 percent of face value. In addition, a local real estate firm has offered to buy FPI's land for twice its book value, less a normal 7 percent commission on the sale price. As an alternative to dissolving FPI, a client of the real estate firm is willing to offer $120,000 for the firm as an ongoing concern. In this case, the seller would pay the normal real estate commission.

a.   Determine the economic value before taxes of the dissolution sale versus sale as ongoing concern alternatives.

b.   If Fox sells FPI for more than his purchase price, he must pay a state plus federal capital gains tax of 30 percent on his profit. In

118

light of this fact, what rate of return on investment of the sale proceeds would make Fox financially indifferent to selling FPI and returning to his former employer, versus continuing to run FPI? (Note: Labor expenses itemized in the income statement do <u>not</u> include a salary for Fox.)

7.2 SOLUTION

a. The economic value of the dissolution sale versus sale as ongoing concern alternatives can be determined as follows:

<u>Dissolution Sale Proceeds</u>
Plant	$ 62,000
Accounts Receivable (0.8 × 20,000)	16,000
Land (0.93 × 40,000)	<u>37,200</u>
	115,200
Debts	<u>(20,000)</u>
	$ 95,200

<u>Ongoing Concern Sale Proceeds</u>
Offer (0.93 x 120,000)	$111,600

Thus, the sale as an ongoing concern dominates the dissolution sale alternative, and constitutes a measure of the economic value of the firm.

b. The before tax interest rate necessary for Fox to be indifferent between selling FPI and returning to his former employer, versus continuing to run FPI, is calculated by comparing FPI's current profits with its current asset value.

First, actual profits can be obtained by adjusting reported profits to reflect Fox's employment opportunity costs.

Reported profits	$85,000
Fox's employment opportunity cost	<u>(75,000)</u>
Adjusted business profits	$10,000

And second, FPI's current post capital gains tax economic value is:

Sale Proceeds	$111,600
Capital gains tax 0.3(111,600 - 80,000)	<u>(9,480)</u>
	$102,120

119

Therefore, FPI's effective current rate of return on realizable economic value is:

$$\frac{\$\ 10,000}{\$102,120} = \underline{0.098} \text{ or } 9.8 \text{ percent}$$

This means that Fox would be indifferent between the two alternatives of maintaining his investment in FPI versus returning to his former employer if investments with taxable returns and risks similar to FPI currently yield 9.8 percent. If they yield more, he would realize an economic gain from selling out.

7.3

Hartford Instruments manufactures a single precision measuring instrument, which it sells to other manufacturers who process it further for ultimate sale to research laboratories. The yearly volume of output is 5,000 units produced and sold. The selling price and cost per unit are shown below:

Selling Price		$250
Costs:		
Direct material	$40	
Direct labor	60	
Variable overhead	30	
Variable selling expenses	25	
Fixed selling expenses	20	175
Unit profit before tax		$ 75

Management is evaluating the alternative of performing the further processing necessary to allow Hartford to sell its entire output directly to university laboratories for $300 per unit. Although no added investment in productive facilities is required, there are additional costs for further processing. These costs are estimated as:

Direct labor	$20 per unit
Variable overhead	$5 per unit
Variable selling expenses	$2 per unit
Fixed selling expenses	$20,000 per year

Should Hartford process the product further?

7.3 SOLUTION

This problem deals with the preferable extent of processing for a product, and should be answered through incremental profit analysis. The analysis deals only with the incremental revenues and costs associated with the decision to engage in further processing.

Incremental revenue per unit ($300 - $250)	$50
Incremental variable cost per unit ($20 + $5 + $2)	<u>27</u>
Incremental profit contribution per unit	$23
Yearly output volume in units	<u>× 5,000</u>
Incremental variable profit per year	$115,000
Incremental fixed cost per year	<u>20,000</u>
Yearly incremental profit	$ 95,000

Since incremental profit is positive, the decision to engage in further processing would be preferable to continuing the present operating policy.

7.4

The Maritime Construction Company has successfully completed a $2 million flood plain control project for a local municipality. Ed Murphy, project manager, believes that the experience gained on the project will allow the company to now complete a similar job for $1.9 million.

a. In percentage terms, what is the learning or experience rate projected by Murphy? (<u>Hint</u>: Learning rates are expressed as a cost savings percentage).

b. Assuming Murphy's learning rate estimate is accurate, how would you explain actual costs of $1.95 million on a second project?

7.4 SOLUTION

a. In this problem, the learning rate projection is made using total costs since the project is the relevant scale of output.

$$\text{Learning rate} = (1 - \frac{\text{Cost}_2}{\text{Cost}_1}) \times 100$$

$$= (1 - \frac{\$1.9}{\$2.0}) \times 100$$

$$= \underline{\underline{5}} \text{ percent}$$

b.   If actual costs were $1.95 million, or $500,000 above the $1.9 million projection, then one of two possible explanations could be offered. A first possibility is that the second project may not have been as efficiently carried out. The same level of operating efficiency must be achieved in both periods if learning curve advantages are to be fully realized. Secondly, higher costs could be due to increases in wage or interest rates, higher material costs, poorer weather conditions, etc. Learning curve calculations are made based on the assumption that all else is held equal in terms of operating conditions.

7.5

Kirby Puckett, sales manager of Spectro Medical Supply Co., has informed the president that if the price of SMS's disposable syringe is reduced, sales and profits will both increase. Currently, sales are 100,000 units per month, variable costs are 40 percent of total revenue, allocated fixed costs are 50 percent of total revenue, with profits making up the remaining 10 percent. The current syringe price is $2. According to Puckett, a price reduction of 10 percent will result in profits one and one-half times what they are now. The firm has large amounts of excess capacity and, therefore, no increase in overhead is expected to accompany an increase in output. Unit variable costs are also expected to remain constant.

a.   How many units must be sold at the new price for the sales manager to be correct?

b.   What point price elasticity is implicit in the sales manager's forecast?

7.5 SOLUTION

a.   Currently,

$$TR = PQ = \$2(100,000) = \$200,000$$

$$\pi = 0.1(\$200,000) = \$20,000$$

$$TFC = 0.5(\$200,000) = \$100,000$$

$$TVC = 0.4(\$200,000) = \$80,000$$

$$AVC = \frac{TVC}{Q} = \frac{\$80,000}{100,000} = \$0.80$$

The projected profit is 150 percent of current profit, or:

$$\pi_P = 1.5(\$20,000)$$

$$= \$30,000$$

The new price is 90 percent of the current price, therefore:

$$P_P = 0.9(\$2)$$

$$= \$1.80$$

The unit profit contribution of the product is price minus variable cost, thus:

$$\pi_C = \$1.80 - \$0.80$$

$$= \$1$$

Dividing fixed costs plus the projected profit by the unit profit contribution determines the projected sales quantity:

$$Q_P = \frac{TFC + \pi_P}{\pi_C}$$

$$= \frac{\$100,000 + \$30,000}{\$1}$$

$$= \underline{\underline{130,000}} \text{ units}$$

b. Following a price decline from $2 to $1.80, the quantity purchased is projected to increase from 100,000 to 130,000. Therefore, the sales manager is projecting:

$$\varepsilon_P = dQ/dP \times P/Q$$

$$= \frac{130,000 - 100,000}{\$1.80 - \$2} \times \frac{\$2}{100,000}$$

$$= \underline{-3} \text{ (Elastic)}$$

7.6

Management of the Cola King Bottling Company, a small regional producer operating in the Pacific Northwest, is considering two alternative expansion proposals:

1. Construct a single bottling plant in Phoenix, Arizona with a capacity of 40,000 cases per month, at a monthly fixed cost of $20,000 and a variable cost of $2.50 per case.

2. Construct 3 plants, 1 each in Phoenix, Arizona; Las Vegas, Nevada; and Albuquerque, New Mexico, with capacities of 15,000, 14,000 and 13,000 respectively; and monthly fixed costs of $11,000, $10,000 and $9,000 each. Variable costs would be only $2.30 per case due to lower distribution costs, but sales from each plant would be limited to demand within the home state. The total estimated monthly sales volume in the southwestern states, 37,000 cases, is distributed as: Arizona, 15,000 cases; Nevada, 14,000 cases; and New Mexico, 8,000 cases.

   a. Using a wholesale price of $4 per case in each state, calculate the breakeven output quantities for each alternative.

   b. Which alternative expansion scheme should Cola King follow?

   c. If sales increase to production capacities, which alternative would prove to be more profitable?

7.6 SOLUTION

a. Single-plant alternative

$$Q = \frac{TFC}{P - AVC}$$

$$= \frac{\$20,000}{\$4 - \$2.50}$$

$$= \frac{20,000}{1.5}$$

$$= \underline{\underline{13,333.33}} \text{ cases}$$

Multiple-plant alternative

$$\text{Phoenix: } Q = \frac{\$11,000}{\$4 - \$2.30}$$

124

$$= \frac{11,000}{1.70}$$

$$= 6,471 \text{ cases}$$

$$\text{Las Vegas: Q} = \frac{\$10,000}{\$1.70}$$

$$= 5,882 \text{ cases}$$

$$\text{Albuquerque: Q} = \frac{\$9,000}{\$1.70}$$

$$= 5,294 \text{ cases}$$

Thus, the breakeven quantity for the multiple-plant option would be:

$$6,471 + 5,882 + 5,294 = \underline{17,647} \text{ cases}$$

Of course, this assumes that the demand is distributed among the states in amounts equal to the breakeven quantities for the individual plants.

b. <u>Single-plant alternative</u>

$$\pi = \text{TR - TC}$$

$$= \text{PQ - TFC - AVC(Q)}$$

$$= \$4(37,000) - \$20,000 - \$2.50(37,000)$$

$$= \underline{\$35,500}$$

<u>Multiple-plant alternative</u>

$$\pi = \text{TR - TC}$$

$$= \text{PQ - TFC - AVC(Q)}$$

$$= \$4(37,000) - \$30,000 - \$2.30(37,000)$$

$$= \underline{\$32,900}$$

Management should elect the single-plant alternative because of the larger profit.

125

c.   <u>Single-plant at full capacity</u>

$$\pi = TR - TC$$

$$= PQ - TFC - AVC(Q)$$

$$= \$4(40,000) - \$20,000 - \$2.50(40,000)$$

$$= \$40,000$$

<u>Multiple-plant at full capacity</u>

	<u>PQ</u>	-	<u>TFC</u>	-	<u>AVC(Q)</u>	=	<u>Profit</u>

Phoenix
Plant $4(15,000) - $11,000 - $2.30(15,000) = $14,500

Las Vegas
Plant $4(14,000) - $10,000 - $2.30(14,000) = 13,800

Albuquerque
Plant $4(13,000) - $9,000 - $2.30(13,000) = 13,100

$$\pi = \$41,400$$

In this case, management should select the multiple-plant alternative because of its larger profit potential.

7.7

Atlas Fasteners, Inc. is currently producing and selling 40,000 units of output. Unfortunately, plant capacity is also 40,000 units and potential orders are being turned down. As a result, the company is considering expanding capacity to 50,000 units. Atlas' product sells for $6 per unit, and management expects to maintain that price if capacity is expanded. Currently, output has a variable cost of $2 per unit and fixed costs are $80,000. Expansion of capacity to 50,000 units will increase fixed costs by 50 percent to $120,000, but variable costs per unit will decline by 40 percent to $1.20.

a.   What is the firm's current breakeven output level?

b.   What is the firm's current degree of operating leverage at 40,000 units?

c.   Considered by itself (that is, assuming that variable cost per unit remains at $2), would the increase in fixed costs associated with

126

expansion increase, decrease, or leave unchanged the degree of operating leverage at 40,000 units?

d. Considered by itself (that is, assuming that fixed costs remain at $80,000), would the decrease in variable costs associated with expansion increase or leave unchanged the degree of operating leverage at 40,000 units?

e. What is the importance of analyzing operating leverage in a decision problem such as this one?

7.7 SOLUTION

a. The breakeven quantity is:

$$Q = \frac{TFC}{P - AVC} = \frac{\$80,000}{\$6 - \$2} = \underline{20,000} \text{ units}$$

b. From the degree of operating leverage formula, we find:

$$DOL = \frac{Q(P - AVC)}{Q(P - AVC) - TFC}$$

$$= \frac{40,000(6 - 2)}{40,000(\$6 - \$2) - 80,000}$$

$$= \underline{\underline{2}}$$

c. Increase. Since,

$$DOL = \frac{Q(P - AVC)}{Q(P - AVC) - TFC}$$

If TFC increases while Q, P and AVC remain constant, then the positive net profit denominator of $80,000 will fall and DOL will increase.

d. Decrease. If AVC decreases while holding Q, P and TFC constant, then both the profit contribution numerator and net profit denominator will rise by the same dollar amount. However, the relative increase in the denominator will be larger and DOL will decrease.

e. The study of operating leverage is important for operating and planning purposes. For example, the level of operating leverage can have an important effect on changes in operating profits, especially when projected changes in output are substantial. Remember:

$$DOL = \frac{\% \Delta \pi}{\% \Delta Q}$$

$$\% \Delta \pi = DOL \times \% \Delta Q$$

If we expect that the $\% \Delta Q$ over the next couple of years will be positive, then we would want the highest DOL possible, thus achieving the highest $\% \Delta \pi$. Unfortunately, we seldom know for certain that changes in output will be positive. A severe recession, for example, can cause output to fall. If this were the case and DOL were high, then we would also experience a large negative change in operating profits. Since the expected change in output has an element of uncertainty attached to it in the real world, the desired level for DOL will depend on the risk attitude of the managers and owners of the firm. By changing fixed and variable costs, we can change the level of DOL to the desired level.

7.8

Better Motor Works (BMW) recently converted an unused assembly plant in Pennsylvania to produce BMW's, adding to the number of foreign-owned auto makers building cars in the U.S. BMW analyses indicate that variable production costs may be described by the function:

$$TVC = \$3,500Q + \$10Q^2$$

Where TVC = total variable costs in thousands of dollars, and Q = output in thousands of cars. While low-priced (\$8,000 average) American-produced BMW's have been enthusiastically accepted by American buyers, BMW is currently well below the industry's theoretical threshold volume.

a. Calculate the breakeven level of yearly output for BMW, assuming that fixed costs are \$500 million.

7.8 SOLUTION

a. From the breakeven formula, we find:

$$Q = \frac{TFC}{P - AVC}$$

$$Q = \frac{\$500,000}{\$8,000 - \left(\frac{\$3,500Q + \$10Q^2}{Q} \right)}$$

128

$$(8,000 - 3,500 - 10Q)(Q) = 500,000$$

$$-10Q^2 + 4,500Q - 500,000 = 0$$

This is a quadratic equation in the form:

$$aQ^2 + bQ + c = 0$$

where a = -10, b = 4,500 and c = -500,000. Its two roots can be obtained from the quadratic formula:

$$Q = \frac{-b \pm \sqrt{b^2 - 4ac}}{2a}$$

$$= \frac{-4,500 \pm \sqrt{4,500^2 - 4(-10)(-500,000)}}{2(-10)}$$

$$= \frac{-4,500 \pm 500}{-20}$$

$$= \underline{\underline{200}}(000) \text{ or } \underline{\underline{250}}(000)$$

Thus, there are dual breakeven points of 200,000 and 250,000 cars.

Here again, a unit's problem may be encountered if one isn't careful in the solution to this problem. All dollar and output values must reflect the fact that TVC is in thousands of dollars and Q is in thousands of cars. Here, a P = $8,000 per car becomes $8,000,000 per unit of Q when expressed in dollars, and $8,000 per unit of Q when expressed in thousands of dollars. Thus, P = $8,000 is the breakeven formula.

129

Theme

This appendix considers important aspects of both short- and long-run cost analyses. Some combination of statistical, accounting and engineering methods is typically employed in attempting to accurately estimate cost-output relations. A number of conceptual and practical data-related problems are often encountered in this estimation process. Among these problems, perhaps identifying the effect on variable cost of changes in output and inflation pose the most serious challenges to managerial economists. Given sufficient reliable cost and output data, perhaps 30 to 40 observations, statistical analyses of nonlinear or even linear models can provide significant insight concerning short- and long-run cost relations. Changes in input prices and technology must be minor, or be appropriately controlled for. An important advantage to the statistical approach lies in its ability to provide data regarding expected costs and the variability of these estimates (standard errors). If the statistical approach isn't feasible, accounting and engineering methods of cost estimation can be profitably employed. Each approach attempts to reconstruct "typical" working conditions in order to project a likely cost-output relation. In most instances, no method has a clear-cut advantage over its alternatives. Thus, accurate cost estimation usually requires using that combination of methods which best fits the individual situation.

Outline

I.   Short-Run Cost Estimation

   A.   Cost Specification and Data Preparation: Most difficulties in cost estimation relate to model specification errors, or to data-related problems. Some specific problems are:

   1.   Conceptual Problems: Relevant costs for decision making are future, not historical, costs. Estimating future costs is made difficult by the fact that the accounting data from which costs are often estimated ignores implicit opportunity costs.

   2.   Cost/Output Matching: In many instances, distinguishing the variable component of total costs is very difficult since some costs vary closely with output (variable costs), while other costs vary with blocks of output (semivariable costs).

   3.   Timing of Costs: In some instances, leads and lags in cost reporting cause a misallocation of costs across reporting periods. Of course, correct cost allocation is the important objective of accrual accounting.

4. Inflation: Since cost estimation is forward-looking, cost estimates embody implicit forecasts of future input price levels. Such forecasting is made difficult by the fact that input prices are affected by supply and demand conditions beyond control of the firm.

5. Observation Period Problems: A consistent definition of inputs and outputs must be maintained if short- or long-run cost analysis is to be possible. This is sometimes quite difficult when operating experience over fairly long time periods is analyzed.

B. Statistical Short-Run Cost Functions: Common forms for short-run cost analysis include:

1. Linear Short-Run Cost Functions: For small changes in output, linear cost functions can provide a good fit of cost/output data. In short-run cost functions the intercept coefficient b_O is typically irrelevant, while the slope coefficient b_1 is an estimate of average variable costs per unit.

2. Quadratic and Cubic Cost Functions: Both quadratic functions (with squared or second power terms) and cubic functions (with cubed or third power terms) can be used to estimate costs when linear functions prove inadequate.

3. Empirically Estimated Short-Run Cost Functions: Studies indicate that most short-run cost functions can be adequately described by linear functions. Typically, empirical studies confirm L-shaped short-run average costs curve rather than U-shaped curves.

II. Long-Run Statistical Cost Estimation

A. Costs to be Estimated: Since all costs are variable in the long-run, the total cost curve must be estimated in long-run analysis. Here, the intercept coefficient can provide an estimate of fixed costs, while the slope coefficient(s) provides an estimate of variable costs per unit. Estimation methods include:

1. Time Series Regression: Here, one firm is examined over a long period of time. However, the applicability of this approach is limited by the difficulty of finding a situation where the scale of the firm has been variable enough to allow statistical estimation of a long-run cost curve while, at the same time, technology and all other factors have remained constant.

2. Cross-Sectional Regression: This involves a cost analysis of different size firms and output levels at one point in time.

    a. Advantages: The problem of price inflation is removed.

    b. Disadvantages:

        1. Since factor prices can vary among regions, unless all firms in the sample are located in the same area, price differences may distort the analysis.

        2. Variations in accounting procedures or means of factor payment among firms may distort the true cost/output relation.

        3. The problem of changing technology is not necessarily avoided since firms may be of varying vintages and therefore have equipment of different ages.

B. Empirical Long-Run Cost Functions: The majority of empirically estimated long-run cost functions exhibit sharply increasing returns to scale at low output levels, but the extent of these scale economies declines as output increases, and constant returns appear to hold at higher output levels.

C. Alternative Long-Run Cost Estimation Techniques: In light of the problems encountered in long-run statistical cost estimation, alternative cost estimation techniques have been developed. Among these alternatives are:

    1. Survivor Technique: Here it is assumed that relatively more efficient firms, those with lower average costs, will survive through time. Therefore, by examining the size makeup of an industry over time, one can determine the nature of its cost-output relation.

        a. Limitations:

            (i) The survivor technique assumes that survival is directly related to minimization of long-run average costs, which implicitly assumes that firms are operating in a very competitive market. This may or may not be true.

       (ii)   It does not indicate the relative inefficiency of greater than or less MES operations.

       (iii)   Because of the very long-run nature of the analysis, the survivor technique is particularly vulnerable to distortions that may result from changing technology.

2.   Engineering Technique: This technique is directly based on the physical relation expressed in the production function of a firm. The cost curve is formulated by multiplying each input in the least-cost combination (for a given output) by its price, and then summing.

    a.   Advantages:

       (i)   Since it is based on currently available technology, it alleviates the possibility of confounding results through improper data observations.

       (ii)   It better reflects the timeless nature of the theoretical cost function.

    b.   Limitations: The reliability of the engineering technique often breaks down when the results are extended beyond the range of existing systems, or from pilot plant operations to full-size production facilities.

III. Estimating Nursing Costs: An Illustrative Cost Estimation Problem

PROBLEMS AND SOLUTIONS

7A.1

Industrial Coatings, Inc. is a leading producer of varnishes, lacquers, enamels, wood fillers and coil coatings. A recent study of weekly total variable cost for its enamel production facility over the last six months (26 observations) revealed the following:

$$\text{Cost} = \$100,000 + \$6Q + 0.0005Q^2$$
$$(50,000) \quad (1.5) \quad (0.0002)$$

$$R^2 = 0.90$$

$$\text{S.E.E.} = 10,000$$

where Q is gallons of enamel, and standard errors are in parentheses.

Explain the relation between enamel production and cost as depicted by this equation. Be specific.

7A.1   SOLUTION

On an overall basis, we note:

i)   Coefficient of determination = $R^2 = 0.9$, implying that 90 percent of total variable cost variation is explained by the quadratic cost model.

ii)   Standard error of the estimate = S.E.E. = 10,000, implying:

$C = \hat{C} \pm 2(10,000)$ with 95 percent confidence.

$C = \hat{C} \pm 3(10,000)$ with 99 percent confidence.

On a more specific basis, we note that $100,000 is not an estimate of fixed costs per week since the analysis included only variable costs. T-statistics for each output variable can also be calculated to test:

$$H_0: b_1 = 0, \text{ and } H_0: b_2 = 0.$$

For b_1: $t = \left| \frac{6}{1.5} \right| = 4 > 3$, thus implying significance with 99% confidence.

134

For b_2: $t = \left| \dfrac{0.0005}{0.0002} \right| = 2.5 > 2$, thus implying significance with 95% confidence.

Furthermore,

Total
Variable Cost = TVC = $100,000 + \$6Q + \$0.0005Q^2$

Average
Variable Costs = AVC = $\dfrac{100,000}{Q} + \$6 + \$0.0005Q$

Thus, we can see that average variable costs will first fall, then rise as output expands. Since average fixed costs always decline as output expands, average total costs for ICI will be "U-shaped".

7A.2

Redi-Serve, Inc. supplies temporary office personnel to industrial and retail clients. A recent study by the accounting department estimates annual administrative and selling costs per business client as:

$$TC = \$30,000 + \$50Q + \$3Q^2$$

$$MC = \$50 + \$6Q$$

where TC is total cost ($), MC is marginal cost ($), and Q is the number of Redi-Serve business clients. Currently, the company provides its services to 80 clients.

a.   Calculate the level of fixed administrative and selling costs per year.

b.   Calculate average administrative and selling costs at Q = 80.

c.   Calculate the output level at which these average costs would be minimized.

7A.2   SOLUTION

a.   The intercept term for the quadratic total cost function above is $30,000. This indicates total fixed costs for administration and selling of $30,000.

b.   Average total cost at Q = 80 are:

$$AC = TC/Q$$

$$= \frac{(\$30,000 + \$50Q + \$3Q^2)}{Q}$$

$$= \frac{30,000}{Q} + 50 + 3Q$$

$$= \frac{30,000}{80} + 50 + 3(80)$$

$$= 375 + 50 + 240$$

$$= \underline{\$665}$$

c. Set MC = AC to determine the AC minimizing output level:

$$MC = AC$$

$$\$50 + \$6Q = \frac{\$30,000}{Q} + \$50 + \$3Q$$

$$3Q = \frac{30,000}{Q}$$

$$Q^2 = 10,000$$

$$Q = \underline{100}$$

(Note: Since AC is rising for Q > 100, Q = 100 is a point of minimum average costs.)

7A.3

The Weedbeater Manufacturing Company markets a line of lawn trimmers. Sales for next year have been forecast at 400,000 units. The standard wholesale price for the trimmer is $46 when sold through independent distributors, and $43 when sold directly to large discount chains. Variable costs associated with the manufacture of the trimmer are:

	Unit Cost Estimate
Direct labor	$25
Raw materials	10
Marketing	3
Warranty	2
	$40

136

a.   Calculate expected total variable costs for 400,000 units.

b.   Assuming that this total variable cost estimate is accurate, what is
the minimum share of total sales that must be made to
independent distributors if a profit contribution target of $1.5
million is to be realized?

7A.3   **SOLUTION**

a.   Calculation of expected total variable costs is:

$$TVC = (C_L + C_{RM} + C_M + C_W)Q$$

$$= (\$25 + \$10 + \$3 + \$2)400,000$$

$$= \underline{\$16,000,000}$$

b.   The minimum share of total sales which must be made to
independent distributors, α, is calculated as follows:

$$\text{Profit Contribution} = \text{Total Revenue} - \text{Total Variable Costs}$$

$$\$1,500,000 = (\$46)(400,000)(\alpha) + (\$43)(400,000)(1 - \alpha) - \$16,000,000$$

$$17,500,000 = 18,400,000\alpha + 17,200,000(1 - \alpha)$$

$$17,500,000 = 18,400,000\alpha + 17,200,000 - 17,200,000\alpha$$

$$300,000 = 1,200,000\alpha$$

$$\alpha = \underline{0.25} \text{ or } 25 \text{ percent}$$

CHAPTER EIGHT: LINEAR PROGRAMMING

Theme

Linear programming is a powerful analytical tool which can be used to solve a broad range of managerial problems. The technique has two highly positive attributes. First, it allows managers to find an optimal problem solution when several operating constraints are in effect. And second, it can be applied when constraints may or may not be binding such as, for example, when resources can be less than fully employed. Both of these features of the linear programming approach are valuable because they reflect actual conditions under which managerial decisions are typically made. A further important advantage of the approach is its generality. Being highly general, linear programming is equally adaptable to problems involving maximization (output, revenue, profits, etc.) or minimization (costs, etc.). In addition, both algebraic and graphic methods can be used to arrive at solution values, as well as aid in their interpretation. Of course, solution of complex linear programming problems requires the aid of electronic computers. Today, user-friendly LP software is widely available for use on personal computers and mainframes alike. The algebraic and graphic techniques described in the chapter will help in the set-up and interpretation of solution values for such programs, and provide an intuitive understanding of the LP method.

Outline

I.   Basic Assumptions

A.   Assumption of Linearity: As its name implies, linear programming is a tool designed to deal with optimization problems involving linear relations. To be applicable in managerial economics, the decision problems addressed must involve:

1.   Constant output prices.

2.   Constant input prices.

3.   Constant returns to scale in production.

Together, these requirements will result in linear objective (output, revenue, cost or profit) functions and constraint conditions.

B.   Relation of Linear Programming to the Lagrangian Technique:

1.   Similarities: Like the Lagrangian technique, linear programming is a powerful method of analysis which is useful in a broad range of constrained optimization prob-

lems. The approach is equally applicable for problems involving maximization or minimization objectives.

2.   Dissimilarities: Unlike the Lagrangian technique, linear programming requires linear objective functions and constraint conditions. It also allows for inequality constraints, i.e., excess capacity.

II. Linear Programming and Production Planning: One Product (Cost Minimization Example)

A.   Production Processes: If it is assumed that a firm's production system exhibits constant returns to scale and that the two inputs employed (L and K) can be combined in only a limited number of combinations, these production combinations (processes) can be represented as linear rays in an LK plane. Given that each production process exhibits constant returns to scale, one can determine output quantities by measuring the length of the ray in question. Be sure to note that equal distances along different process rays do not necessarily imply equal output quantities.

B.   Production Isoquants: Joining points of equal output on the production rays produces a set of isoquant curves composed of linear segments which represent all possible combinations of L and K that can be used to produce a given quantity of output.

C.   Isocost Lines: An isocost line shows all L and K combinations which will result in a given level of total costs where $TC = P_L \times L + P_K \times K$, and P_L and P_K are prices for L and K, respectively. Since isocost lines are linear, they can be easily drawn by simply connecting their two endpoints. These endpoints can be found by dividing a given level of total cost by each input price, i.e., TC/P_L and TC/P_K. Alternatively, we can simply express the budget constraint in the equivalent linear form $L = (TC/P_L) - (P_K/P_L)K$ where the intercept is (TC/P_L), and the slope is $-(P_K/P_L)$.

D.   Least Cost Input Combinations: Adding an isocost curve to a set of isoquants permits one to determine a point of tangency between them. This tangency point indicates the least cost method of producing output.

E.   Optimal Input Combinations with Limited Resources: Frequently, managers are faced with production decisions in which there are resource limitations that constrain the options available. Adding such resource constraints to a production process ray diagram delineates a feasible space for the problem solution and can assist a decision maker in choosing among various production alternatives.

III. **Linear Programming and Production Planning: Multiple Products (Profit Maximization Example)**

A. Specification of the Objective Function: Assuming a two product production problem for a firm attempting to maximize profits, the objective function can be expressed as:

$$\text{Maximize } \pi = \begin{array}{c}\text{Per unit}\\\text{profit}\\\text{contribution}\\\text{of product X}\end{array} \times Q_X + \begin{array}{c}\text{Per unit}\\\text{profit}\\\text{contribution}\\\text{of product Y}\end{array} \times Q_Y$$

B. Specification of the Constraint Equations: For each resource, a constraint equation is expressed as:

$$\begin{array}{c}\text{Quantity}\\\text{of resource}\\\text{used}\\\text{in producing}\\\text{one unit}\\\text{of X}\end{array} \times Q_X + \begin{array}{c}\text{Quantity}\\\text{of resource}\\\text{used}\\\text{in producing}\\\text{one unit}\\\text{of Y}\end{array} \times Q_Y \leq \begin{array}{c}\text{Amount of}\\\text{resource}\\\text{available}\\\text{for use in}\\\text{production}\\\text{of X}\\\text{and Y}\end{array}$$

C. Non-Negativity Requirement: In order to prevent economically irrelevant results, all variables in a linear programming problem are constrained to non-negative values.

IV. **Graphic Specification and Solution of the Linear Programming Problem (Profit Maximization Example Continued)**

A. Determining the Feasible Space: Constraint equations are graphed in the first quadrant to identify the feasible space of the program.

B. Graphing the Objective Function: The objective function is graphed as a set of isoprofit curves, each illustrating all possible combinations of output X and output Y that result in a constant amount of profit. (See isocost line discussion, II. C., for graphing technique.)

C. Graphic Solution of the Linear Programming Problem: When a set of isoprofit curves is superimposed on the feasible space determined by the constraints, the optimal solution is the point of tangency between a corner of the feasible space and the highest possible isoprofit line.

140

1. Reasons that the optimal solution is always at a corner of the feasible space:

    a. Given the linearity assumption, the feasible space must always be a convex figure and the objective function will be maximized or minimized by moving as far through it as possible to a point where one or more constraints are binding, which is by definition a boundary of the feasible space.

    b. Even when the highest obtainable isoprofit curve lies along a boundary face of the feasible space, either corner at the end of the line segment provides an optimal solution to the problem.

2. Implications of corner solutions: We can ignore the infinite number of points lying within the feasible space and concentrate on analyzing only the corner points when attempting to solve a linear programming problem.

V. Algebraic Specification and Solution of the Linear Programming Problem (Profit Maximization Example Continued)

A. Rationale: Algebraic methods can be combined effectively with graphic methods to find solutions for linear programming problems that are too complex to be solved simply through graphic analysis.

B. Slack Variables: Slack variables represent excess (unused) input capacity at optimal solution points. By introducing slack variables into constraint equations these equations become equalities rather than inequalities (i.e., $\leq$ or $\geq$).

    1. Slack variables whose value is zero at the optimal solution represent inputs that are limiting factors in production.

    2. Slack variables with positive values at the optimal solution provide measures of excess capacity in the related factor.

C. Algebraic Solution: For solution of any linear program, or any system of equations, the number of constraint equations ("known relations") must be at least as large as the number of unknown variables. This is seldom true for linear programs with slack variables. This problem can be resolved, however, by knowledge that at the corners of the feasible space, enough of the slack variables take on zero values so that the number of

141

unknown variables is equal to the number of constraint equations. Algebraic analysis can then be used to solve for remaining unknown variable values.

1. From graphic analysis, we know:

   a. The optimal output occurs at a corner point.

   b. At each corner point, the number of non-zero variables is equal to the number of constraint equations. Hence, solution values for all variables can be obtained algebraically at each corner point.

2. Given a determinate system of equations for each corner point, the corner solution that produces the maximum profit is the constrained profit maximizing output combination.

D. Slack Variables at the Solution Point: At each corner solution, the values of slack variables have a ready interpretation.

   1. When a given constraint is binding, its associated slack variable equals zero.

   2. When a given constraint is not binding, its associated slack variable exceeds zero.

E. Complex Linear Programming Problems: While the graphic and combined algebraic-graphic methods of linear program solutions are highly useful, they are limited in application to quite simple examples. Linear programming problems with very large numbers of variables and constraints can be readily solved using electronic computers.

VI. Constrained Cost Minimization: An Additional Linear Programming Example

A. Motivation: Constrained cost minimization problems are frequently encountered in managerial decision making, and while the principles for solving such a linear programming problem are identical to those found in the product mix problem examined above, it is useful to work through such a problem to gain facility in using the technique.

B. The Problem Statement: The cost minimization problem is set up and solved in precisely the same fashion as the product mix problem.

142

PROBLEMS AND SOLUTIONS

8.1

Production of a product Q requires use of two inputs X and Y. Furthermore, these inputs must be combined in a fixed ratio with each unit of Q requiring 5 units of X and 9 units of Y.

a. What combination of X and Y would be used to produce 4 units of Q?

b. Assume that a firm has 26 units of X and 27 units of Y available. How much Q can be produced?

c. Determine the marginal products of X and Y in part b.

d. Are input prices irrelevant to the calculation of optimal input proportions in this problem?

8.1 SOLUTION

a. Since inputs must be combined in the ratio 5X to 9Y for each unit produced, production of 4 units of Q requires:

$$Q \times \frac{X}{Q} = 4(5) = \underline{\underline{20}} \text{ units of X}$$

$$Q \times \frac{Y}{Q} = 4(9) = \underline{\underline{36}} \text{ units of Y}$$

b. With 26 units of X, 5.2 units of Q could be produced before X is exhausted since:

$$Q = \frac{X}{X/Q}$$

$$= \frac{26}{5}$$

$$= 5.2$$

With 27 units of Y, 3 units of Q could be produced before Y is exhausted since:

$$Q = \frac{Y}{Y/Q}$$

$$= \frac{27}{9}$$

Clearly, Y will be exhausted before X, and Y is the scarce resource since it limits production to only 3 units of Q. Thus, with 26 units of X and 27 units of Y available, 3 units of Q will be produced, and:

X Utilized	X Surplus	Y Utilized	Y Surplus
$X = Q(X/Q)$ $= 3(5)$ $= 15$	$26 - 15 = 9$	$Y = Q(Y/Q)$ $= 3(9)$ $= 27$	$27 - 27 = 0$

c. Since Q requires inputs in the required ratio 5X to 9Y,

$$Q = (1/5)X \quad \text{When X is scarce}$$

$$Q = (1/9)Y \quad \text{When Y is scarce}$$

This implies

Input	Marginal Product	When
X	$MP_X = 1/5$	X is scarce $(X < (5/9)Y)$
X	$MP_X = 0$	X is redundant (Surplus) $(X \geq (5/9)Y)$
Y	$MP_Y = 1/9$	Y is scarce $(Y < (9/5)X)$
Y	$MP_Y = 0$	Y is redundant (Surplus) $(Y \geq (9/5)X)$

Since X is redundant in part b, the $MP_X = 0$. Additional X will just add to excess capacity. Since Y is scarce in part b, the $MP_Y = 1/9$. An additional unit of Y would increase Q by 1/9.

d. Yes. When inputs must be combined in some fixed ratio, say 5X to 9Y, input prices are irrelevant to the calculation of optimal input proportions because there is no substitutability between inputs.

144

8.2

Biogenetics, Inc., can produce a new high-yield crop culture, product X, using any of three possible production processes. In order to produce one unit of X, the following combinations of laboratory and greenhouse hours are required.

Process	Laboratory Hours	Greenhouse Hours
1	4	1
2	3	2
3	2	4

The selling price for X is well-established at $P_X = \$40$. Furthermore, Biogenetics pays a variable rental fee of $6 per laboratory hour and $5 per greenhouse hour. Using the following notation:

X = the number of units of output

X_1 = the number of units of X produced by process 1

X_2 = the number of units of X produced by process 2

X_3 = the number of units of X produced by process 3

P_X = fixed selling price per unit of X

VC_1 = variable cost per unit of X_1

VC_2 = variable cost per unit of X_2

VC_3 = variable cost per unit of X_3

a. Draw the Biogenetic's process rays on a laboratory hours-greenhouse hours graph.

b. On the above graph, draw isoquants for production levels of 10, 15, and 20.

c. Draw an isocost curve and visually determine what the least cost production process would be for any given output level.

d. On a new graph, draw the process rays. Allow for a laboratory constraint of 120 hours and a greenhouse constraint of 80 hours.

e. On the graph constructed in part d, draw some isoprofit curves and determine the level of maximum profits, given the laboratory and greenhouse constraints. (This can be done graphically and/or algebraically.)

8.2 SOLUTION

a,b.   See Biogenetics graph (1).

c.   In order to draw the relevant isocost line, we note:

$$\text{Total Cost} = \$6(\text{Laboratory hours}) + \$5(\text{Greenhouse hours})$$

$$= 6L + 5G$$

$$6L = TC - 5G$$

$$L = 1/6\, TC - 5/6\, G$$

Isocost lines are parallel to each other; extending the isocost curves out to any isoquant would indicate (visually) that process 2 would be the least cost process.

d,e.   See Biogenetics graph (2).

Profit for process 1,

$$\pi_1 = P_X X_1 - VC_1(X_1)$$

$$= P_X X_1 - (\$6(L) + \$5(G))(X_1)$$

Since P_X and the costs of laboratory and greenhouse hours are fixed, unit profit will also be fixed. With process 1, unit profit will be \$11. That is, if $X_1 = 1$:

$$\pi_1 = \$40 - (\$6(4) + \$5(1))(1)$$

$$= 40 - 29$$

$$= \$11$$

For example, a profit level of \$100 involves: $X_1 = 9.09$, $L_1 = 36.36$, and $G_1 = 9.09$.

Profit for process 2,

$$\pi_2 = \$40 X_2 - (\$6(L) + \$5(G)) X_2$$

per unit profit will be \$12. That is, if $X_2 = 1$,

146

$$\pi_2 = \$40 - (\$6(3) + \$5(2))(1)$$

$$= 40 - 28$$

$$= \$12$$

For example, a profit level of \$100 involves: $X_2 = 8.33$, $L_2 = 24.99$, and $G_2 = 16.66$.

Profit for process 3,

$$\pi_3 = \$40X_3 - (\$6(L) - \$5(G))X_3$$

per unit profit will be \$8. That is, if $X_3 = 1$,

$$\pi_3 = \$40 - (\$6(2) + \$5(4))(1)$$

$$= 40 - 32$$

$$= \$8$$

For example, a profit level of \$100 involves: $X_3 = 12.5$, $L_3 = 25$, and $G_3 = 50$.

According to the isoprofit curve $\pi = \$100$, process 2 is the most profitable. The laboratory and greenhouse constraints also intersect process 2, so it appears that we can maximize profits by using only that process. Furthermore, both constraints will be binding.

Process 2 uses 3L and 2G for each output, so:

$$3X_2 \leq 120$$

$$2X_2 \leq 80$$

Since both constraints are binding, we can use the equality form:

$$
\begin{array}{rl}
(1) & 3X_2 = 120 \\
-(2) & \underline{2X_2 = 80} \\
& X_2 = \underline{\underline{40}}
\end{array}
$$

At $X_2 = 40$, $L_2 = \underline{\underline{120}}$, $G_2 = \underline{\underline{80}}$, and:

147

$$\pi_2 = P_X X_2 - 6L_2 - 5G_2$$

$$= \$40(40) - \$6(120) - \$5(80)$$

$$= 1,600 - 720 - 400$$

$$= \underline{\underline{\$480}}$$

For comparison purposes, it is interesting to note that $\pi = \$480$ would involve:

Using Process 1:

$X_1 = 43.63, L_1 = 174.52, G_1 = 43.63$.
(Note: See point X).

Using process 3:

$X_3 = 60, L_3 = 120, G_3 = 240$. (Note: See point Z).

However, only point Y on the Process 2 ray is feasible given the greenhouse and laboratory constraints. Points X and Z, which would also give the firm $480 in profits, are not feasible since they lie outside the feasible region.

(Note: Part of the isoprofit curve $\pi_0 = \$480$ (Curve XYZ) is superimposed on the laboratory constraint line from points Y to Z.)

8.2
Biogenetics graph (1).

LABORATORY
HOURS, L

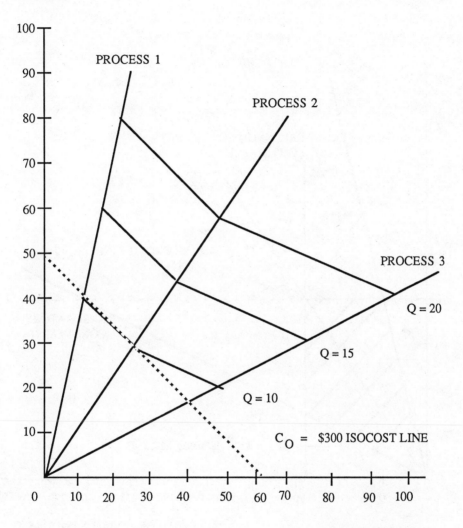

GREENHOUSE HOURS, G

149

8.2

Biogenetics graph (2).

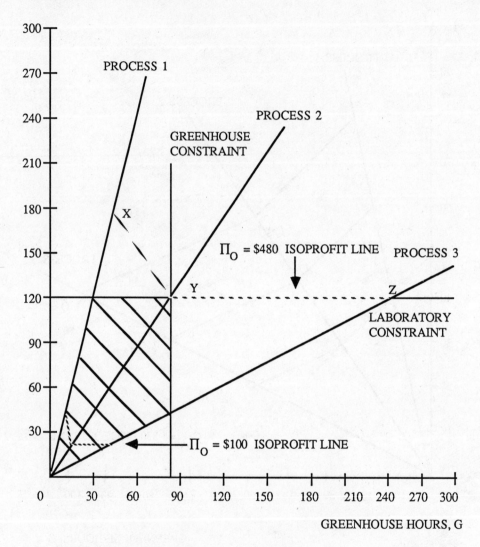

150

8.3

The Investors' Balanced Fund is an open-end investment company (mutual fund) designed to meet the needs of investors planning for future retirement. IBF seeks to provide current income plus capital growth by investing in a diversified portfolio of high-quality stocks and investment-grade bonds. The fund's bylaws state that at least 25 percent of the portfolio must be invested in bonds in order to reduce downside risk during bear markets. The fund's growth potential is maintained by a requirement that the share of the portfolio invested in common stocks must be at least as large as the share devoted to bonds. Like most mutual funds, IBF is prohibited from using leverage (borrowing) to enhance investor returns. Without leverage, stock and bond investments cannot exceed 100 percent of IBF's portfolio. And finally, the fund's investment management committee currently projects an expected return of 10 percent on stocks and 8 percent on bonds.

a. Set up and interpret the linear programming problem IBF would use to determine the optimal portfolio percentage holdings in stocks (S) and bonds (B). Use both the inequality and equality forms of the constraint conditions.

b. Use a graph to determine the optimal solution, and check your answer algebraically. Interpret the solution.

c. Holding all else equal, how much would the expected return on bonds have to rise before the optimal investment policy determined in part a would change?

d. What is the maximum share of the portfolio that could be converted into cash if management projects a downturn in both stock and bond prices?

8.3 SOLUTION

a. In this problem, the goal is to maximize expected return, R, subject to the various stock, bond and leverage constraints. The relevant linear programming problem is:

Maximize: $R = 0.1S + 0.08B$

Subject to: $B \geq 0.25$

$S - B \geq 0$ (or $S \geq B$)

$S + B \leq 1$

or, in equality form:

$$(1) \quad B - L_B = 0.25 \quad \text{(Bond constraint)}$$

$$(2) \quad S - B - L_S = 0 \quad \text{(Stock constraint)}$$

$$(3) \quad S + B + L_L = 1 \quad \text{(Leverage constraint)}$$

$$S, B, L_S, L_B, L_L \geq 0$$

Here, R is expected return, S is the portfolio share in common stocks, B is the portfolio share in bonds. L_S, L_B, and L_L are slack variables, representing excess stock investments, excess bond investments, and "slack leverage" or cash holdings, respectively.

b. From the graph, we see that the bond investment (1) and leverage (3) constraints are binding and, therefore, that $L_B = L_L = 0$ at point X. Thus,

$$(1) \quad B - 0 = 0.25$$

$$(2) \quad S - B - L_S = 0$$

$$(3) \quad S + B + 0 = 1$$

From (1),

$$(1) \quad B + 0 = 0.25$$

$$B = \underline{\underline{0.25}}$$

From (3),

$$(3) \quad S + 0.25 + 0 = 1$$

$$S = \underline{\underline{0.75}}$$

From (2),

$$(2) \quad 0.75 - 0.25 - L_S = 0$$

$$L_S = \underline{\underline{0.5}}$$

And the expected return is:

$$R = 0.1S + 0.08B$$

$$= \quad 0.1(0.75) + 0.08(0.25)$$

$$= \quad \underline{0.095} \text{ or } 9.5 \text{ percent}$$

Solution values can be interpreted as follows:

S = 0.75   The optimal portfolio percentage in stocks is 75 percent.

B = 0.25   The optimal share of the portfolio in bonds is 25 percent.

$L_B = 0$ At optimum, IBF is holding the minimum percentage of bonds.

$L_S = 0.5$ At optimum, IBF is holding a 50 percent greater share of its portfolio in stocks than the minimum required in light of its bond holdings.

$L_L = 0$ At optimum, IBF is not employing leverage, and the fund is fully invested (holds no cash).

R = 0.095   Maximum expected return given constraints.

c.   The isoreturn line $S = (R_O/R_S) - (R_B/R_S)B$, where R_O is any return level, and R_S and R_B are returns on stocks and bonds, respectively. The isoreturn line in this problem has a slope equal to $-(R_B/R_S) = -(0.08/0.1) = -0.8$. Holding all else equal, this slope will become more negative as the return on bonds rises (or return on stocks falls). Similarly, this slope will move closer to zero as the return on bonds falls (or return on stocks rises).

Holding all else equal, if R_B falls to slightly less than 10 percent, the optimal feasible point will shift from point X(0.25B, 0.75S) to point Z(0.5B, 0.5S), since the isoreturn line slope will then be steeper than -1, the slope of the leverage constraint, S = 1 - B. Thus, a rise from 8 to more than 10 percent, or <u>at least 2 percent</u>, is necessary before the optimal solution derived above would change.

d.   The bond investment constraint requires that a minimum of 25 percent of the overall portfolio be invested in bonds. From the stock constraint, we know that stock investments must be at least as large as bond investments. Therefore, a minimum 50 percent of the overall portfolio must be invested in stocks (25 percent) plus bonds (25 percent), and the maximum share of the portfolio which could be converted into cash is <u>50 percent</u> (point Y on the graph.)

8.3

Investors' Balanced Fund graph.

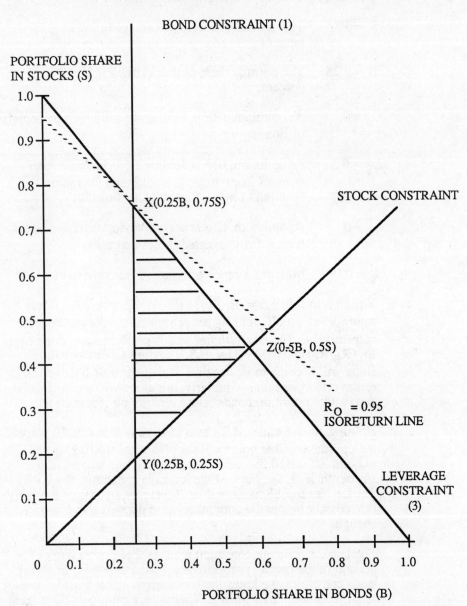

154

The Michigan Boat Company manufactures two models of boats--an 8-foot jet ski, model X, and a 12-foot family sailboat, model Y. The market for both models is competitive, so Michigan can sell all the boats it can produce at the going prices of $6,000 for the jet ski and $8,000 for the sailboat. Since variable costs are $3,300 per unit for the jet ski and $4,400 for the sailboat, the profit contributions are $2,700 and $3,600, respectively.

Fractional inputs and outputs are permissible and are carried over to the next monthly production period. All inputs included as variable costs are available in unlimited quantities at constant prices, and the firm's production process provides constant returns to scale. However, three resources, the power engine assembly shop, the dry dock, and the boat assembly shop are limited. The number of boat-unit-hours of each of these resources, together with the requirements for each model, is given in the table below.

	Boat-unit-hours available per month	Hours Required per Boat	
		Jet ski X	Sailboat Y
Boat assembly (A)	9,600	600	1,200
Dry dock (D)	3,000	300	300
Engine shop (E)	6,300	900	0

a. Set up and interpret the linear programming problem Michigan would use to determine the company's optimal output mix. You can use a graph to help set up the model, but solve it algebraically for the values at the optimal corner as determined by the graph. Use the equality form of the constraint conditions.

b. If dry-dock capacity is increased by 20 percent, would the output of sailboats increase or decrease? (Note: This can be seen easily from the graph.)

8.4 SOLUTION

a. The problem requires that we find the profit maximizing output combination. Thus, the primal linear programming problem using the equality form of the constraint conditions is:

Maximize: $\pi = \$2,700X + \$3,600Y$

Subject to:

(1) $600X + 1,200Y + S_A = 9,600$ (Assembly constraint)

(2) $300X + 300Y + S_D = 3,000$ (Dry dock constraint)

(3) $900X + 0Y + S_E = 6,300$ (Engine shop constraint)

$$X, Y, S_A, S_D, S_E \geq 0$$

Here, X and Y represent jet ski and sailboat output, respectively. S_A, S_D and S_E represent excess capacity of assembly, dry dock, and engine shop resources, respectively. The total monthly profit contribution is represented by π.

To determine the optimal combination of X and Y, we graph the constraints and objective function for the linear programming problem. As shown below, the shaded region represents the feasible space. To learn which constraints are binding at the optimal solution, we graph the isoprofit line:

$$\pi = \$2,700X + \$3,600Y$$

$$3,600Y = \pi - 2,700X$$

$$Y = (\pi/3,600) - (2,700/3,600)Y$$

which has a slope = $-2,700/3,600 = -0.75$. Graphing succeeding isoprofit lines, we find the optimal solution occurs at the point Z where constraints (1) and (2) are binding. Thus, $S_A = S_D = 0$.

Then, adding (1) plus negative 2 times (2):

$$(1) \quad 600X + 1,200Y = 9,600$$

$$+ (-2) \times (2) \quad \underline{-600X - 600Y = -6,000}$$
$$600Y = 3,600$$

$$Y = \underline{6} \text{ sailboats}$$

And substituting Y = 6 into (1) yields:

$$(1) \quad 600X + 1,200(6) = 9,600$$

$$600X = 2,400$$

156

$$X = \underline{\underline{4}} \text{ jet skis}$$

And finally, from the objective function we find:

$$\pi = \$2,700X + \$3,600Y$$

$$= 2,700(4) + 3,600(6)$$

$$= \underline{\underline{\$32,400}}$$

Therefore, Michigan's maximum monthly profit contribution is $32,400

b.   Referring back to the graph, we can see that if dry dock capacity were increased, this would amount to a parallel shift of constraint (2) upwards and to the right. The appropriate corner solution would shift down along the boat assembly constraint (1), which would become the binding constraint, until constraint (3) became binding. This would mean a _reduction_ of sailboats and an increase in jet skis as Michigan took advantage of its unused engine shop capacity.

Michigan Boat Company graph.

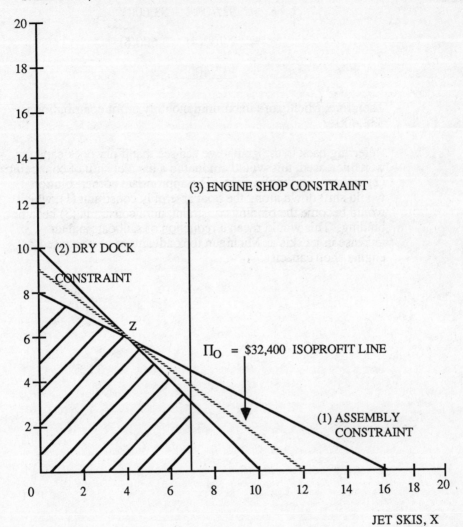

8.5

Mathew's Arms Company is a specialized producer of small firearms (shotguns) for use by sportsmen in small game hunting as well as target (skeet) competition. Currently, two shotgun models are produced. The hunting, H, model retails for $1,000, while the target, T, model retails for $1,200. Both are offered to consumers by retailers at a 100 percent markup on their cost from MAC. MAC's variable production costs are $350 for the H model, and $500 for the T model.

Each model uses scarce woodworking, W, and metalworking, M, capacity. The H model requires 2 hours each of woodworking and metalworking, while the T model requires only 1 hour of woodworking but 5 hours of metalworking. In addition, each T model requires 2 hours of hand finishing, F. MAC currently has a monthly capacity of 1,000 hours for woodworking, 1,500 hours for metalworking, and 500 hours for hand finishing.

a. Set up the linear programming problem that MAC might use to determine optimal output levels for the H and T models in light of an operating philosophy of profit maximization. Be sure to completely interpret the program, and use the equality form of the constraint conditions.

b. Solve and completely interpret the solution values.

c. How would the optimal output levels determined above differ if MAC had an operating philosophy of sales rather than profit maximization? Explain.

8.5 SOLUTION

a. Prior to specifying the linear programming problem, we must calculate MAC's profit contribution from the H and T models. These values are:

$$\begin{array}{l} \text{H Unit Profit} \\ \text{Contribution} \end{array} = \pi_H = 0.5(1,000) - 350 = \$150$$

$$\begin{array}{l} \text{T Unit Profit} \\ \text{Contribution} \end{array} = \pi_T = 0.5(1,200) - 500 = \$100$$

Using the equality form of the constraint conditions, the relevant linear programming problem can then be written:

Maximize $\pi^* = \$150H + \$100T$

Subject to:

$$(1)\ 2H + 1T + S_W = 1,000 \qquad \text{(Woodworking}$$

159

constraint)

$$(2)\ 2H + 5T + S_M\ =\ 1,500 \qquad \text{(Metalworking constraint)}$$

$$(3)\ 0H + 2T + S_F\ =\ 500 \qquad \text{(Hand finishing constraint)}$$

$$H, T, S_W, S_M, S_F\ \geq\ 0$$

Here, H and T represent output of each model of shotgun. S_W, S_M and S_F represent excess capacity of woodworking, metalworking, and hand finishing inputs, respectively.

b.   To learn which constraints are binding at the optimal solution we graph the isoprofit line:

$$\pi\ =\ \$150H + \$100T$$

$$150H\ =\ \pi - 100T$$

$$H\ =\ (\pi/150) - (100/150)T$$

which has a slope = -100/150 = -0.67. Graphing succeeding isoprofit lines, we find the optimal solution occurs at the point X where constraints (1) and (2) are binding and $S_W = S_M = 0$.

Taking (1) minus (2):

$$(1)\ 2H + 1T\ =\ 1,000$$

$$- (2)\ \underline{2H + 5T\ =\ 1,500}$$
$$-4T\ =\ -500$$

$$T\ =\ \underline{\underline{125}}$$

Substituting T = 125 into (1):

$$(1)\quad 2H + 1(125)\ =\ 1,000$$

$$2H\ =\ 875$$

$$H\ =\ \underline{\underline{437.5}}$$

Substituting T = 125 into (3) yields:

160

$$(3) \quad 2(125) + S_F = 500$$

$$S_F = \underline{\underline{250}}$$

And finally, solving the objective function:

$$\pi = \$150H + \$100T$$

$$= 150(437.5) + 100(125)$$

$$= \underline{\underline{\$78,125}}$$

Summarizing from above, and an interpretation of solution values reads:

Solution	Interpretation
H = 437.5	437.5 hunting models will be produced.
T = 125	125 target models will be produced.
$S_W = 0$	No excess woodworking capacity.
$S_M = 0$	No excess metalworking capacity.
$S_F = 250$	250 hours of excess hand finishing capacity available.
$\pi = \$78,125$	Maximum profit given input constraints.

c. <u>No</u>. In this problem, output levels would remain the same with an operating strategy of revenue or profit maximization. This is easily seen if one considers the revenue function:

$$R = \$500H + \$600T$$

or

$$H = (R/500) - (600/500)T$$

This function has a slope = -600/500 = -1.2 which is somewhat "steeper" than the profit function shown above, but will still intersect the feasible region at the point X when maximized. Of course, this result will not always hold true. In most instances, a change in the objective function will lead to a change in short-run operating policy. To determine the magnitude of this change, we

161

must graph the alternate objective function to determine its point of intersection with the feasible space. Like a change in the feasible space caused by a change in one or more constraint conditions, changes in the objective function typically, but not always, lead to a change in the optimal operating decision.

8.5

Mathews Arms graph.

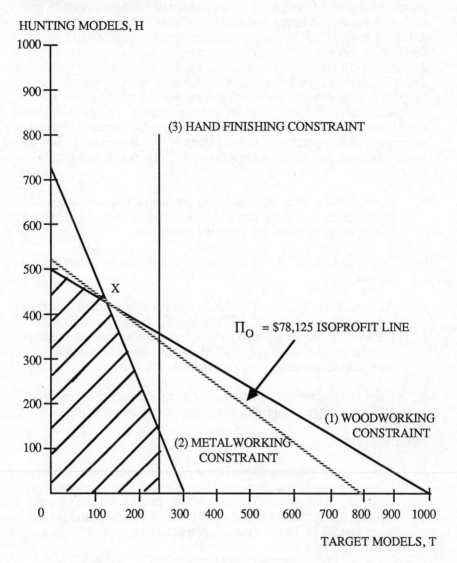

HUNTING MODELS, H

(3) HAND FINISHING CONSTRAINT

X

Π_O = $78,125 ISOPROFIT LINE

(1) WOODWORKING
CONSTRAINT

(2) METALWORKING
CONSTRAINT

TARGET MODELS, T

8.6

Denver Custom Homes (DCH) uses two different types of crews on home construction projects. *A* crews consist of master carpenters and skilled carpenters, whereas *B* crews include skilled carpenters and unskilled labor. Each home involves framing (F), roofing (R), and finish carpentry (FC). During recent months, *A* crews have demonstrated a capability for framing one home, while roofing two, and doing finish carpentry for no more than four homes per month. Capabilities for *B* crews are framing three homes, roofing two, and completing finish carpentry for one during a month. DCH has agreed to build ten homes during the month of July, but subcontracted 10 percent of framing and 20 percent of finish carpentry requirements. Labor costs are $60,000 per month for *A* crews, and $45,000 per month for *B* crews.

a. Formulate the linear programming problem DCH would use to minimize its total labor costs in July, showing both the inequality and equality forms of the constant conditions.

b. Solve the linear programming problem and interpret your solution values.

c. Assuming that DCH can both buy and sell subcontracting services at prevailing prices of $8,000 per unit for framing and $14,000 per unit for finish carpentry, would you recommend the company alter its subcontracting policy? If so, how much could the company save through such a change?

d. Calculate the minimum increase in *A* crew costs necessary to cause DCH to change its optimal employment combination for July.

8.6   SOLUTION

a. The problem requires minimization of total labor costs subject to constraints on home framing (F), roofing (R), and finished carpentry (FC) outputs. DCH's subcontracting policy reduces output requirements for F from 10 to 9 (= 10×0.9) and for FC from 10 to 8 (= 10×0.8) units, respectively.

Thus, the linear programming problem is:

Minimize: Total cost = $60,000A + $45,000B

Subject to: (1) $1A + 3B \geq 9$

(2) $2A + 2B \geq 10$

(3) $4A + 1B \geq 8$

Or, in equality form:

(1) $1A + 3B - L_F = 9$ (Framing constraint)

(2) $2A + 2B - L_R = 10$ (Roofing constraint)

(3) $4A + 1B - L_{FC} = 8$ (Finished carpentry constraint)

$A, B, L_F, L_R, L_{FC} \geqq 0$

b.   By graphing the constraints and the lowest possible isocost line, we find at the optimal point X that $L_R = L_{FC} = 0$.

Thus,   (1) $1A + 3B - L_F = 9$

(2) $2A + 2B - 0 = 10$

(3) $4A + 1B - 0 = 8$

Then, taking 2 times (2) times (3),

$2 \times (2)$ $4A + 4B = 20$

-3 $\underline{4A + 1B = \quad 8}$

$3B = 12$

$B = \underline{\underline{4}}$

From (3),

(3) $4A + 1(4) = 8$

$A = \underline{\underline{1}}$

From (1),

(1) $1(1) + 3(4) - L_F = 9$

$L_F = \underline{\underline{4}}$

And, from the objective function:

Total cost $= \$60,000(1) + \$45,000(4)$

$$= \underline{\underline{\$240{,}000}}$$

Solution values can be interpreted as follows:

$A = 1$ Optimal number of type A crews.

$B = 4$ Optimal number of type B crews.

$L_F = 4$ Excess capacity of four house framings per month.

$L_R = 0$ No excess roofing capacity at the optimal employment level.

$L_{FC} = 0$ No excess finished carpentry capacity at the optimal employment level.

$C = \$240{,}000$ Minimum possible total labor cost given output constraints.

c.   <u>Yes</u>. A change in the company's subcontracting policy is in order. DCH currently has excess capacity sufficient to allow it to frame an additional 4 homes per month. By laying off its current framing subcontractor and doing required framing "in-house," the company could save $8,000 per month. In addition, DCH could offer its own subcontracting services for 3 additional homes for a total of $24,000. Thus, the company could reduce total labor costs <u>$32,000</u> by altering its subcontracting policy.

d.   In general, the isocost relation for this problem is:

$$C_0 = C_A A + C_B B$$

Where C_0 is any monthly labor cost level, and C_A and C_B are monthly crew costs for A and B crews, respectively. In terms of the graph shown below, A is on the vertical axis and B is on the horizontal axis. Thus, rearranging our isocost formula, we find:

$$A = C_0/C_A - (C_B/C_A)B$$

Where C_0/C_A is the intercept and $-(C_B/C_A)$ is the slope coefficient.

The slope of the isocost line will fall (become less negative) as C_A increases, holding C_B constant. If C_A increases by slightly more than <u>$120,000</u>, the optimal feasible point will shift from point X (4B, 1A) to point Y (8B, 0A), since the isocost line slope will then

166

become less than -1/4, the slope of the third constraint ($A = 2 - (1/4)B$). Thus, an increase in C_A from \$60,000 to \$180,000, or a tripling in the cost of employing A crews, would be necessary before DCH would change its current minimal use of A crews and employ B crews exclusively.

$$C_0 = C_E T_E + C_w T_w$$

250

$PW = C_0 / T_w$

$$\left(\frac{\$500}{50}\right) - \left(\frac{r^s}{50}\right)$$

8.6
Denver Custom Homes graph.

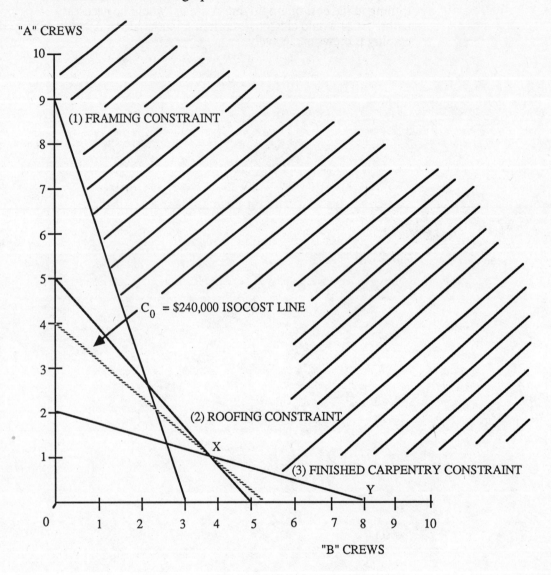

"A" CREWS

(1) FRAMING CONSTRAINT

C_0 = $240,000 ISOCOST LINE

(2) ROOFING CONSTRAINT

X

(3) FINISHED CARPENTRY CONSTRAINT

Y

"B" CREWS

CHAPTER NINE: MARKET STRUCTURE, I: PERFECT COMPETITION AND MONOPOLY

Theme

In previous chapters, managerial decisions were studied independent of market structure considerations. In actual practice, however, the competitive environment faced by the firm is a factor of utmost importance. In perfectly competitive markets characterized by many buyers and sellers of an identical product, firms take market prices as given and make production decisions accordingly. When the firm can greatly expand or reduce output without affecting market prices, then price equals marginal revenue. Profit maximization requires setting marginal revenue, and hence price, equal to marginal cost. Vigorous price competition requires that firms produce in a least-cost fashion, and eliminates the potential for excess or economic profits. In monopoly markets characterized by a single seller of a differentiated product, the firm is the industry. Hence, by setting price (output), the firm also sets industry output (price). The downward sloping monopoly demand curve contrasts sharply with the horizontal demand curve faced by firms in perfectly competitive markets. Monopoly gives rise to the potential for excess profits, even in long-run equilibrium. The effects of market structure on managerial decisions will be examined further in Chapter Ten where monopolistic competition and oligopoly are examined. Broader efficiency and equity implications of market structure are the subject of Chapter Twelve.

Outline

I.   **The Contrast Between Perfect Competition and Monopoly**

      A.   Market Structure: The competitive environment in the market for any product is described as the market structure faced by the firm. This environment is described in terms of the number of buyers and sellers (actual plus potential entrants), barriers to entry and exit, capital requirements, nonprice competition, and so on.

      B.   Perfect Competition: A perfectly competitive market is characterized by a large number of buyers and sellers of an identical product.

      C.   Monopoly: Monopoly is characterized by a single seller of a highly differentiated product.

II.   **Factors That Determine the Level of Competition**

      A.   Effect of Product Characteristics on Market Structure: Market competition will tend to increase with product standardization. In addition, when distribution costs are low, broad geographic markets and active competition are possible.

B. Effect of Production Characteristics on Competition: Industries whose production function exhibits increasing returns to scale are sometimes characterized by less competition than are industries where constant or decreasing returns are prevalent.

C. Effect of Entry and Exit Conditions on Competition: When entry and exit are easy, the threat of potential entry can effectively limit prices and profits for current competitors.

    1. A barrier to entry is any advantage for industry incumbents over new rivals.

    2. A barrier to exit is any limit on asset redeployment by incumbents.

D. Effect of Buyers on Competition: Competition will tend to be most vigorous when numerous highly informed buyers are present.

    1. Monopsony describes a market with one buyer.

III. Pure Competition

A. Definition: Pure competition exists when individual producers in a market have no influence over prices. Basic requirements for pure competition are:

    1. Large numbers of buyers and sellers.

    2. Product homogeneity.

    3. Free entry into and exit from the market.

    4. Perfect dissemination of information.

B. Market Price Determination: The industry supply curve is the summation of the quantities that individual firms are willing to supply at different prices. The industry demand curve is determined by the aggregate quantity that individual purchasers will buy at each price. Together, industry supply and demand conditions determine market prices.

    1. The Firm's Demand Curve: Under pure competition, a firm's output decision does not affect price. The demand curve faced by the firm is a horizontal line intersecting the

170

vertical axis at the market price. Price equals marginal revenue.

    C.   The Firm's Price/Output Decision: Management must determine the output that maximizes profit, given the prevailing market price.

        1.   Decision Rule: A profit maximizing firm in a competitive market will operate at that point where the market price (and MR) is equal to MC.

        2.   No Economic Profits: Above-normal profits can exist in the short-run, but in the long-run, those profits will attract competitors and drive down prices and eliminate above-normal profits.

        3.   Long-Run Equilibrium Conditions: Prices are stable, and each firm is operating at the minimum point on its short-run and long-run average cost curve. Hence,

$$P = AR = MR = MC = AC$$

    D.   The Firm's Supply Curve: In the short run, the competitive firm's supply schedule will correspond with the portion of the marginal cost curve that lies above the average variable cost curve.

IV. Monopoly

    A.   Definition: Monopoly exists when a single firm is the sole producer of a good or service that has no close substitute.

    B.   Price/Output Decision Under Monopoly: Management must determine that price and output combination that will maximize profits.

        1.   The Firm's Demand Curve: The firm *is* the industry. Thus, the downward sloping industry demand curve is identical to the firm demand curve. The monopolist can set either price or quantity, the value of the other being determined by the relation expressed in the demand function.

        2.   Economic Profits: Monopolists operate at the point where MR = MC, so long as average variable costs are covered. With P = AR > AC, economic profits result.

171

C. Long-Run Equilibrium Under Monopoly: Economic profits can persist even in the long-run for a monopolist protected by barriers to entry or exit.

    1. A natural monopolist emerges in an industry where long-run average costs are declining at the intersection of industry supply and demand curves.

D. Regulation of Monopoly: Monopolies can be efficient, but monopoly can also lead to excess profits and under production. Hence, a dilemma for regulation is created.

V. Countervailing Power: The Monopoly/Monopsony Confrontation

A. Definition: Countervailing power is any economic influence that creates a closer balance of power between previously unequal sellers and buyers.

VI. Market Structure and Competitive Strategy

A. Importance: To develop an effective competitive strategy, it is important to assess the degree to which product markets involve elements of perfect competition or monopoly.

B. Market Niche: A market niche is a segment of a market that can be successfully exploited given the special capabilities of a given firm or individual.

PROBLEMS AND SOLUTIONS

9.1

Demand conditions for household chemical spray treatments to control insects and other pests in the St. Louis, Missouri market area are described as follows:

Spray Treatments per year	Price
0	$25
1	24
2	23
3	22
4	21
5	20
6	19
7	18

The marginal cost of service is stable at $20 per spray treatment.

a.   Use the indicated price and output data to complete the following table.

Spray Treatments per year	Price	Total Revenue	Marginal Revenue
0	$25		
1	24		
2	23		
3	22		
4	21		
5	20		
6	19		
7	18		

b.   Determine price and the level of service per customer if a perfectly competitive market structure is present.

c.   Determine price and the level of service if the city grants a single firm a monopoly franchise.

173

a.

Output (000)	Price	Total Revenue	Marginal Revenue
0	$25	$0	--
1	24	24	$24
2	23	46	22
3	22	66	20
4	21	84	18
5	20	100	16
6	19	114	14
7	18	126	12

b.   In a perfectly competitive industry, P = MR, so the optimal activity level occurs where P = MC. Here, <u>P = MC = $20</u> at <u>Q = 5</u> treatments per year.

c.   A monopoly will maximize profits by setting MR = MC. Here, MR = MC = $20 at <u>Q = 3</u> treatments and <u>P = $22</u>.

9.2

Demand and Supply conditions in the perfectly competitive domestic oil industry are:

$$Q_S = 10P \qquad \text{(Supply)}$$

$$Q_D = 1,000 - 40P \qquad \text{(Demand)}$$

where Q is quantity in millions of barrels, and P is price per barrel.

a.   Graph industry supply and demand curves.

b.   Determine both graphically and algebraically the equilibrium industry price/output combination.

9.2 SOLUTION

a.

Price ($ per Barrel)

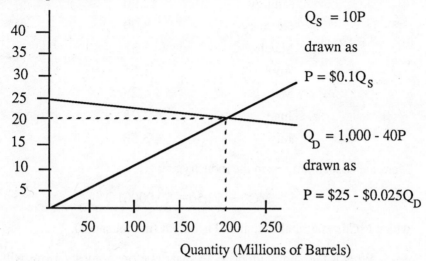

$Q_S = 10P$

drawn as

$P = \$0.1Q_S$

$Q_D = 1,000 - 40P$

drawn as

$P = \$25 - \$0.025Q_D$

Quantity (Millions of Barrels)

b. From the graph, we see that $Q_D = Q_S = 200(000,000)$ at a price of $20 per barrel. Thus, $P = \$20$ and $Q = 200(000,000)$ is the equilibrium price-output combination.

Algebraically,

$$Q_D = Q_S$$

$$1,000 - 40P = 10P$$

$$50P = 1,000$$

$$P = \underline{\$20}$$

Both demand and supply equal 200(000,000) since:

Demand: $Q_D = 1,000 - 40(20) = \underline{200}\,(000,000)$

Supply: $Q_S = 10(20) = \underline{200}\,(000,000)$

9.3

The market price for 256K-DRAM chips used in computers and "intelligent" electronics fluctuates widely depending on changes in world-wide demand and supply conditions in this perfectly competitive

175

industry. Market prices for a recent seven month period were as follows:

Month	Price
January	$2.90
February	3.00
March	3.35
April	3.55
May	4.25
June	3.75
July	3.50

Marginal cost conditions in the industry are:

$$MC = \$2.50 + \$0.00001Q$$

where MC is marginal cost and Q is output (in thousands).

a. What is the minimum price necessary before domestic firms will supply chips?

b. Calculate the domestic supply of chips per month.

9.3 SOLUTION

a. $2.50. Given MC = $2.50 + $0.00001Q, a minimum price of $2.50 must be obtained before and domestic supply would be forthcoming.

b. In a perfectly competitive industry, P = MC. Therefore, when price is expressed as a function of output, the industry supply curve equals the marginal cost curve:

$$P = MC = \$2.50 + \$0.00001Q$$

To express quantity as a function of price, we note:

$$P = \$2.50 + \$0.00001Q$$

$$0.00001Q = -2.50 + P$$

$$Q = -250,000 + 100,000P$$

Therefore, domestic supply per month is:

Month	Supply (000)
January	$Q = -250{,}000 + 100{,}000(2.90) = 40{,}000$
February	$Q = -250{,}000 + 100{,}000(3.00) = 50{,}000$
March	$Q = -250{,}000 + 100{,}000(3.35) = 85{,}000$
April	$Q = -250{,}000 + 100{,}000(3.55) = 105{,}000$
May	$Q = -250{,}000 + 100{,}000(4.25) = 175{,}000$
June	$Q = -250{,}000 + 100{,}000(3.75) = 125{,}000$
July	$Q = -250{,}000 + 100{,}000(3.50) = 100{,}000$

9.4

Solar Systems, Inc., produces and sells solar heat panels for hot water heaters in a perfectly competitive industry and has the following total and marginal cost functions:

$$TC = \$500Q - \$10Q^2 + Q^3$$

$$MC = \$500 - \$20Q + \$3Q^2$$

where TC is total cost (in thousands of dollars) and Q is output (in thousands of units). Included in this cost function is a normal return of 15 percent on invested capital.

a. Assuming that the firm and the industry are in equilibrium, what is the price charged by Solar Systems for its product?

b. What is the value of economic profits, average cost, and marginal cost at this equilibrium price?

c. Graph the marginal revenue, marginal cost, and average cost curves.

d. What is the supply function for Solar Systems' output?

9.4 SOLUTION

a. If the firm and the industry are in equilibrium, then P = AC where average costs are minimized. To find the point of minimum average costs, we set MC = AC where:

$$MC = AC$$

$$\$500 - \$20Q + \$3Q^2 = \frac{\$500Q - \$10Q^2 + Q^3}{Q}$$

$$500 - 20Q + 3Q^2 = 500 - 10Q + Q^2$$

$$2Q^2 = -10Q$$

$$2Q = 10$$

$$Q = 5(000)$$

At Q = 5(000),

$$AC = 500 - 10Q + Q^2$$

$$= 500 - 10(5) + 5^2$$

$$= \$475$$

Therefore, since P must equal AC:

$$P = AC$$

$$= \underline{\$475}$$

(Note: average cost is rising for Q > 5, so Q = 5 is a point of minimum average costs.)

b. In equilibrium, economic profits equal zero, and average cost equals marginal cost.

$$\pi = TR - TC$$

$$= PQ - 500Q + 10Q^2 - Q3$$

$$= \$475(5) - \$500(5) + \$10(5^2) - \$1(5^3)$$

$$= \underline{\$0}$$

$$AC = \$500 - \$10Q + Q^2$$

$$= 500 - 10(5) + 5^2$$

$$= 500 - 50 + 25$$

$$= \underline{\$475}$$

$$MC = \$500 - \$20(5) + \$3(5)^2$$

178

$$= \underline{\underline{\$475}}$$

c.   Solar Systems graph.

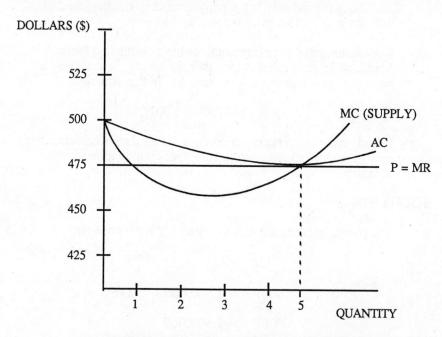

d.   A competitive firm's supply function is defined by that portion of the marginal cost curve lying above the average variable cost curve. Since Solar Systems' total cost function does not contain a fixed cost component, average costs and average variable costs are identical. Thus, Solar Systems' supply curve would be that portion of its marginal cost curve lying above the average cost curve.

9.5

Otto Maddux, Inc., a Chicago-based supplier of micro-electronic products, has retained an independent management consulting firm to provide advice concerning supply and demand conditions in the industry. Using Department of Commerce data, the consultant estimates:

$$Q_S = 4,000P \qquad \text{(Supply)}$$

$$Q_D = 1,500,000 - 2,000P \qquad \text{(Demand)}$$

a. Assuming the industry is perfectly competitive, calculate the industry equilibrium price/output combination.

b. Now assume that import restrictions have eliminated Otto Maddux's leading competitors, thereby giving the company a monopoly position in its home market. In this situation,

$$MR = \$750 - \$0.001Q$$

Based on the same supply conditions stated above, calculate the new monopoly equilibrium price/output combination for the industry.

9.5 SOLUTION

a. The perfectly competitive industry equilibrium price is:

$$Q_S = Q_D$$

$$4,000P = 1,500,000 - 2,000P$$

$$6,000P = 1,500,000$$

$$P = \underline{\$250}$$

At $P = \$250$, industry equilibrium output is:

$$Q_S = 4,000(\$250)$$

$$= \underline{1,000,000}$$

b. The new monopoly equilibrium price/output combination will be found at the profit maximizing activity level where MC = MR. Here it is important to recognize that the industry supply curve represents the horizontal sum of the marginal cost curves for individual producers. Therefore, when the industry is transformed into a monopoly, the industry supply curve represents the relevant marginal cost curve:

$$Q_S = 4,000P \qquad \text{(Supply)}$$

$$MC = P = \$0.00025Q$$

And the profit maximizing activity level is where:

$$MC = MR$$

$$\$0.00025Q = \$750 - \$0.001Q$$

$$0.00125Q = 750$$

$$Q = \underline{\underline{600,000}}$$

$$P = \$750 - \$0.0005(600,000)$$

$$= \underline{\underline{\$450}}$$

From parts a and b, we see that import restrictions reduce the level of industry output from 1,000,000 to 600,000 units, and increase prices from $250 to $450 per unit. Generally speaking, monopolists offer consumers too little output at too high a price.

9.6

Prescription Pharmaceuticals, Ltd. enjoys an exclusive patent on a drug used to treat peptic ulcers. Total and marginal revenue relations for the product are:

$$TR = \$100Q - \$0.0002Q^2$$

$$MR = \$100 - \$0.0004Q$$

Marginal costs for production and distribution are stable at $20 per unit. All other costs have been fully amortized.

a.   As a monopoly, calculate Prescription Pharmaceuticals' output, price, and profits at the profit maximizing activity level.

b.   What price and profit levels would prevail following expiration of patent protection based on the assumption that perfectly competitive pricing would result?

9.6 SOLUTION

a.   Set MR = MC to find the profit maximizing activity level:

$$MR = MC$$

$$\$100 - \$0.0004Q = \$20$$

$$0.0004Q = 80$$

$$Q = \underline{\underline{200,000}}$$

$$P = TR/Q$$

$$= (\$100Q - \$0.0002Q^2)/Q$$

$$P = TR/Q \qquad = 100 - 0.0002Q$$

$$= 100 - 0.0002(200,000)$$

$$= \underline{\underline{\$60}}$$

$$\pi = TR - TC$$

$$= \$60(200,000) - \$20(200,000)$$

$$= \underline{\underline{\$8,000,000}}$$

b. In a perfectly competitive industry, P = MR = MC in equilibrium. Thus, after expiration of patent protection, $\underline{P = MC = \$20}$ would result. Since MC = AC, P = MC implies that $\underline{\pi = 0}$.

9.7

The Steam Boiler Inspection and Insurance Company is the leading underwriter of boiler and machinery insurance. Market demand and marginal revenue relations for the company's insurance are:

$$P = \$7,500 - \$1.1Q$$

$$MR = \$7,500 - \$2.2Q$$

All costs are variable, and average $2,000 per policy (Q).

a. Calculate the profit-maximizing price/output combination and economic profits if the company enjoys a monopoly due to state licensing requirements.

b. Calculate the profit-maximizing price/output combination if a relaxation of entry restrictions transforms the industry into one that is perfectly competitive.

182

9.7

a.   The profit maximizing price/output combination is found by setting MR = MC. Since AVC is constant, MC = AVC = $2,000. Therefore:

$$MR = MC$$

$$\$7,500 - \$2.2Q = \$2,000$$

$$2.2Q = 5,500$$

$$Q = \underline{\underline{2,500}}$$

$$P = \$7,500 - \$1.1(2,500)$$

$$= \underline{\underline{\$4,750}}$$

$$\text{Economic Profits} = PQ - AVC \times Q$$

$$= \$4,750(2,000) - \$2,000(2,500)$$

$$= \underline{\underline{\$6,875,000}}$$

(Note: As a monopolist, SBII is the industry).

b.   In a perfectly competitive market, P = MC. In this instance where AVC is constant and, therefore, MC = AVC, perfectly competitive equilibrium will occur when:

$$P = MC = AVC$$

$$\$7,500 - \$1.1Q = \$2,000$$

$$1.1Q = 5,500$$

$$Q = \underline{\underline{5,000}}$$

$$P = \$7,500 - \$1.1(5,000)$$

$$= \underline{\underline{\$2,000}}$$

$$\text{Economic Profits} = PQ - AVC \times Q$$

$$= \$2,000(5,000) - \$2,000(5,000)$$

$$= \underline{\underline{\$0}}$$

In words, the transformation of the industry from monopoly to perfect competition has brought a $2,750 reduction in price and a 2,500 unit expansion in output. At the same time, economic profits have been eliminated.

CHAPTER TEN: MARKET STRUCTURE, II: MONOPOLISTIC COMPETITION AND OLIGOPOLY

Theme

This chapter extends our analysis of the effect of market structure considerations on managerial decisions by studying monopolistic competition and oligopoly market settings. Like competition in perfectly competitive markets, monopolistic competition involves large numbers of buyers and sellers. Given the presence of at least some product differentiation, each seller enjoys some discretion in the setting of prices. However, vigorous price and product competition from firms offering close substitutes eliminates the potential for above-normal or economic profits in long-run equilibrium. Oligopoly markets involve competition among only a handful of competitors. Products offered could be homogeneous, as in aluminum and steel, or differentiated, as in soft drinks and cigarettes. In both instances, fewness in the number of competitors stems from the presence of meaningful barriers to entry due to capital costs, advertising or research and development requirements, economies of scale in production or distribution, or other factors. Competition among the few has the potential to result in excess profits if so-called "competitors" make implicit or explicit agreements not to compete. For this reason, the number and size distribution of rivals in various markets is an important matter of concern for regulatory bodies at the state and federal levels. Nevertheless, it is important to remember that high market share provides no guarantee of lasting success. Competition among the few is often vigorous, and today's "winners" often find themselves tomorrow's "also-rans."

Outline

I.   **The Contrast Between Monopolistic Competition and Oligopoly**

    A.   Monopolistic Competition: This market structure is characterized by a large number of sellers of a differentiated product.

    B.   Oligopoly: Oligopoly is a market structure characterized by few sellers.

II. **Monopolistic Competition**

    A.   Definition: Monopolistic competition exists when a large number of firms offer close but not identical substitutes. Thus, elements of pure competition and pure monopoly are involved.

    B.   Price/Output Decisions Under Monopolistic Competition: Profit maximization requires that firms operate at a point where marginal revenue equals marginal cost. However, monopolistic competition causes zero economic profits in the long-run since $P = AR = AC$.

1.   Equilibrium prices will be found within the range:

   a.   High-price/low-output solution: The tangency between the LRAC curve and new firm demand curve created through a parallel leftward shift in the original (monopoly) demand curve.

   b.   Low-price/high-output solution: The tangency between the minimum LRAC point and a new horizontal firm demand curve. This is also the perfectly competitive solution.

2.   Cost of Product Diversity: Average costs will be higher with monopolistic competition than in the case of pure competition. This can be viewed as a cost of product diversity.

III. Oligopoly

A.   Definition: Oligopoly is a market structure characterized by fewness in the number of sellers. Individual price/output decisions often produce reactions on the part of competitors.

B.   Price/Output Decisions Under Oligopoly: Under oligopoly, a price change by one firm will induce price changes by other firms. Therefore, by changing its price, a firm shifts from one demand curve to another, rather than moving along a single demand curve.

1.   Economic Profits: Despite oligopolists' uncertainty regarding the reactions of competitors, economic profits are typical since $P = AR > AC$.

C.   Cartel Arrangements: A cartel is an explicit (overt) or implicit (covert) agreement among competitors not to compete in order to enhance their collective profitability.

D.   Price Leadership: With price leadership, one firm tacitly establishes itself as the industry leader, and all other firms follow its pricing policy. The leader faces a price/output problem similar to a monopolist, while the other firms face a competitive price/output problem under the "dominant firm" price leadership model.

E.   Kinked Demand Curve: According to the Kinked Demand Curve Theory of Oligopolist Pricing, rival firms are assumed to follow any decrease in price in order to maintain their respective market shares, but refrain from following price increases, thereby allowing their market shares to increase at the expense of the firm making the initial price increase. The discontinuity in the marginal revenue curve associated with the kink in the demand curve explains the price rigidity characteristic of some oligopolist markets.

IV.   Nonprice Competition

A.   Rationale: Competitors are often able to quickly match a firm's price cut. Therefore, oligopolists tend to use nonprice competition to boost demand (product diversity, advertising, etc.).

B.   The Optimal Level of Advertising: Profit maximization requires that the marginal revenue derived from advertising, or any other nonprice method of competition, be set equal to its marginal cost.

V.   Defining Market Structure

A.   The Economic Censuses: Economic censuses by the U.S. Department of Commerce provide a comprehensive view of economic activity across a number of important sectors. These data are of immense value to firms, government regulators, and academic researchers.

B.   The Census Classification System: Census data are organized in ever increasing levels of detail from broad industry groups to narrow product classifications.

C.   Market Concentration: Concentration ratios are an empirical measure of the degree of concentration or centralization in productive resources within industries. Most commonly, concentration ratios are measured at the four firm level using four-digit industry sales data. By definition:

$$CR_i = \sum_{i=1}^{N} X_i$$

where CR is a concentration ratio for the ith number of firms and X_i is a relative percentage measure of firm input or output (employment, sales, etc.). For example, if the four largest firms account for 80 percent of industry sales, then the four firm concentration ratio (CR_4) would be 80, since concentration is usually expressed in percentage terms.

187

1. Limitations: Among the important limitations of concentration ratio data are:

   a. Only domestic production is considered, thereby ignoring possible foreign competition.

   b. Only national concentration ratios are published. This ignores the regional character of many markets.

   c. Competitive pressures are measured only imperfectly since even a small number of firms in an industry will sometimes compete vigorously.

2. Advantages: Despite their limitations, concentration ratios have generally provided an attractive empirical measure of the varying competitive pressures faced by firms in industry.

VI. Competitive Strategy in Imperfectly Competitive Markets

A. Importance: The design of an effective competitive strategy involves a careful consideration of the likely reaction of actual and potential competitors.

VII. Competitive Strategy at Columbia Drug Stores, Inc.: An Illustrative Market Structure Analysis Problem

PROBLEMS AND SOLUTIONS

10.1

Indicate whether each of the following statements is true or false and why.

a. Equilibrium in oligopoly markets requires that firms be operating at the point where marginal revenue equals marginal cost.

b. A high ratio of distribution cost to total cost tends to increase competition by widening the geographic area over which any individual producer can compete.

c. The price elasticity of demand will tend to fall as new competitors introduce substitute products.

d. An efficiently functioning cartel would achieve the monopoly price/output combination.

e. An increase in price advertising will tend to increase the slope of firm demand curves.

10.1 SOLUTION

a. <u>True</u>. Stable equilibrium in all market structures requires that firms operate at the point where marginal revenue equals marginal cost.

b. <u>False</u>. A low ratio of distribution cost to total cost tends to increase competition by widening the geographic area over which any individual producer can compete.

c. <u>False</u>. The price elasticity of demand will tend to rise as new competitors introduce substitute products.

d. <u>True</u>. A perfectly functioning cartel would achieve the monopoly price-output combination.

e. <u>False</u>. An increase in price advertising will tend to increase the slope of individual firm demand curves.

10.2

Information Systems, Inc. is a small supplier of computer software information systems to hospitals.

a. Use ISI's price, output, and weekly total cost data to complete the following table:

Price	Output	Total Revenue	Marginal Revenue	Total Cost	Marginal Cost	Average Cost
$7,500	0	$0	--	$2,500	--	--
5,000	1			5,000		
3,500	2			7,000		
2,800	3			8,100		
2,400	4			9,600		
2,000	5			12,500		
1,700	6			16,500		

b.   What is the monopolistically competitive high-price/low-output equilibrium?

c.   What is the monopolistically competitive low-price/high-output equilibrium?

10.2   SOLUTION

a.

Price	Output	Total Revenue	Marginal Revenue	Total Cost	Marginal Cost	Average Cost
$7,500	0	$0	--	$2,500	--	--
5,000	1	5,000	$5,000	5,000	$2,500	$5,000
3,500	2	7,000	2,000	7,000	2,000	3,500
2,800	3	8,400	1,400	8,100	1,100	2,700
2,400	4	9,600	1,200	9,600	1,500	2,400
2,000	5	10,000	400	12,500	2,900	2,500
1,700	6	10,200	200	16,500	4,000	2,750

b.   The monopolistically competitive high-price/low-output equilibrium is at P = AC = $3,500, Q = 2 and π = TR - TC = 0. No excess profits are being earned, MR = MC = $15, and there would be no incentive for either expansion or contraction since MR = MC = $2,000. Such an equilibrium is typical of monopolistically competitive industries where each individual firm retains some pricing discretion in the long-run.

c.   The monopolistically competitive low-price/high-output equilibrium is at P = AC = $2,800, Q = 4 and π = TR - TC = 0. No excess profits are being earned, MR = MC = $9, and there

190

would be no incentive for either expansion or contraction. This is similar to the perfectly competitive equilibrium. (Note that MR < MC and average cost is rising for $Q > 4$.)

10.3

CATV, Inc. has been granted an exclusive license to operate a cable television system in Jackson, Wyoming. Recent operating experience in similar locations suggests a close relation between the monthly price for basic service and the number of subscribers.

a. Complete the following table based on CATV's projected price, output, and monthly total cost data:

Price	Output (000)	Total Revenue	Marginal Revenue ($000)	Total Cost ($000)	Marginal Cost ($000)
$50	0			$0	
40	1			20	
30	2			40	
25	3			60	
20	4			80	
15	5			100	

b. Calculate the equilibrium monopoly price/output combination and profit level.

c. Calculate the equilibrium price/output combination and profit level if competitive bidding for the franchise resulted in a perfectly competitive market outcome.

10.3 SOLUTION

a.

Price	Output (000)	Total Revenue	Marginal Revenue ($000)	Total Cost ($000)	Marginal Cost ($000)
$50	0	$0	--	$0	--
40	1	40	$40	20	$20
30	2	60	20	40	20
25	3	75	15	60	20
20	4	80	5	80	20
15	5	75	-5	100	20

191

b. The profit maximizing activity level is found where MR = MC. As a monopoly, MR = MC = $20,000 at the Q = 2(000) activity level. This implies P = $30 and π = TR - TC = $$60 - $40 = $20,000 per month.

c. The perfectly competitive equilibrium occurs where P = MC = AC and zero excess profits are earned, and TR = TC. Here, MR = MC = $20(000) and TR = TC = $80(000) at Q = 4(000) units per month, with P = $20 and π = TR - TC = $0 per month.

10.4

No-reservation (shuttle) airline passenger service is currently provided in the Washington, D.C. to New York city-pair market by only three firms. Weekly output measured in passengers flown and the marginal cost per passenger are as follows:

Weekly Output (000,000)	Marginal Cost of Service:		
	Apple Airlines, Inc. (A)	Big Bird, Inc. (B)	Chancy Airlines, Ltd. (C)
1	$40	$20	$50
2	30	25	40
3	25	30	45
4	35	35	55
5	50	40	65
6	60	50	75

The current fare (market price) of $45 cannot be raised given the threat of competitor entry. Nevertheless, each airline is able to greatly expand service without lowering prices. Thus, P = MR = $45.

a. Calculate current industry output and the market share of each airline.

b. Calculate industry output if the introduction of a high-speed passenger train forces airline industry prices down to $35.

10.4 SOLUTION

a. Each industry participant will produce to the point where MR = MC, but never where MR < MC. Given P = MR = $45, each firm will produce such that MC = MR = $45. A total Q = 12 units will be produced as follows:

192

Firm	Output	Market Share
Apple Airlines (A)	4	33%
Big Bird, Inc.	5	42%
Chancy Airlines, Ltd. (C)	3	25%
Total	12	100%

b.   Following a decrease in industry prices to P = MR = $35, industry output will fall to $\underline{Q = 8}$ distributed as follows:

Firm	Output	Market Share
Apple Airlines (A)	4	44%
Big Bird, Inc. (B)	4	44%
Chancy Airlines, Ltd. (C)	1	12%
Total	9	100%

Note that a fare reduction has a disproportionately severe effect on Chancy, the high-cost carrier.

10.5

Racine Foundry, Inc. is a medium-sized foundry specializing in heavy duty pipe for industrial use. Racine's demand and cost information are as follows:

$$P = \$4,500 - Q \qquad \text{(Demand)}$$

$$MR = \$4,500 - \$2Q \qquad \text{(Marginal Revenue)}$$

$$TC = \$150,000 + \$400\,Q \qquad \text{(Total Cost)}$$

$$MC = \$400 \qquad \text{(Marginal Cost)}$$

where Q is output (thousand feet of heavy gauge pipe), P is price and TC is total costs. The total cost function includes a normal return of 12 percent on capital resources

a.   Determine the profit-maximizing price/output combination and profit level.

b.   Compute price, output and profits under the assumption that the Racine seeks to maximize revenue. Assuming that Racine operates in a monopolistically competitive industry, is the industry in equilibrium?

c.   If not, what output, price, and economic profits will occur in equilibrium? Assume equilibrium occurs through a parallel leftward shift in the demand curve. (Hint: The slope of the average cost curve = $-150,000/Q^2$.)

d.   Calculate Racine's new equilibrium demand curve.

10.5   SOLUTION

a.   Set MR = MC to determine the profit maximizing level of output:

$$MR = MC$$

$$\$4,500 - \$2Q = \$400$$

$$2Q = 4,100$$

$$Q = \underline{2,050}\ \text{units}$$

$$P = \$4,500 - Q$$

$$= 4,500 - 2,050$$

$$= \underline{\$2,450}$$

$$\pi = TR - TC$$

$$= \$4,500Q - Q^2 - \$150,000 - \$400Q$$

$$= -\$150,000 + \$4,100Q - Q^2$$

$$= -150,000 + 4,100(2,050) - 2,050^2$$

$$= \underline{\$4,052,500}$$

(Note: profits are decreasing for Q > 2,050, thus Q = 2,050 is a profit maximum).

b.   Set MR = 0 to determine the revenue maximizing level of output:

$$MR = \$0$$

$$4,500Q - 2Q = 0$$

$$2Q = 4,500$$

$$Q = \underline{2,250}$$

$$P = \$4,500 - Q$$

194

$$= 4{,}500 - 2{,}250$$

$$= \underline{\underline{\$2{,}250}}$$

e.

$$\pi = -\$150{,}000 + \$4{,}100Q - Q^2$$

$$= -150{,}000 + 4{,}100(2{,}250) - 2{,}250^2$$

$$= \underline{\underline{\$4{,}012{,}500}}$$

<u>No</u>, the industry is not in equilibrium. Under monopolistic competition, only normal profits can be earned in equilibrium. Racine is earning substantial economic profits.

(Note: Total revenue is falling for $Q > 2{,}250$, thus $Q = 2{,}250$ is a revenue maximum.)

c. Racine's economic profits will attract new firms to the foundry industry. These new firms will attract business away from Racine, with the result being that Racine's demand curve will shift in a leftward direction until $P = AC$ and economic profits are eliminated. This process is described graphically below. (Note: Here there is no low-price/high-output equilibrium point since the AC curve declines continuously, i.e., there is no minimum AC point).

Algebraically, we can determine equilibrium output, price and profit by following a few simple steps:

<u>Step 1</u>: The problem specifies that the demand curve shifts in a parallel fashion, so the demand curve intercept changes but the slope remains constant and equal to -1, so the new demand curve is $Q = a - P$. We do not need to determine the intercept a at this point since we are only interested in the slope of the new demand curve.

<u>Step 2</u>: Find tangency between AC curve and the demand or AR curve. This occurs where the slope of the AC curve (given as $-150{,}000/Q^2$) equals the slope of the new demand curve:

$$\frac{\text{Average cost}}{\text{curve slope}} = \frac{\text{New demand}}{\text{curve slope}}$$

$$\frac{-150{,}000}{Q^2} = -1$$

195

$$Q^2 = 150,000$$

$$Q = \sqrt{150,000}$$

$$Q = \underline{\underline{387.3}} \text{ units}$$

Step 3: In equilibrium,

$$P = AC$$

$$= \frac{\$150,000 + \$400Q}{Q}$$

$$= \frac{150,000 + 400(387.3)}{387.3}$$

$$= \underline{\underline{\$787.30}}$$

d. Step 4: Since $P = AR = AC$, excess profits in equilibrium are zero.

We know that $Q = 387.3$, $P = \$787.30$, and $\pi = 0$. We also know $P = \$787.30$ and $Q = 387.3$ is one point on the new demand curve $Q = a - P$ (where $b = -1$). Thus,

$$387.3 = a - 787.3$$

$$a = 1174.6$$

And, therefore, $Q = 1174.6 - P$ is Racine's new equilibrium demand curve.

196

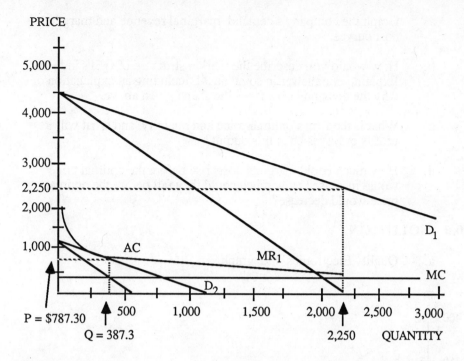

PRICE

5,000

4,000

3,000

2,250
2,000

1,000

AC

MR₁

MC

D₁

D₂

P = $787.30

500   1,000   1,500   2,000   2,500   3,000

Q = 387.3

2,250   QUANTITY

10.6

Quality Electronics, Inc. faces the following segmented demand curve for a new printed circuit board:

<u>Over the range 0-50,000 units:</u>

$$P_1 = \$300 - \$5Q$$

$$MR_1 = \$300 - \$10Q$$

<u>When output exceeds 50,000 units:</u>

$$P_2 = \$400 - \$15Q$$

$$MR_2 = \$400 - \$30Q$$

The company's total and marginal cost functions are:

$$TC = \$250 + \$100Q + \$2.5Q^2$$

$$MC = \$100 + \$5Q$$

where P is price (in dollars), Q is output (in thousands) and TC is total cost (in thousands of dollars).

197

a. Graph the company's demand, marginal revenue and marginal cost curves.

b. How would you describe the market structure of QEI's industry? Explain your answer in some detail, including an explanation of why the demand curve takes the shape given above.

c. What is the firm's optimal price and quantity, and what will its profits or losses be at this output?

d. How much could marginal costs rise before the optimal price would increase? How much could they fall before the optimal price would decrease?

10.6 SOLUTION

a. Quality Electronics, Inc. graph.

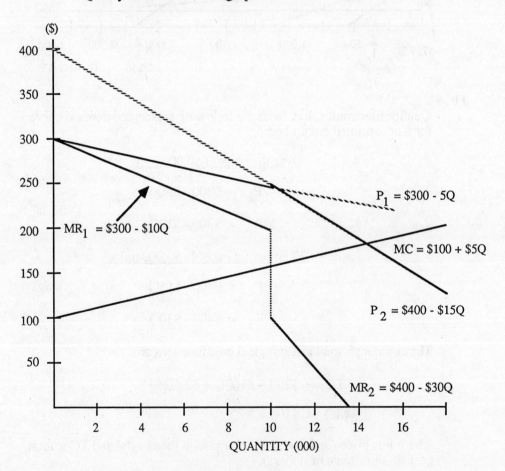

b. The firm is in an oligopolistic industry. It faces a kinked demand curve meaning that competitors will react to price reductions by cutting their own prices, thereby causing the segment of the demand curve below the kink to be relatively inelastic. Price increases are not followed, causing the portion of the demand curve above the kink to be relatively elastic.

c. An examination of the graph indicates that the marginal cost curve passes through the gap in the marginal revenue curve. Graphically, this indicates that optimal P = $\underline{\underline{\$250}}$ and Q = $\underline{\underline{10}}$(000).

Analytically,

$$MR_1 = \$300 - \$10Q \qquad\qquad Q \leq 10,000$$

$$MR_2 = \$400 - \$30Q \qquad\qquad Q \geq 10,000$$

$$MC = \$100 + \$5Q$$

If we solve for the output levels where MR = MC we see that $MR_1 > MC$ over the range $Q \leq 10$(000), and $MR_2 < MC$ for the range $Q \geq 10$(000). Therefore, we know QEI will produce 10(000) units of output and market them at P = $250. And finally,

$$\pi = PQ - TC$$

$$= \$250(10) - \$250 - \$100(10) - \$2.5(10^2)$$

$$= \underline{\underline{\$1,000}}(000) \text{ or } \$1,000,000$$

d. At Q = 10(000),

$MR_1 = \$300 - \$10Q$ $\qquad\qquad\qquad\qquad$ $MR_2 = \$400 - \$30Q$

$\quad = 300 - 10(10)$ $\qquad\qquad\qquad\qquad\qquad = 400 - 30(10)$

$\quad = \$200$ $\qquad\qquad\qquad\qquad\qquad\qquad\quad = \$100$

This implies that if marginal costs at Q = 10(000) exceed $200, the optimal price would increase.

Conversely, if marginal costs at Q = 10(000) fall below $100, the optimal price would decrease. So long as marginal costs at Q

= 10(000) are in the range of $100 to $200, QEI will have no incentive to change its price.

10.7

Computer Management Corporation specializes in the development of management information and decision assistance computer programs that it markets throughout the United States. CMC has just finished development of a new software package that will permit small retail firms to computerize their inventory management at a lower cost than has previously been possible. The company is now confronted with the problem of setting a price for the product in the face of uncertain demand. On the basis of sales data for similar software packages CMC has marketed in the past, management believes that demand for the product will be greatly influenced by the reactions of other computer software companies to the introduction of CMC's new product. A minimal reaction will result in the monthly demand and marginal revenue functions:

$$P = \$150 - \$0.1Q$$

$$MR = \$150 - \$0.2Q$$

A major reaction will lead to the more elastic curves:

$$P = \$130 - \$0.4Q$$

$$MR = \$130 - \$0.8Q$$

CMC's total monthly cost for marketing this product is composed of $3,000 additional administrative expenses and $50 per unit for production and distribution costs. That is, the relevant total cost and marginal cost functions are given by the expression:

$$TC = \$3,000 + \$50Q$$

$$MC = \$50$$

a. What is the profit maximizing price for CMC's product, assuming no competitor reaction?

b. Calculate this price based on the assumption competitors will react.

c. In light of CMC's cost conditions, and absent any substantial barriers to entry, which scenario is more likely?

10.7   SOLUTION

a. With no competitor reaction, we find:

200

$$MR = MC$$

$$\$150 - \$0.2Q = \$50$$

$$0.2Q = 100$$

$$Q = \underline{\underline{500}}$$

$$P = \$150 - \$0.1(500)$$

$$= \underline{\underline{\$100}}$$

b.   With a competitor reaction, we find:

$$MR = MC$$

$$\$130 - \$0.8Q = \$50$$

$$0.8Q = 80$$

$$Q = \underline{\underline{100}}$$

$$P = \$130 - \$0.4(100)$$

$$= \underline{\underline{\$90}}$$

c.   <u>Competitor reaction</u>. We note that:

$$MC = \$50$$

Therefore, CMC prices of P = $100 (in part a) or P = $90 (In part b) are both substantially above marginal costs, and thus are likely to attract substantial entry. Entrants have a significant opportunity to gain excess profits by pirating CMC's software. Still, the industry does not have the potential to achieve a stable perfectly competitive long-run equilibrium since average costs will decline continuously as output expands. Therefore, a monopolistically competitive long-run equilibrium where P = AC > MC and no excess profits seems likely.

Of course, in real world markets where software packages enjoy copyright protection, and assuming that copyright laws are effectively enforced, software publishing companies may have at least a short-run opportunity to earn above-normal profits.

10.8

In the inland waterways shipping industry, bulk carriers (barges) are chartered on an annual basis to haul grain, oil, ore, and other bulk commodities. As far as the shippers are concerned, the service provided by barges of any given class are homogeneous products. Industry demand for carriers varies over time, depending on grain and oil movements. At present, industry demand is estimated using the following linear approximation as:

$$Q = 40,000 - 0.2P$$

The industry consists of one large firm, Mississippi Barge Transport Company (MBT), and ten smaller firms of roughly equal size. MBT is the industry leader with regard to pricing decisions, and its marginal cost curve is given by the following linear approximation:

$$MC_L = -\$20,000 + \$6Q$$

The following firms' marginal cost curve, derived by summing the MC curves of the ten follower firms, is given by the linear approximation:

$$MC_F = \$44,000 + \$4Q$$

It must be stressed that these curves are approximations, empirically derived over a limited range of outputs. If observations were available over the full range of outputs, the curves would not be linear. However, these are good approximations over probable output ranges.

MBT has several interesting characteristics. First, it controls most port facilities, and has a reputation for fairness and good business judgment. Following firms are permitted to use these facilities on a fee basis, but this permission could be terminated. And finally, MBT has great financial strength. Should the need arise, it could conduct an extended price war.

a.   Construct a graph showing

    (i)   The industry demand curve,

    (ii)   The leader's and the followers' marginal cost curves.

    (iii)   The leader's demand and marginal revenue curves. To construct this graph, make the following calculations and use them to help draw the relevant curves:

        Q_F, when P = \$113,333
        Q_F, when P = \$ 60,000

Q_L, when P = $113,333

Q_L, when P = $ 60,000

b. What price will MBT establish, and what will be its output at this price?

c. How many units of output will the following firms supply?

d. Is price leadership as described here consistent with the kinked demand curve theory of oligopoly behavior?

e. Reconsider your graph. Could a price leadership situation exist, given the other facts of this problem, if MC_L were to lie above MC_F for all output quantities where the MC_F curve is below the industry demand curve?

10.8 SOLUTION

a(i) The industry demand curve is simply:

$$Q = 40,000 - 0.2P$$

$$0.2P = 40,000 - Q$$

$$P = \$200,000 - \$5Q$$

(ii) The following firms will take price as a given, then determine their outputs by setting MR = MC. Since followers take P as given, then P = MR = AR, and each following firm faces a horizontal demand curve once the leader establishes a price. Therefore, MC = MR = P, or P = MC.

When P = $113,333, the followers set P = 113,333 = MC_F:

$$P = \$113,333 = \$44,000 + \$4Q_F = MC_F$$

$$4Q_F = 69,333$$

$$Q_F = 17,333$$

When P = $60,000,

$$P = \$60,000 = \$44,000 + \$4Q_F = MC_F$$

$$4Q_F = 16,000$$

203

$$Q_F = 4,000$$

From this, we have two points on the linear MC_F curve, and thus, can easily graph it.

(iii)   Whatever market demand is not supplied by followers, the leader can supply. Therefore, the leader's demand is comprised of residual demand. When P = \$113,333, followers supply 17,333, which is the entire amount demanded at this price. Thus, the leader can supply only zero, since:

Leader demand = Market demand - Follower supply

$$Q_L = 17,333 - 17,333$$

$$= 0$$

Therefore, we have established one point on the leader's demand curve--the vertical axis intercept, P = \$113,333 and Q_L = 0. When P = \$60,000, followers supply 4,000 units. The leader will then supply:

$$Q_L = 28,000 - 4,000$$

$$= 24,000$$

We have thus established another point on the leader's demand curve: P = \$60,000 and Q_L = 24,000. With these two points we can construct the leader's demand curve. Note that at any P < \$44,000, followers drop out and the leader has the entire market demand to itself. Thus, D_L is kinked at P = \$44,000. However, note that these calculations are probably not valid because we are working with linear approximations.

We can also find the leader's demand curve directly:

$$Q_L = \text{Total demand - Followers' supply}$$

where followers' supply S_F, is given by the relations:

$$MC = P = \$44,000 + \$4Q$$

    or

$$Q = 0.25P - 11,000$$

and, therefore, leader demand is:

$$Q_L = 40{,}000 - 0.2P - (0.25P - 11{,}000)$$

$$= 51{,}000 - 0.45P$$

or

$$P = \$113{,}333 - \$2.22Q$$

We also note that:

$$MR_L = dTR/dQ = \$113{,}333 - \$4.44Q$$

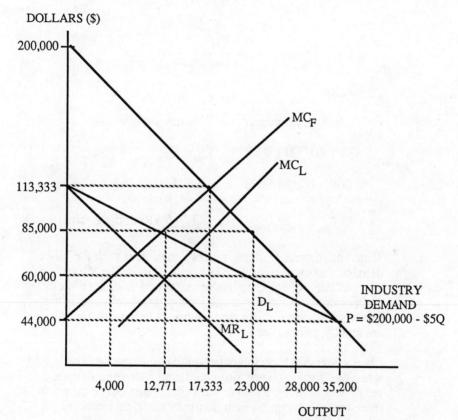

b. In order to determine a profit maximizing output level, MBT will set $MR_L = MC_L$, where:

$$MR_L = \$113{,}333 - \$4.44Q_L = -\$20{,}000 + \$6Q_L = MC_L$$

$$10.44Q_L = 133{,}333$$

$$Q_L = \underline{12{,}771} \text{ units}$$

$$P_L = \$113{,}333 - \$2.22Q$$

$$= 113{,}333 - 2.22(12{,}771)$$

$$= \underline{\$84{,}981}$$

c. The following firms will take the \$85,000 price as given, and will supply:

$$S_F = 0.25P - 11{,}000$$

$$= 0.25(84{,}981) - 11{,}000$$

$$= \underline{10{,}245}$$

To check,

Industry demand = Industry supply

$$Q_T = 40{,}000 - 0.2P = Q_L + Q_F$$

$$40{,}000 - 0.2(84{,}981) = 12{,}771 + 10{,}245$$

$$\underline{23{,}004} \overset{\checkmark}{\approx} \underline{23{,}016} \text{ (Rounding error)}$$

d. This type of price leadership is not consistent with the kinked demand theory of oligopoly behavior. Under the kinked demand curve theory, no leader exists and prices are sticky. Under dominant firm price leadership, prices change as the leader's MC curve shifts, and followers behave as though they are strictly price-takers.

Price leadership theory is often quite consistent with reality when one firm is clearly dominant, and following firms are small factors in the market. Kinked demand curve theory is more realistic when no firm dominates, and all firms are relatively large.

e. If MC_L lies above MC_F at the point where $MR_L = MC_L$, the only change that would occur is that the leader would then supply less than half the total market. This situation could still be consistent with price leadership, as explained in part d.

206

However, the larger and more dominant the leader, the more likely price leadership is to exist.

10.9

The industry supplying precision cast parts to mechanical robot manufacturers is comprised of one large firm and a number of small firms. The large firm acts as a price leader and sets the industry price. The small firms are price followers and can sell all they want at the industry price. The demand curve for the industry is:

$$Q = 2,000 - 0.1P$$

The total and marginal cost curves for the large firm and the aggregate curves for the smaller firms are as follows:

$$TC_L = \$10,000 + \$2,000Q_L \qquad MC_L = \$2,000$$

$$TC_S = \$1,000Q_S + \$20Q_S^2 \qquad MC_S = \$1,000 + \$40Q_S$$

a.   What is the aggregate supply curve of the price followers?

b.   Determine the relevant demand curve for the large firm.

c.   Determine the price/output combination that maximizes the price leader's profit. (Note: If $TR_L = \$16,200Q_L - \$8Q_L^2$ then $MR_L = \$16,200 - \$16Q_L$).

d.   What output would be supplied by the smaller firms?

10.9   Solution

a.   Since price followers take prices as given, they operate at the output level at which their marginal costs equal price. Therefore,

$$P = MC_S$$

$$= \$1,000 + \$40Q_S$$

or

$$Q_S = -25 + 0.025P.$$

b)   The demand curve for the large firm can be calculated algebraically by subtracting the supply curve of the price-following firms from the total industry demand, i.e., $Q_L = Q -$

Q_S. Since the supply curve for the price followers is $Q_S = -25 + 0.025P$,

$$Q_L = Q - Q_S$$

$$= 2,000 - 0.1P - (-25 + 0.025P)$$

$$= 2,025 - 0.125P,$$

or

$$P_L = \$16,200 - \$8Q_L$$

c) Set

$$MR_L = MC_L$$

$$\$16,200 - \$16Q_L = \$2,000$$

$$16Q_L = 14,200$$

$$Q_L = \underline{\underline{887.5}}$$

$$P = \$16,200 - \$8(887.5)$$

$$= \underline{\underline{\$9,100}}$$

d) The total quantity supplied by both the large and small firms can be found by substituting the price of $9,100 into the industry demand equation.

$$Q = 2,000 - 0.1P$$

$$= 2,000 - 0.10(9,100)$$

$$= 2,000 - 910$$

$$= 1,090$$

The total quantity supplied will be 1,090 units. The small firms should supply $1,090 - 887.5 = 202.5$ units. At this quantity, their marginal costs will equal their marginal revenue:

$$MC_S = MR_S$$

$$\$1,000 + \$40Q = 9,100$$

208

$$40Q = 8,100$$

$$Q = \underline{\underline{202.5}}$$

CHAPTER ELEVEN: PRICING PRACTICES

Theme

In this chapter, economic theory is used to analyze a number of commonly encountered pricing practices. Markup on cost and markup on price methods, by far the most prevalent pricing practices employed by firms, are examined in detail and shown to be highly compatible with profit maximization. In addition to markup pricing, the relevance of incremental analysis in pricing practice is also analyzed. Here we see how businesses actually use the marginal cost concept for pricing purposes. And finally, price discrimination and multiple product pricing methods are analyzed as ways for firms to deal with pricing problems posed by multiple markets and multiple outputs. When firms sell in more than one market, a difference in profit maximizing output prices will result if market demand elasticities vary. By charging higher prices in markets with relatively more inelastic demand, firms are said to be price discriminating. When joint products are produced in variable proportions, efficient pricing requires that marginal revenue be set equal to marginal cost for each product. With joint products A and B produced in fixed proportions where $Q = A = B$, efficient pricing requires that the sum of marginal revenues derived from each product be set equal to the marginal cost of producing the composite product.

Outline

I. Markup Pricing

A. Markup Pricing: In markup pricing, the average variable costs of producing and marketing a particular product are estimated, and then a percentage mark-up is applied to provide for a required profit margin.

1. Markup on Cost: The markup on cost formula is:

$$\text{Markup on cost} = \frac{\text{Price - Cost}}{\text{Cost}}$$

2. Markup on Price: The markup on price formula is:

$$\text{Markup on price} = \frac{\text{Price - Cost}}{\text{Price}}$$

B. The Role of Costs in Markup Pricing: The standard cost or fully allocated cost concept is often applied in markup pricing policies.

1. Standard Costs: Fully allocated costs are determined by first estimating the per unit direct costs, then allocating the

firm's expected indirect expenses assuming a standard output level.

    2.   Potential Problems: Most standard costs are based on historical accounting costs which can be misleading if not properly adjusted for changes in the price level or modified to reflect opportunity costs. Care must also be taken to ensure that only relevant marginal costs are considered.

C.   The Role of Demand in Markup Pricing: Firms set different markups for different products on the basis of competitive pressure and demand elasticities. Care must be exercised to ensure that markups used in markup pricing result in optimal prices.

D.   Markup Pricing and Profit Maximization: Markup pricing is an efficient means for achieving the profit maximization objective.

    1.   Optimal markup on cost formula: The profit maximizing markup on cost is:

$$\text{Optimal markup on cost} = \frac{-1}{\varepsilon_P + 1}$$

where ε_P is the price elasticity of demand.

    2.   Optimal markup on price formula: The profit-maximizing markup on price is:

$$\text{Optimal markup on price} = \frac{-1}{\varepsilon_P}$$

    3.   Empirical evidence strongly suggests that firms employ markup pricing strategies in a manner that is entirely consistent with profit maximization.

II. Incremental Analysis in Pricing

A.   Definition: Incremental profit analysis, a practical counterpart to marginal profit analysis, deals with the incremental relation between the changes in revenues and costs associated with a particular managerial decision.

B.   The Time Factor in Incremental Analysis: Long-run profit or value maximization requires that both transitory and enduring cost and demand influences be considered. Thus, some decisions with negative short-run consequences may prove value maximizing in the long-run.

III. Price Discrimination

Question 11.5

A. Definition: Price discrimination exists whenever different classes of customers are charged different prices for the same product, or when a multiproduct firm prices closely-related products in such a manner that the differences in their prices are not proportional to the differences in their marginal costs of production and distribution. Analytically, price discrimination exists whenever:

$$\frac{P_1}{P_2} \neq \frac{MC_1}{MC_2}$$

   1. Objective: The objective of price discrimination is to enhance seller profits by setting $MR = MC$ for each customer or customer group. In so doing, sellers capture a greater share of the total value of output.

   2. Consumers' Surplus: Consumers' surplus is the difference between the prices paid and the value of output to consumers. Price discrimination results in a transfer of consumers' surplus to producers (sellers).

B. Requirements for Profitable Price Discrimination:

   1. The firm must be able to segment the market for a product. Not only must multiple markets exist, but reselling from one market to another must be prevented.

   2. Different price elasticities of demand for the product must exist in the various submarkets.

Question 11.6

C. Types of Price Discrimination: Price discrimination can be encountered in the:

   1. First degree: Different prices (markups) for each consumer. This creates maximum profits for sellers.

   2. Second degree: Different prices (markups) based on customer use rates.

   3. Third degree: Different prices (markups) for each customer type defined on the basis of age, sex, income, etc. This is the most common type of price discrimination.

212

D. Profit Maximization under Price Discrimination: A firm that can segment its market will maximize profits by operating in such a way that marginal revenue equals marginal cost in each market segment.

IV. Multiple-Product Pricing

A. Background: Although multiple product pricing requires the same basic analysis as that for a single product, the analysis is complicated by interrelations between output demand and production costs.

B. Demand Interrelations: Revenues generated by one product sometimes affect sales of other products.

C. Production Interrelations: Products are sometimes produced in a fixed or variable ratio. They may compete for the resources of the firm or be complementary.

D. Joint Products Produced in Fixed Proportions: If two or more products must be produced in a fixed ratio, they are are joint products and must be considered as a package of output.

   1. Profit Maximizing Decision Rule: For joint products A and B where $Q = A = B$, profit maximization requires setting relevant:

   $$MR_A + MR_B = MC_Q$$

E. Joint Products Produced in Variable Proportions: If two or more products can be produced in variable proportions, they can be treated as individually separate outputs.

   1. Profit Maximizing Decision Rule: Since the firm can vary the proportions in which the products are produced, it is possible to construct separate marginal cost relations for each of the products. Optimal price-output determination requires:

   $$MR_A = MC_A \text{ and } MR_B = MC_B$$

PROBLEMS AND SOLUTIONS

11.1

Air California, Ltd., is a regional airline serving a large number of west coast markets. Using recent operating data, the company wants to determine a profit maximizing price for service provided between the Orange County and Sacramento airports. During recent weeks, the company found that a one-way fare reduction from $75 to $69 had increased route traffic from 43 to 53 passengers per flight. On average, the company projects a cost per departure of $2,194.20.

a. Calculate the arc price elasticity of demand for the airline service.

b. Using the arc price elasticity of demand as the best available estimate of the point price elasticity, and in light of operating costs, will the new $69 fare result in an optimal markup on cost? If so, why? If not, why not?

11.1 SOLUTION

a.

$$E_P = \frac{Q_2 - Q_1}{P_2 - P_1} \times \frac{P_2 + P_1}{Q_2 - Q_1}$$

$$= \frac{53 - 43}{\$69 - \$75} \times \frac{\$69 + \$75}{53 + 43}$$

$$= \underline{-2.5}$$

b. <u>Yes</u>. The marginal cost per passenger is $41.40 (= 2,194.20/53). Given P = $69, the implied markup on cost is:

$$\text{Markup on cost} = \frac{\text{Price - Cost}}{\text{Cost}}$$

$$= \frac{\$69 - \$41.40}{\$41.40}$$

$$= \underline{0.67} \text{ or } 67 \text{ percent}$$

We see from Table 11.2 in the text that this is an optimal markup given $\varepsilon_P = -2.5$. Given MC = $41.40, the optimal price is:

$$P = MC \left(\frac{1}{1 + \dfrac{1}{\varepsilon_P}} \right)$$

$$= \$41.40 \left(\frac{1}{1 + \dfrac{1}{-2.5}} \right)$$

$$= \underline{\underline{\$69}}$$

Alternatively, using the optimal markup on cost formula:

$$\text{Optimal Markup on Cost} = \frac{-1}{\varepsilon_P + 1}$$

$$= \frac{-1}{-2.5 + 1}$$

$$= \underline{\underline{0.67}} \text{ or } 67 \text{ percent}$$

11.2

Last week, Hammond's Grocery offered a 25¢ coupon on 12-packs of Diet Cola, regularly priced at $4. Coupons were used on 40 percent of all purchases, and resulted in an increase from 400 to 490 cases sold.

a. Using the regular $4 price as a base, calculate the point price elasticity of demand for Diet Cola. Assume the price cut was entirely responsible for the change in sales.

b. Calculate the optimal markup on cost for Diet Cola.

c. If Hammond's marginal cost per unit is $3 plus 20¢ in handling costs, calculate Hammond's profit maximizing price on Diet Cola.

d. Using P = $4 and Q = 400 as a base and the point price elasticity of demand formula, calculate expected unit sales, revenues and profits at the profit maximizing activity level. (Note: For simplicity, assume MC = AVC).

11.2 SOLUTION

a. Since coupons were used on 40 percent of all purchases, the average price reduction was 10¢ (= 0.4 × 25¢). Thus,

$$\varepsilon_P = \Delta Q / \Delta P \times P/Q$$

$$= \frac{(490 - 400)}{(\$3.90 - \$4)} \times \frac{\$4}{400}$$

215

$$= \underline{\underline{-9}}$$

b. Given $\varepsilon_P = -9$, the optimal markup on cost is:

$$\text{Optimal Markup on Cost} = \frac{-1}{\varepsilon_P + 1}$$

$$= \frac{-1}{-9 + 1}$$

$$= \underline{\underline{0.125}} \text{ or } 12.5 \text{ percent}$$

c. With an optimal markup of 12.5 percent, Hammond's profit maximizing price on Diet Cola is:

$$\text{Markup} = \frac{\text{Price} - \text{Cost}}{\text{Cost}}$$

$$0.125 = \frac{\text{Price} - \$3.20}{\$3.20}$$

$$0.40 = \text{Price} - 3.20$$

$$\text{Price} = \underline{\underline{\$3.60}}$$

d. Expected unit sales at the profit maximizing activity level can be calculated using the point price elasticity formula:

$$\varepsilon_P = dQ/dP \times P/Q$$

$$-9 = \frac{(Q_2 - 400)}{(\$3.60 - \$4)} \times \frac{\$4}{400}$$

$$3.60 = 0.01(Q_2 - 400)$$

$$360 = Q_2 - 400$$

$$Q_2 = \underline{\underline{760}} \text{ cases}$$

$$TR = PQ$$

$$= \$3.60(760)$$

$$= \underline{\underline{\$2,736}}$$

216

$$\pi \ = \ TR - TC$$

$$= \ (P - AVC)Q$$

$$= \ (\$3.60 - \$3.20)760$$

$$= \ \underline{\underline{\$304}}$$

11.3

Car-Rent, Inc. recently offered $50 off its regular $325 weekly price on unlimited mileage subcompact car rentals. Due to the success of the promotion, sales rose from 20 to 40 rentals. The company finds that incremental costs per rental average $243.75.

11.3 SOLUTION

a.
$$E_P \ = \ \frac{Q_2 - Q_1}{P_2 - P_1} \times \frac{P_2 + P_1}{Q_2 + Q_1}$$

$$= \ \frac{40 - 20}{\$275 - \$325} \times \frac{\$275 + \$325}{\$40 + 20}$$

$$= \ \underline{\underline{-4}}$$

b.   <u>No</u>. Given relevant costs of $243.75 per unit, markup on price is:

$$\text{Markup on price} \ = \ \frac{\text{Price - Cost}}{\text{Price}}$$

$$= \ \frac{\$275 - \$243.75}{\$275}$$

$$= \ \underline{\underline{0.11}} \text{ or 11 percent}$$

We see from the optimal markup on price formula that this is too low since:

$$\text{Optimal Markup on Price} \ = \ \frac{-1}{\varepsilon_P}$$

$$= \ \frac{-1}{-4}$$

$$= \ \underline{\underline{0.25}} \text{ or 25 percent}$$

217

The original $325 price is optimal, and the promotion should be discontinued.

$$\text{Original markup on price} = \frac{\text{Price - Cost}}{\text{Price}}$$

$$= \frac{\$325 - \$243.75}{\$325}$$

$$= 0.25$$

11.4

Last year, Body Beautiful Health Centers, Inc. reduced its annual membership rate by four percent. After accounting for changes in other important factors, the company could only attribute a six percent gain in unit sales to this price reduction.

a. Calculate the point price elasticity of demand for memberships.

b. In light of marginal costs per member of $500, calculate the optimal membership price and markup on price.

11.4 SOLUTION

a.
$$\varepsilon_P = \frac{\text{Percentage change in unit sales}}{\text{Percentage change in price}}$$

$$= \frac{0.06}{-0.04}$$

$$= \underline{-1.5}$$

b. Given MC = $500, the optimal price is:

$$P = MC \left(\frac{1}{1 + \dfrac{1}{\varepsilon_P}} \right)$$

$$= \$500 \left(\frac{1}{1 + \dfrac{1}{-1.5}} \right)$$

$$= \underline{\$1,500}$$

From the optimal markup on price formula, we find:

218

$$\text{Optimal Markup on Price } = \frac{-1}{\varepsilon_P}$$

$$= \frac{-1}{-1.5}$$

$$= \underline{0.67} \text{ or } 67 \text{ percent}$$

Thus, a membership price of $1,500 involves an optimal markup of $1,000 or 67%.

11.5

The Columbia Power Tools Company manufactures a battery-powered saw. Due to increased demand during the past few years, CPT has increased plant capacity for the saw to 300,000 units. The firm's expected output for next year was 250,000 units, but it has received a special order for 100,000 units from a firm outside its normal market. The standard selling price is $50 per unit, but this firm has offered $40 per unit for the special order. Relevant cost data for the saw are as follows:

	Per Unit
Raw materials	$20
Direct labor	10
Variable overhead	3
Fixed overhead	2

Using the incremental profit framework, should CPT accept the special order?

11.5   SOLUTION

Incremental Revenue calculation:

Price per unit	$ 40
Units	× 100,000
Incremental revenue	$4,000,000

219

Incremental Cost Calculation:

Raw materials	$2,000,000
Direct labor	1,000,000
Variable overhead	300,000
Opportunity cost:	
Capacity is 300,000 units; 50,000 units of next year's expected demand will have to be foregone if the order is accepted:	
Sales revenue 2,500,000	
Variable costs 1,650,000	
Profit lost on foregone orders	850,000
Incremental Cost	$4,150,000
Incremental Profit	-$150,000

The firm should not accept the special order, since the incremental profit from the special order is negative.

11.6

The Modern Appliance Company manufactures an electric mixer-juicer. Sales of the appliance have increased steadily during the previous five years and, because of a recently completed expansion program, annual capacity is now 500,000 units. Production and sales for next year are forecast at 400,000 units, and projected standard production costs are estimated as:

Materials	$3.00
Direct labor	2.00
Variable indirect labor	1.00
Overhead	1.50
Standard costs per unit	$7.50

In addition to production costs, Modern projects fixed selling expenses and variable warranty repair expenses of 75¢ and 60¢ per unit, respectively. Modern is currently receiving $10 per unit from its wholesale customers (primarily retail appliance stores), and expects this price to hold during the coming year.

After making these projections, Modern received an inquiry about the purchase of a large quantity of mixers-juicers from a discount department store chain. The discount chain's inquiry contained two purchase offers:

Offer 1.   The chain would purchase 80,000 units at $7.30 per unit. These units would bear the Modern label and the Modern warranty would be provided.

Offer 2.   The chain would purchase 120,000 units at $7 per unit. These units would be sold under the buyer's private label and Modern would not provide warranty service.

a.   Evaluate the effect of each offer on pretax net income for next year.

b.   Should other factors be considered in deciding whether to accept one of these offers?

c.   Which offer, if either, should Modern accept? Why?

11.6   SOLUTION

a.   The incremental net income from the offers can be determined as follows:

	Offer 1		Offer 2	
Unit price		$7.30		$7.00
Unit variable costs:				
Materials	$3.00		$ 3.00	
Direct labor	2.00		2.00	
Variable indirect labor	1.00		1.00	
Variable warranty expense	0.60		---	
Unit variable costs		$6.60		$ 6.00
Unit incremental profit		$0.70		$1.00
Units to be sold		× 80,000		× 120,000
Total variable profit on units sold at special price		$56,000		$120,000

Less variable profit
 lost on regular sales:

Regular price	$10.00	
Regular variable cost	- 6.60	
Regular variable profit	$ 3.40	
Units which cannot be sold at regular price if offer 2 is accepted	× 20,000	
Opportunity cost of lost regular sales		$ 68,000
Incremental profit	$56,000	$ 52,000

b.   Other factors to be considered by Modern include:

 1.   The image of Modern's quality may be affected by sales of the appliance in the discount chain with Modern's label.

 2.   Other buyers may demand the reduced price if Modern accepts offer 1, and the discount chain undercuts them at the retail price.

 3.   The sales lost if Modern accepts offer 2 may affect future orders from regular customers.

c.   It depends upon how you evaluate the factors discussed in part b above. The incremental profits of offer 1 exceed those of offer 2, but other factors might well dictate that offer 1 not be accepted.

11.7

The Midcontinent Railroad Company runs a freight train daily between Indianapolis and Chicago. It has two major users of this service: Indiana Steel Companies and Midwestern Agriculture. The demand for freight cars by each market is given by the equations:

$$P_1 = \$550 - \$5Q_1 \text{ (Indiana Steel Companies demand)}$$

$$P_2 = \$300 - \$1.25Q_2 \text{ (Midwestern Agriculture demand)}$$

P_i is the price charged by Midcontinent for hauling one freight car of materials between Indianapolis and Chicago, and Q_i represents the number of cars demanded by each user. Midcontinent's total cost function for the daily train service is given by:

$$TC = \$10,000 + \$50Q$$

where Q is the number of freight cars hauled on a particular trip.

222

a. What conditions are necessary for profitable price discrimination by Midcontinent?

b. What profit maximizing rule will Midcontinent employ to set prices as a price discriminator? Graphically determine the profit maximizing quantity of freight service Midcontinent will supply, show how it will divide this quantity between the steel and agricultural markets, and indicate the corresponding prices to be charged each company. Show that marginal revenue is equal in the two markets.

c. Assume that Midcontinent is prevented by law from engaging in price discrimination. What is the profit maximizing rule for determining profit and output under these conditions? Graphically determine Midcontinent's profit maximizing output and price under these conditions.

11.7 SOLUTION

a. In order for price discrimination to be profitable, Midcontinent must first be able to segment the market and prevent resale from one segment to another. Second, the elasticity of demand in one segment of the market must be lower than in the other if price discrimination is to be profitable.

b. With price discrimination, the profit maximizing rule is to equate marginal revenue with marginal cost in each market. Such an equality exists at points X and Y in the steel and agricultural market graphs, respectively. This indicates how total output (150 freight cars) should be allocated between steel (50 freight cars) and agriculture (100 freight cars), and the different prices to be charged each user.

The freight unit price for steel is $300, while that for agriculture is $175. Marginal revenue in each market is $50 and is equal to marginal cost.

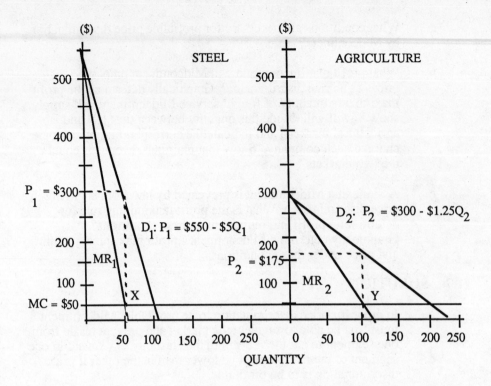

c. Without price discrimination, the profit maximizing rule is to equate aggregate marginal revenue with marginal cost (point Z on graph). Here a vertical line from Z intersects the aggregate demand curve (point Y) determining the equal price ($200) to be charged in each market. A horizontal line at that price level will intersect the individual submarket demand curves (points W and X) and indicate the quantity of service (70 and 80 freight cars for steel and agriculture, respectively) that will be sold in each market.

The important point to remember is that total output and total costs are identical with and without price discrimination. However, since price discrimination allows the seller to charge higher average prices by setting MR = MC in each market, price discrimination will always increase seller profits.

224

11.7

Midcontinent Railroad Company graph.

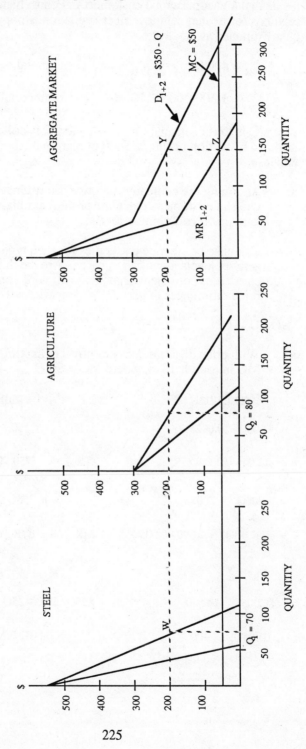

11.8

Envirotec Corporation is an insulation contractor serving both residential and commercial customers in Pennsylvania. Demand relations for treated cellulose fiber insulation, a popular product, have been estimated as:

$$Q_R = 400,000 - 400P_R \qquad \text{(Residential demand)}$$

$$Q_C = 1,200,000 - 1,600P_C \qquad \text{(Commercial demand)}$$

where Q is tons of insulation installed and P is dollars. Each ton of installed insulation results in $600 of marginal labor and materials expense.

a. Assuming the company can price discriminate between its two types of customers, calculate profit maximizing price, output and total profit contribution levels.

b. Calculate point price elasticities for each type of customer at the activity levels identified in part a. Are the differences in these elasticities consistent or inconsistent with your recommended price differences in part a? Why or why not?

11.8 SOLUTION

a. With price discrimination, profits are maximized by setting MR = MC in each market, where MC = $600.

Residential	Commercial

$P_R = \$1,000 - \$0.0025Q_R$ $\qquad$ $P_C = \$750 - \$0.000625Q_C$

$TR_R = (1,000 - 0.0025Q_R)Q_R$ $\qquad$ $TR_C = (750 - 0.000625Q_C)Q_C$

$\quad = 1,000Q_R - 0.0025Q_R^2$ $\qquad$ $\quad = 750Q_C - 0.000625Q_C^2$

$MR_R = dTR_R/dQ_R = 1,000 - 0.005Q_R$ $\qquad$ $MR_C = dTR_C/dQ_C = 750 - 0.000125Q_C$

$MR_R = MC$ $\qquad\qquad\qquad$ $MR_C = MC$

$\$1,000 - \$0.005Q_R = \$600$ $\qquad$ $\$750 - \$0.00125Q_C = \$600$

$0.005Q_R = 400$ $\qquad\qquad\qquad$ $0.00125Q_C = 150$

$\underline{Q_R = 80,000}$ $\qquad\qquad\qquad$ $\underline{Q_C = 120,000}$

226

and

$$P_R = \$1,000 - \$0.0025(80,000) \qquad P_C = \$750 - \$0.000625(120,000)$$

$$= \underline{\$800} \text{ per ton} \qquad\qquad = \underline{\$675} \text{ per ton}$$

The profit contribution earned by the company is:

$$\pi = P_R Q_R + P_C Q_C - AVC(Q_R + Q_C)$$

$$= \$800(80,000) + \$675(120,000) - \$600(80,000$$

$$+ \$120,000)$$

$$= \underline{\$25,000,000}$$

b.   Yes. A higher price for residential customers is consistent with the lower degree of price elasticity observed in that market.

	Residential	Commercial

$$\varepsilon_P = dQ_R/dP_R \times P_R/Q_R \qquad \varepsilon_P = dQ_C/dP_C \times P_C/Q_C$$

$$= -400 \times (\$800/80,000) \qquad = -1,600 \times (\$675/120,000)$$

$$= \underline{-4} \qquad\qquad\qquad = \underline{-9}$$

11.9

Iota Enterprises produces two products in a joint production process. The products are produced in fixed proportions in a 1:1 ratio. The cost functions for this production process are:

$$TC = \$50 + \$2Q + \$2Q^2$$

$$MC = \$2 + \$4Q$$

where Q is a unit of output consisting of one unit of Product A and one unit of Product B.

a.   Assuming the demand and marginal revenue curves for Iota's two products are:

	Product A	Product B

$$P_A = \$352 - Q_A \qquad\qquad P_B = \$100 - 3Q_B$$

$$MR_A = \$352 - \$2Q_A \qquad MR_B = \$100 - \$6Q_B$$

what are the optimal sales quantities and prices for each of these products? (Assume unsold production can be costlessly dumped.)

b. Assume now that Iota incurs an added disposal cost of $\$20Q^*$, where Q^* is the number of units of A and/or B manufactured but not sold. What are the optimal sales quantities and product prices under these conditions?

11.9   SOLUTION

a. We can begin analysis of this problem by examining the optimal activity level of Iota, assuming the firm manufactures and sells equal quantities of A and B. In this situation, since each unit of production generates revenues for both products A and B, we set:

$$MR = MR_A + MR_B = MC$$

$$\$352 - \$2Q + \$100 - \$6Q = \$2 + \$4Q \quad \text{(Since } Q_A = Q_B = Q\text{)}$$

$$12Q = 450$$

$$Q = \underline{\underline{37.5}}$$

Thus, profit maximization with equal sales of each product requires that the firm operate at the level $Q = 37.5$. Marginal revenues for the two products would be:

$$MR_A = \$352 - \$2Q_A = 352 - 2(37.5) = \$277$$

$$MR_B = \$100 - \$6Q_B = 100 - 6(37.5) = -\$125$$

Despite the fact that $MR_A + MR_B = \$277 - \$125 = \$152 = 2 + 4(37.5) = MC$, the negative marginal revenue for B invalidates this solution. With the negative marginal revenue for B, this solution is obviously incorrect if Iota can dispose of B, or otherwise hold it off the market, without incurring additional costs. In this case, Iota would sell B only up to the point where its marginal revenue is zero since with production for A, the relevant marginal cost of B is zero.

$$MR_B = MC_B$$

228

$$\$100 - \$6Q_B = \$0$$

$$6Q_B = 100$$

$$Q_B = \underline{16.67}$$

and

$$P_B = \$100 - \$3(Q_B)$$

$$= 100 - 3(16.67)$$

$$= \underline{\$49.99}$$

Determination of the optimal production and sales level for A is found by equating the marginal revenue from A, the only product being sold from the marginal production unit, with the marginal cost of production.

$$MR_A = MC_A = MC_Q$$

$$\$352 - \$2Q = \$2 + \$4Q \qquad \text{(Since } Q_A = Q)$$

$$6Q = 350$$

$$Q_A = \underline{58.33}$$

and

$$P_A = \$352 - Q_A$$

$$= 352 - 58.33$$

$$= \underline{\$293.67}$$

Here, note that $MR_A + MR_B = \$235.33 = MC$, but unlike before, $MR_A = MC_A$ and $MR_B = MC_B$ as well. Thus, Iota should produce 58.33 units of output, selling all 58.33 units of A at a price of $293.67. Only 16.67 units of B will be sold at a price of $49.99, with the remaining 41.67 units being destroyed or otherwise held off the market.

b. The solution to part a indicates that only disposal of B needs to be examined. In this situation, it will be more profitable for Iota to continue selling B so long as the negative marginal revenue is less than $20, the per unit disposal cost. Alternatively, the marginal cost of selling as opposed to dumping B is -$20. Thus, we can determine the maximum sales quantity for B under these conditions as:

$$MR_B = MC_B - \text{Disposal cost saving}$$

$$\$100 - \$6Q_B = \$0 - \$20$$

$$6Q_B = 120$$

$$Q_B = \underline{\underline{20}}$$

$$P_B = \$100 - \$3Q_B$$

$$= 100 - 3(20)$$

$$= \underline{\underline{\$40}}$$

The optimal production level is found by setting MR_A equal to MC_Q plus the disposal cost of the unsold B being produced and dumped at the margin.

$$MR_A = MC_Q + \text{Disposal cost} = MC_A$$

$$\$352 - \$2Q = \$2 + \$4Q + \$20 \quad (\text{Since } Q_A = Q)$$

$$6Q = 330$$

$$Q_A = \underline{\underline{55}}$$

$$P_A = \$352 - \$55 = \underline{\underline{\$297}}$$

Once again, $MR_A + MR_B = MC$, with $MR_A = MC_A$ and $MR_B = MC_B$. Iota will produce 55 units of output selling all 55 units of A produced. Twenty units of B will be sold, and 35 units of B will be disposed of.

11.10

Nisswa Petroleum, Inc. operates oil and gas producing wells in the Overthrust Belt region. On average, for each barrel of oil pumped to the surface, one thousand cubic feet of natural gas is also recovered. Therefore, the company views oil and gas as joint products where each unit of production involves 1 bbl: 1 mcf. Marginal costs are $15 per unit of production.

While each output is sold in perfectly competitive commodity markets, transport, handling and related costs have the effect of reducing the net price received by Nisswa. Thus, the net price/output and marginal revenue relations for oil is:

$$P_O = \$20 - \$0.000075Q_O$$

$$MR_O = dTR_O/dQ_O = \$20 - \$0.00015Q_O$$

and for gas is:

$$P_G = \$3 - 0.000025Q_G$$

$$MR_G = \$3 - \$0.00005Q_G$$

where Q_O is barrels of oil and Q_G is mcf of natural gas sold per month.

a.   Calculate the profit maximizing price/output combination for oil and gas under current conditions.

b.   Now assume that instability in the world oil market has caused the demand for domestic oil to double. Holding all else equal, calculate the new optimal price/output combination for oil and gas.

11.10 SOLUTION

a.   We begin analysis of this problem by examining the optimal activity level for Nisswa based on the assumption that all production of each byproduct will be sold.

For profit maximization set,

$$MR = MR_O + MR_G = MC$$

$$\$20 - \$0.00015Q + \$3 - \$0.00005Q = \$15 \text{ (Since } Q = Q_O = Q_G)$$

$$0.0002Q = 8$$

$$Q = \underline{40,000}$$

Thus, profit maximization with all production being sold requires that the firm produce 40,000 units of production involving 40,000 bbls of oil and 40,000 mcf of natural gas. Under this assumption, marginal revenues for each byproduct are:

$$MR_O = \$20 - \$0.00015(40,000) = \$14$$

231

$$MR_G = \$3 - \$0.00005(40,000) = \$1$$

Clearly, each byproduct is making a positive contribution to marginal costs. Since MR = \$14 + \$1 = \$15 = MC, Nisswa has no incentive to alter production from the $Q = Q_O = Q_G = 40,000$ optimal production and sales level.

And finally, relevant prices are:

$$P_O = \$20 - \$0.000075(40,000) = \underline{\underline{\$17}} \text{ per bbl}$$

$$P_G = \$3 - \$0.000025(40,000) = \underline{\underline{\$2}} \text{ per mcf}$$

b. A doubling (or 100 percent increase) in oil demand means that a given quantity could be sold at twice the original price. Alternatively, 2 times the original quantity demanded could be sold at a given price. Therefore, the new oil demand and marginal revenue curves can be written:

$$P_O' = 2(\$20 - \$0.000075Q_O) \qquad MR_O' = 2(\$20 - \$0.00015Q_O)$$

$$= \$40 - \$0.00015Q_O \qquad\qquad = \$40 - \$0.0003Q_O$$

Now, assuming all output is sold, we set:

$$MR' = MR_O' + MR_G = MC$$

$$\$40 - \$0.0003Q + \$3 - \$0.00005Q = \$15 \text{ (Since } Q = Q_O = Q_G)$$

$$0.00035Q = 28$$

$$Q = 80,000$$

Thus, profit maximization with sale of all production requires that the firm produce and sell $Q = Q_O = Q_G = 80,000$. Under this assumption, marginal revenues for the two products are:

$$MR_O' = \$40 - \$0.0003(80,000) = \$16$$

$$MR_G = \$3 - \$0.00005(80,000) = -\$1$$

Even though $MR' = MR_O' + MR_G = \$15 = MC$, the above

$Q = 80,000$ solution is suboptimal. $MR_O' = \$16 > \$15 = MC$ implies that a $1 profit contribution was earned on each unit of production when just considering oil sales. This means that Nasri would like to expand production beyond $Q = 80,000$ just in order to sell more oil. The negative marginal revenue on gas is "holding down" oil production at the margin.

Nasri will only sell gas up until the point where $MR_G = 0$ since, given expanded production to sell oil, the marginal cost of gas is zero. Set,

$$MR_G = MC_G$$

$$\$3 - \$0.00005Q_G = \$0$$

$$0.00005Q_G = 3$$

$$Q_G = \underline{\underline{60,000}}$$

$$P_G = \$3 - \$0.000025(60,000)$$

$$= \underline{\underline{\$1.50}} \text{ per mcf}$$

The optimal production and sales level for oil is found by setting $MR_O' = MC_O = MC$, since oil is the only product being sold from the marginal unit of production.

$$MR_O' = \$40 - \$0.0003Q_O = \$15$$

$$0.0003Q_O = 25$$

$$Q_O = \underline{\underline{83,333}}$$

$$P_O = \$40 - \$0.00015(83,333) = \underline{\underline{\$27.50}} \text{ per bbl}$$

Therefore, Nisswa will produce 83,333 units of production and sell all 83,333 bbls of oil produced at $27.50 per bbl, but only 60,000 mcf of gas at $1.50 per mcf. The remaining 23,333 mcf of gas produced will be flared off (burned or dumped) at the well site, or otherwise held off the market (stored for future sale).

233

(Note: A doubling in oil demand doesn't have the effect of
doubling oil prices given the resulting increase in production).

234

CHAPTER TWELVE:
THE ROLE OF GOVERNMENT IN THE MARKET ECONOMY

Theme

An important element of the competitive environment today is the growing importance of government involvement in the market economy. Recent changes in the method and scope of government regulation, including moves toward deregulation, affect the entire spectrum of economic activity, from industrials, to financial institutions (banks, savings and loans, insurance, etc.), to power and transportation utilities. Both state and federal regulation and antitrust policy constitute important constraints on many managerial decisions. As a result, their analysis constitutes an important aspect of managerial economics. In this chapter, the role of government in the market economy is analyzed by considering the economic and political rationale for regulation, including: grant policy which provides firms with positive incentives for "desirable" activity, tax policy which constrains the nature of goods and services that are marketed and the processes used to produce them, direct regulation of firms possessing substantial market power, and antitrust policy designed to maintain a "workable" level of competition in the economy. And finally, some problems of current methods of regulation are investigated in order to illuminate the causes of deregulation and various possibilities for improving regulatory processes.

Outline

I. **The Rationale for Regulation**

    A.   Economic Considerations: Government regulation is sometimes justified on the basis of its ability to correct various market imperfections which lead to inefficiency and waste. The two types of market imperfections most often thought to cause "market failure" are structural and incentive problems.

        1.   Market Failure: The failure of unregulated market activity to provide desired goods and services at competitive prices. Most often, market failure is thought to be caused by:

            a.   Structural problems: too few buyers or sellers.

            b.   Incentive problems: externalities such as pollution, etc.

    B.   Political Considerations: Government regulation is also sometimes justified on the basis of political considerations. Primary among such considerations are desires to:

1. Preserve Consumer Choice: A wide variety in production enhances personal freedom.

2. Limit Economic and Political Power: Unchecked economic and political power could threaten basic liberties.

II. Regulatory Response to Incentive Failures

A. Operating Right Grants: Service "in the public interest" is often promoted by offering firms valuable operating rights in return for specific operating concessions (e.g., public service broadcasts for local TV licenses).

B. Patent Grants: The patent monopoly (17 years in length) is granted to firms in order to promote valuable research and development.

C. Subsidies: A rapidly growing method of public support for desired business activity is implicit or outright subsidy. A prominent example is the growing use of tax-free financing (municipal bonds at low interest rates) for private investment and housing projects.

D. Tax Policies: Taxes or fines can be assessed on a regular or intermittent basis in order to encourage firms to minimize undesirable externalities such as air, water, or noise pollution.

E. Operating Controls: Operating controls are various government directives designed to compel desirable business activity under penalty of law.

F. Who Pays?: In dealing with this issue, both the incidence and burden of regulatory costs must be considered. The point of cost incidence is where, for example, taxes are collected, tolls are paid or pollution reducing expenditures are made. The burden of these costs, however, may be passed on to customers through higher output prices, to workers through lower wages, or suppliers through lower input prices. The ability of producers to pass on regulatory costs depends on product demand elasticities:

1. Elastic demand: With perfectly elastic demand, producers including firm owners, employees and suppliers bear all regulatory costs.

2. Inelastic demand: With perfectly inelastic demand, consumers bear all regulatory costs.

3. Most common result: Elasticities of demand are seldom perfectly elastic or perfectly inelastic. In most cases, both

producers and consumers share the burden of regulatory costs.

III. Regulatory Response to Structural Failures

    A.   The Dilemma of Natural Monopoly: A natural monopoly exists if average production costs in an industry decline continuously as output expands. This situation presents a dilemma for policy makers since:

        1.   Efficiency Potential: A monopolist has the potential to achieve lower average costs than would a group of smaller competitors.

        2.   Inefficiency Risk: A monopolist can have only limited motivation for efficiency. Inefficiency and waste can result.

    B.   Utility Price Regulation: Utility price regulation attempts to achieve the efficiency potential of natural monopoly, while limiting inefficiency risks. Typically, monopoly is allowed but regulators set $P = AC$ in order to encourage output expansion and thereby lowering average costs, while limiting monopoly profits. Audits of operating costs are also undertaken in an effort to limit excessive expenditures.

    C.   Problems in Utility Regulation: Significant problems in utility regulation exist which limit its effectiveness. Among such problems are:

        1.   Pricing Problems: Defining a pricing schedule that will promote both equity and efficiency objectives is difficult given the large number of utility customer classifications.

        2.   Output Level Problems: Because demand and cost functions are unknown, determining optimal output levels is very difficult.

        3.   Inefficiency: Reducing inefficiency and waste through regulatory surveillance is difficult since only actual, not necessarily minimum, costs are observed.

        4.   Investment Level: Regulation can lead to suboptimal input combinations by encouraging excessive or insufficient levels of capital investment.

        5.   Regulatory Lag and Political Problems: Utility rate increases made necessary by inflation are often delayed or inadequate due to their political unpopularity. These and

other political pressures can thus reduce utility operating efficiency.

6. Cost of Regulation: An important drawback to current methods of utility regulation is their cost. These costs include government administrative costs, as well as company expenditures necessary for compliance.

D. Windfall Profits Taxes: Windfall profits taxes are sometimes used to reduce profits due to unanticipated changes in demand caused by influences beyond firm control (e.g., oil windfall profits due to OPEC price increases).

E. Small Company Tax Preferences: Various tax preferences for small as opposed to large businesses have been imposed for both economic and political reasons during recent years.

IV. Antitrust Policy

A. Basic Statutes: Antitrust policy is based on two statutes and their amendments:

1. Sherman Act (1890)

2. Clayton Act (1914)

B. Overview of Antitrust Law: Antitrust law is an example of case law. In case law, judicial interpretation is relied upon in determining prohibited behavior. Thus, legal precedent is extremely important. (Note: In statutory law specific acts such as murder are explicitly prohibited by the legislative branch.)

C. Sherman Act (1890): The Sherman Act was the first piece of federal antitrust legislation.

1. Section 1: Forbade every contract, combination or conspiracy in restraint of trade and was aimed at cartels or cartel-like behavior.

2. Section 2: Forbade monopolizing or any effort explicitly designed to drive competitors out of business.

3. The imprecise nature of the Sherman Act reduced its effectiveness.

D. Clayton Act (1914): The Clayton Act was designed to overcome some of the ambiguity of the Sherman Act by explicitly prohibiting certain behavior.

238

1. Section 2: Forbade price discrimination between firms which tended to lessen competition. This section was later amended by the Robinson-Patman Act (1936). It is important to remember that price discrimination among consumers, such as senior citizen discounts for bus service, is legal.

2. Section 3: Made leases or any sales contracts which lessened competition illegal. This provision was aimed at so-called tying contracts.

3. Section 7: Forbade stock mergers for monopoly. The Celler-Kefauver Act (1950) closed the asset acquisition loophole.

E. Enforcement: Responsibility for antitrust law enforcement lies with the Antitrust Division of the Department of Justice and the Federal Trade Commission.

   1. Criminal Proceedings: Criminal proceedings under the Sherman Act are pursued by the Justice Department with fines, imprisonment or injunctive relief being sought.

   2. Civil Proceedings: Civil proceedings under the Clayton Act are typically pursued by the FTC with "cease and desist" orders being sought.

F. Economic Analyses in Antitrust Actions: Antitrust policy is only brought to bear when significant harm to competition is perceived. Thus, economic analyses of market structures are an important aspect of any antitrust action.

V. The Regulated Environment: A Second Look

A. Costs of Regulation: An important consideration in any review of regulatory policy is the expense involved in terms of administrative and economic resource allocation costs. Total cost estimates run well into the billions of dollars per year.

B. The Size-Efficiency Problem: Regulation and antitrust policy are sometimes criticized for attacking large firms whose superior size and profitability were fairly obtained as a result of superior efficiency.

C. The "Capture" Problem: Economists have suggested that regulation is sometimes carried out for the benefit of regulated firms rather than for the benefit of society as a whole. In such instances, the regulatory process is said to be "captured" by the regulated.

D.   The Deregulation Movement: Dissatisfaction with the high costs
     and low public benefits of many regulations gave birth to a
     deregulation movement during the early 1970s.

E.   Rationalizing the Regulatory Process: Regulation is a tool which
     can be used to further the public interest, but only when
     regulation-induced incentives are understood and carefully
     accounted for.

PROBLEMS AND SOLUTIONS

12.1

The Orion Fertilizer Company takes raw mineral phosphate and converts it into a phosphate-based fertilizer. Recently, representatives from local agriculture and cattle interests have been at odds with the fertilizer industry regarding the effect of a pollutant which Orion and other fertilizer firms emit into the air as a result of the conversion process. The agriculture and cattle interests are aware of the need for phosphate fertilizer, but argue that during the production process flourine gas is released into the air. This pollutant then settles on the citrus crops and grass in a wide area surrounding production facilities, retards the growth of crops and results in an inferior fruit product. The pollutant also settles on grass eaten by cattle, and produces an arthritic condition retarding their growth. These agriculture and cattle interests have petitioned the State Environmental Protection Agency for immediate pollution controls on Orion's conversion process. These controls would affect annual fixed and variable costs of the fertilizer industry and would also add $30 million to their total asset base of $210 million.

Orion and other firms in the fertilizer industry agree that something needs to be done to stop the pollution. These firms realize that any changes which affect Orion will ultimately have to be followed by the industry in general. These changes could reduce the 10 percent "fair" rate of return on investment which has been earned by the industry. Although they agree with the idea of pollution control, the fertilizer industry argues that an immediate pollution abatement program, similar to the one suggested by the agriculture and cattle interests, would lower industry profits, hamper future capital expansion, lower output, and force employee layoffs. The fertilizer industry advocates a slower program involving some abatement devices to be installed immediately, but with major abatement emphasis to be placed on new facilities. This more gradual process will supposedly have a smaller impact on profits, output, and employment; and would add only $5 million to the total asset base of the industry.

To verify the claims of the fertilizer industry, an independent committee acceptable to both sides was established to determine the relevant economic data. As a result of their analysis, the following demand, marginal revenue, total cost, and marginal cost curves were established for the industry:

$$P = \$35,000 - \$0.5Q \qquad \text{(Demand)}$$

$$MR = \$35,000 - Q \qquad \text{(Marginal Revenue)}$$

$$TC = \$100,000,000 + \$8,000Q + Q^2 \quad \text{(Total cost)}$$

$$MC = \$8,000 + \$2Q \qquad \text{(Marginal Cost)}$$

where P is price and MR is marginal revenue in dollars per hundred tons, Q is hundreds of tons of fertilizer, and TC is total cost and MC is marginal cost in dollars (before capital costs).

If the controls advocated by the agriculture and cattle interests were immediately implemented, the fertilizer industry's cost curves would be adjusted to:

$$TC_1 = \$106,000,000 + \$8,200Q + \$1.1Q^2$$

$$MC_1 = \$8,200 + \$2.2Q$$

If the controls advocated by the fertilizer industry were implemented, the cost curve would be adjusted to:

$$TC_2 = \$101,000,000 + \$8,050Q + Q^2$$

$$MC_2 = \$8,050 + \$2Q$$

a.   What is the current profit maximizing price/output combination, level of profits, and rate of return on investment in the fertilizer industry?

b.   What would be the profit maximizing price/output combination, level of profits, and rate of return on investment in the fertilizer industry if the agriculture and cattle interests' recommendations were implemented?

c.   What would be the profit maximizing price/output combination, level of profits, and rates of return on investment in the fertilizer industry if their own recommendations were implemented?

d.   Which recommendation should be implemented?

12.1 SOLUTION

a.   Set MR = MC to find the profit maximizing output level where:

$$MR = MC$$

$$\$35,000 - Q = \$8,000 + \$2Q$$

$$3Q = 27,000$$

$$Q = \underline{9,000} \text{ (00) or 900,000 tons}$$

$$P = \$35,000 - \$0.5Q$$

$$= 35,000 - 0.5(9,000)$$

$$= \underline{\$30,500} \text{ per hundred tons (or \$305/ton)}$$

$$\pi = \$35,000Q - \$0.5Q^2 - \$100,000,000 - \$8,000Q - Q^2$$

$$= -\$100,000,000 + \$27,000Q - \$1.5Q^2$$

$$= -\$100,000,000 + \$27,000(9,000) - \$1.5(9,000^2)$$

$$= \underline{\$21,500,000}$$

$$\text{Return on investment} = \frac{\pi}{\text{Total assets}}$$

$$= \frac{\$21,500,000}{\$210,000,000}$$

$$= 0.102 \text{ or } 10.2 \text{ percent}$$

(Note: Profits are falling for $Q > 9,000$, so $Q = 9,000$ is a point of maximum profits.)

b. Set $MR = MC_1$ to find the profit maximizing output level:

$$MR = MC_1$$

$$-35,000 - Q = \$8,200 + \$2.2Q$$

$$3.2Q = 26,800$$

$$Q = \underline{8,375}\,(00) \text{ or } 837,500 \text{ tons}$$

$$P = \$35,000 - \$0.5(8,375)$$

$$= \underline{\$30,813} \text{ per hundred tons (or \$308.13/ton)}$$

$$\pi = TR - TC_1$$

$$= -\$106,000,000 + \$26,800(8,375)$$

$$- \$1.6(8,375^2)$$

$$= \underline{\underline{\$6,225,000}}$$

$$\text{Return on investment} = \frac{\pi}{\text{Total assets}}$$

$$= \frac{\$6,225,000}{\$240,000,000}$$

$$= \underline{\underline{0.0259}} \text{ or 2.59 percent}$$

(Note: Profits are falling for $Q > 8,375$, so $Q = 8,375$ is a point of maximum profits).

c.   Set $MR = MC_2$ to find the profit maximizing output level:

$$MR = MC_2$$

$$\$35,000 - Q = \$8,050 + \$2Q$$

$$3Q = 26,950$$

$$Q = \underline{\underline{8,983.33}} \text{ (00) or 898,333 tons}$$

$$P = \$35,000 - \$0.5(8,983.33)$$

$$= \underline{\underline{\$30,508}} \text{ per hundred tons (or \$305.08/ton)}$$

$$\pi = TR - TC_2$$

$$= -\$101,000,000 + \$26,950(8,983.33)$$

$$-\$1.5(8,983.33^2)$$

$$= \underline{\underline{\$20,053,336}}$$

$$\text{Return on investment} = \frac{\pi}{\text{Total assets}}$$

$$= \frac{\$20,053,336}{\$215,000,000}$$

$$= \underline{\underline{0.093}} \text{ or 9.3 percent}$$

244

(Note: Profits are falling for Q > 8,983.33, so Q = 8,933.33 is a point of maximum profits).

d. Obviously, there is no easy answer. While several issues might be raised, some of the more important considerations include:

1. Output and Price: As a result of implementating the agriculture and cattle interests' recommendations, price per ton would be $3.05 higher and industry output would be 60,800 tons lower than if the fertilizer industry's recommendations were implemented.

2. Since output would be much lower with TC_1 than with TC_2, the increase in unemployment in the fertilizer industry would probably be less with the fertilizer industry proposal.

3. The return on investment with TC_1 would fall to less than 3 percent, while with TC_2 it would fall to only 9.3 percent. The former decrease could substantially hamper the raising of funds needed for capital expansion in the fertilizer industry.

4. What is the difference in the short-term and long-run effectiveness of the two pollution abatement programs recommended by the opposing industries?

12.2

The Mid-Ohio Electric Power Company is under review by the state regulatory commission under whose jurisdiction it operates. Relevant demand, marginal revenue, and cost curves including a "fair" rate of return agreed upon by both the firm and the commission are as follows:

$$P = \$100 - \$0.5Q \qquad \text{(Demand)}$$

$$MR = \$100 - Q \qquad \text{(Marginal revenue)}$$

$$TC = \$1,000 + \$5Q \qquad \text{(Total cost)}$$

$$MC = \$5 \qquad \text{(Marginal cost)}$$

where P is price (in dollars), Q is output (in thousands of megawatt hours), TC is total cost (in thousands of dollars), and MC is marginal cost (in thousands of dollars).

a. If the firm were operating as a pure monopolist, what would be its optimal price/output solution and level of economic profits?

245

b. What price should the commission set if it wishes to eliminate economic profits?

12.2 SOLUTION

a. Set MR = MC to find the profit maximizing output level:

$$MR = MC$$

$$\$100 - Q = \$5$$

$$Q = \underline{\underline{95}}(000) \text{ or } 95,000 \text{ megawatt hours}$$

$$P = \$100 - \$0.5Q$$

$$= 100 - 0.5(95)$$

$$= \underline{\underline{\$52.50}}$$

$$\pi = -\$1,000 + \$95(95) - \$0.5(95^2)$$

$$= \underline{\underline{\$3,512.50}}\,(000) \text{ or } \$3,512,500$$

(Note: Profit falls for Q > 95, so Q = 95 is a point of maximum profits).

b. To preclude monopoly profits, the commission should set:

$$P = AR = AC = \frac{TC}{Q}$$

$$\$100 - \$0.5Q = \frac{(\$1,000 + \$5Q)}{Q}$$

$$100Q - 0.5Q^2 = 1,000 + 5Q$$

$$-0.5Q^2 + 95Q - 1,000 = 0$$

This is a quadratic equation of the form:

$$aQ^2 + bQ + c = 0$$

where a = -0.5, b = 95 and c = -1,000. Its two roots can be obtained using the quadratic formula where:

246

$$Q = \frac{-b \pm \sqrt{b^2 - 4ac}}{2a}$$

$$= \frac{-95 \pm \sqrt{(95^2) - 4(-0.5)(-1,000)}}{2(-0.5)}$$

$$= \frac{-95 \pm \sqrt{9,025 - 2,000}}{-1}$$

$$= \frac{-95 \pm 83.82}{-1}$$

$$= 11.18(000) \text{ or } \underline{\underline{178.82}}(000) \begin{array}{l} \text{or } 178,820 \\ \text{megawatt hours} \end{array}$$

Where the "upper" Q is the relevant solution since regulatory commissions generally seek the "largest quantity of service consistent with the public interest." Therefore,

$$P = \$100 - \$0.5Q$$

$$= 100 - 0.5(178.82)$$

$$= \underline{\underline{\$10.59}}$$

$$\pi = -1,000 + 95(178.82) - 0.5(178.82^2)$$

$$= \underline{\underline{0}}$$

12.3

The St. Thomas Paper Company produces newsprint at a plant located in the Fox River Valley of northern Wisconsin. Each ton of newsprint produced, Q_N, creates one ton byproduct of wastewater sludge, Q_S. Currently, there is a limited recycling demand for sludge, and any excess can be costlessly dumped into the Fox River. Monthly demand, marginal revenue, and cost relations facing the company are:

Newsprint	Sludge
$P_N = \$55 - \$0.005Q_N$	$P_S = \$10 - \$0.01Q_S$
$MR_N = \$55 - \$0.01Q_N$	$MR_S = \$10 - \$0.02Q_S$

$$TC = \$40,000 + \$5Q + \$0.005Q^2$$

247

$$MC = \$5 + \$0.01Q$$

a. Calculate optimal output, pollution, price and profit levels for the company.

b. Calculate the minimum fine necessary to compel the company to stop polluting. Explain your answer.

12.3 SOLUTION

a. Solution to this problem requires that one look at various production and sales options available to the firm. If all output were sold, the optimal level of output would be calculated as:

$$MR_N + MR_S = MC$$

$$\$55 - \$0.01Q + \$10 - \$0.02Q = \$5 + \$0.01$$

$$0.04Q = 60$$

$$Q = \underline{\underline{1,500}} \quad (\text{And } Q = Q_N = Q_S)$$

To be optimal, marginal revenue must equal marginal cost for each output. At $Q = 1,500$, we note that:

$$MR_N = \$55 - \$0.01Q$$

$$= 55 - 0.01(1,500)$$

$$= \$40$$

$$MR_S = \$10 - \$0.02Q$$

$$= 10 - 0.02(1,500)$$

$$= -\$20$$

While, $MR_N + MR_S = \$40 - \$20 = \$20 = MC_Q$, this is not an optimal solution because marginal revenue does not equal marginal cost for each output. Since $MR_N > MC_Q$, the company would like to expand output just to sell newsprint. Since $MR_S < 0$, total revenue would rise if fewer tons of sludge were sold. Given that the motivation for increased output is to sell more newsprint, the optimal level of output is determined by setting:

$$MR_N = MC_N = MC_Q$$

248

$$\$55 - \$0.01Q = \$5 + \$0.01Q$$

$$0.02Q = 50$$

$$Q = \underline{\underline{2,500}} \text{ tons (And } Q = Q_N = Q_S)$$

$$P_N = \$55 - \$0.005Q_N$$

$$= 55 - 0.005(2,500)$$

$$= \underline{\underline{\$42.50}}$$

Given output production for newsprint, sludge is "free" and $MC_S = \$0$. Therefore, optimal sales of sludge are:

$$MR_S = MC_S$$

$$\$10 - \$0.02Q_S = \$0$$

$$0.02Q_S = 10$$

$$Q_S = \underline{\underline{500}} \text{ tons of sludge sold}$$

$$Q_S^* = 2,500 - 500$$

$$= \underline{\underline{2,000}} \text{ tons of sludge dumped}$$

$$P_S = \$10 - \$0.01Q_S$$

$$= 10 - 0.01(500)$$

$$= \underline{\underline{\$5}}$$

$$\pi = TR_N + TR_S - TC$$

$$= \$55Q_N - \$0.005Q_N^2 + \$10Q_S$$

$$- \$0.01Q_S^2 - \$40,000 - \$5Q - \$0.005Q^2$$

$$= 55(2,500) - 0.005(2,500^2)$$

$$+ 10(500) - 0.01(500^2)$$

$$-\,40,000 - 5(2,500)$$

$$-\,0.005(2,500^2)$$

$$=\quad \underline{\underline{\$25,000}}$$

b. In part a, we saw that $MR_S = -\$20$ if all output were sold. This means that total profits also fell by \$20 on the last unit of sludge sold since $MC_S = \$0$. A dumping fine of \$20 would make the firm indifferent to dumping and paying a fine, or selling all of its sludge. Note that at $Q_S = 1,500$, $P_S = \$10 - \$0.01Q_S = 10 - 0.01(1,500) = -\$5$. This means that a \$20 dumping fine will cause the company to pay sludge users \$5 per ton to take sludge off its hands. This is similar to the situation faced by some municipalities who pay utilities to burn their garbage for fuel.

Therefore, any fine <u>greater than \$20</u> would cause all sludge to be sold. Dumping would then cease.

12.4

Red River Chemical Corporation produces two products in a joint production process. The two chemicals (A and B) must be produced in the constant 1:1 ratio. Red River Chemical has long followed the practice of dumping its wastes including excess production into the Red River, and currently incurs no cost from this activity. Cost functions for Red River Chemical are:

$$TC \;=\; \$100 + \$10Q + \$4Q^2$$

$$MC \;=\; \$10 + \$8Q$$

where Q represents a unit of production consisting of 1 unit of A and 1 unit of B.

a. Demand and marginal revenue curves for the two products are:

$$P_A \;=\; \$600 - Q_A$$

$$MR_A \;=\; \$600 - \$2Q_A$$

$$P_B \;=\; \$100 - Q_B$$

$$MR_B \;=\; \$100 - \$2Q_B$$

What would be the optimal price/output combination for the two products, assuming Red River Chemical operates as a profit maximizing firm?

b. Assume now that the State Pollution Control Board imposes pollution abatement requirements, including a fine on waste disposal that resulted in Red River Chemical's cost function shifting to:

$$TC = \$100 + \$20Q + \$4Q^2 + \$10Q_A{}^* + \$10Q_B{}^*$$

$$MC = \$20 + \$8Q + 10^*$$

where $Q_A{}^*$ and $Q_B{}^*$ are excess quantities of A and B that are dumped in the Red River, resulting in a $10 fine, 10^*. What are the optimal prices and sales levels for the firm's products now?

c. In light of state-mandated pollution abatement requirements, determine the smallest fine per unit of B dumped that would cause Red River to stop dumping excess production altogether.

12.4   SOLUTION

a. Solution to this problem requires that one look at the production and sales options available to the firm. One option is to produce and sell equal quantities of products A and B. In this case, we consider:

$$MR_A + MR_B = MC$$

$$\$600 - \$2Q + \$100 - \$2Q = \$10 + \$8Q \quad \text{(Since } Q_A = Q_B = Q)$$

$$12Q = 690$$

$$Q = 57.5 \text{ units}$$

Thus, the profit maximizing output level for production and sale of equal quantities of A and B would be 57.5 units. However, one must check to be sure that the marginal revenues of both products are positive at this sales level before claiming that this is an optimal activity level. Marginal revenues for each output evaluated at 57.5 units are:

$MR_A = \$600 - \$2(57.5)$ $\qquad\qquad\qquad MR_B = \$100 - \$2(57.5)$

$\qquad = \$485$ $\qquad\qquad\qquad\qquad\qquad = -\$15$

We see that $MR_A + MR_B = \$485 - \$15 = \$470 = MC$. However, since the marginal revenue for product B is negative, and since Red River can costlessly dump excess production, the sale of 57.5 units of product B is suboptimal. Output of product A is being "held down" by the negative marginal revenue associated with sales of product B. This invalidates the entire solution developed above. The problem must be set up in such a way as to recognize that Red River Chemical will stop selling product B at the point where its marginal revenue becomes zero since, given production for product A, the marginal cost of product B is zero. Set:

$$MR_B = MC_B$$

$$\$100 - \$2Q_B = \$0$$

$$2Q_B = 100$$

$$Q_B = \underline{\underline{50}} \text{ units}$$

Thus, 50 units of product B is the maximum that will be sold. Any excess units will be dumped in the Red River. The price for B at 50 units is:

$$P_B = \$100 - Q_B$$

$$= 100 - 50$$

$$= \underline{\underline{\$50}}$$

To determine the optimal production level of product A, set the marginal revenue of A equal to the marginal cost of producing another unit of the output package.

$$MR_A = MC_A = MC_Q$$

$$\$600 - \$2Q = \$10 + \$8Q \qquad (\text{Since } Q_A = Q)$$

$$10Q = 590$$

$$Q = \underline{\underline{59}}$$

and

$$P_A = \$600 - Q_A$$

252

$$= 600 - 59$$

$$= \underline{\underline{\$541}}$$

The firm will maximize profits by producing 59 units of output, selling 59 units of product A at a price of $541 and 50 units of product B at a price of $50. Nine units of B will be dumped.

b. Part b is solved in a manner similar to part a. Be careful to note, however, that the imposition of pollution abatement requirements has altered Red River's total cost function, as has the imposition of fines on waste disposal. As a first step, one must determine whether production and sale of equal quantities of the two products is optimal. For this case, we consider:

$$MR_A + MR_B = MC$$

$$\$600 - \$2Q + \$100 - \$2Q = \$20 + \$8Q \text{ (Since } Q_A = Q_B = Q)$$

$$12Q = 680$$

$$Q = 56.67 \text{ units}$$

Checking the marginal revenues of A and B at 56.67 units, we find:

$$MR_A = \$600 - \$2Q_A$$

$$= 600 - 2(56.67)$$

$$= \$486.67$$

$$MR_B = \$100 - \$2Q_B$$

$$= 100 - 2(56.67)$$

$$= -\$13.34$$

Here again, $MR_A + MR_B = \$486.67 - \$13.34 = \$473.33 = MC$. However, because the marginal revenue of product B is negative and larger in absolute value than the fine associated with dumping excess units, production and sale of 56.67 units of product B cannot be optimal. As in part a, we must determine the maximum quantity of B that will be sold and then recalculate the optimal production level and sales of product A. Because it costs the firm a $10 fine for every unit of B dumped into the river, the sale of any units of B with marginal revenues greater than a -$10 will result in increased profits. Therefore, the maximum sales quantity for B is determined by setting $MR_B = -$10.$

$$MR_B = MC_B - \text{Fine savings}$$

$$\$100 - \$2Q_B = \$0 - \$10$$

$$2Q_B = 110$$

$$Q_B = \underline{\underline{55}} \text{ units}$$

and

$$P_B = \$100 - \$55$$

$$= \underline{\underline{\$45}}$$

To determine the optimal quantity of A, one sets the marginal revenue of A equal to the marginal cost of producing one more unit of the output package, recognizing that there is a $10 added cost associated with the dumping of the marginal unit of B produced.

$$MR_A = MC_Q$$

$$\$600 - \$2Q = \$20 + \$8Q + \$10 \quad (\text{Since } Q_A = Q)$$

$$10Q = 570$$

$$Q_A = \underline{\underline{57}} \text{ units}$$

and

$$P_A = \$600 - Q_A$$

$$= 600 - 57$$

$$= \underline{\underline{\$543}}$$

Thus, given the conditions in part b, Red River Chemical maximizes profit by producing 57 units of the output package, selling 57 units of A at $543, 55 units of B at $45, and dumping 2 units of B into the river.

c.   In part b above, we saw that the profit maximizing output level for the firm if it produced and sold equal quantities of the two

254

products was 56.67 units, and that the marginal revenue of product b was -$13.34 at that sales level. Thus, any fine less than $13.34 will cause the firm to produce added units of the output package since the lower cost of dumping and paying the fine would make the sale of additional units of A profitable. A fine greater than $13.34 would be larger than necessary since all dumping will cease with a fine of that amount.

12.5

Vegi-Fruit Farms, Inc. is the major employer in Lakeland County, Arizona. VFF produces avocados, the demand and marginal revenue curves for which are:

$$P = \$1,000 - \$0.02Q$$

$$MR = \$1,000 - \$0.04Q$$

where Q is the quantity demanded per year (in tons). Production of each unit of output requires 100 hours of labor, 0.25 hour of capital equipment time, and $50 of raw materials. VFF has a total of 5,000 hours of capital equipment time available each year, and can purchase all the labor and materials it desires. The capital equipment investment by VFF is $30,000,000, and the firm has a required rate of return on capital of 15 percent. Assume for simplicity that these are the only costs incurred by VFF.

a.   You have been retained by the State Unemployment Service to evaluate the impact on employment at VFF of a proposed extension of the state minimum wage law to agricultural employers such as VFF. As a first step in the analysis, develop the short-run demand curve for labor by VFF.

b.   VFF currently pays $3.35 per hour for migrant labor. Calculate the short-run impact on employment of a new $4 per hour state minimum wage law.

c.   Would the long-run impact on unemployment differ significantly from the short-run impact? Justify your answer.

12.5 SOLUTION

a.   Solution of this problem requires construction of VFF's cost functions. The total revenue function is:

$$TR = PQ$$

$$= (\$1,000 - \$0.02Q)Q$$

$$= \$1,000Q - \$0.02Q^2$$

255

The total cost function is constructed as follows:

$$TC = \text{Fixed cost} + (\text{Per unit material cost}) \times Q$$
$$+ (\text{Per unit labor cost}) \times Q$$

$$\text{Fixed cost} = 0.15 \times 30{,}000{,}000$$
$$= \$4{,}500{,}000$$

Per unit material cost = \$50

Per unit labor cost = $100P_L$,

where P_L is the labor wage rate

Therefore, VFF's total cost function is:

$$TC = \$4{,}500{,}000 + \$50Q + 100P_LQ$$

and,

$$MC = \text{Per Unit Material Cost} + \text{Per Unit Labor Cost}$$
$$= \$50 + 100\,P_L$$

For profit maximization, set MR = MC, where:

$$MR = MC$$
$$\$1{,}000 - \$0.04Q = \$50 + 100\,P_L$$
$$100P_L = 950 - 0.04Q$$
$$P_L = \$9.5 - \$0.0004Q$$

Since 100 hours are required in the production of each unit of Q, $L = 100Q$ or $Q = L/100$. Therefore, the short-run demand for labor equation can be written:

$$P_L = \$9.5 - \$0.0004(L/100)$$
$$= \$9.5 - \$0.000004L$$

or

$$L = 2,375,000 - 250,000P_L$$

b. Employment levels at \$3.35 and \$4 per hour can be calculated using the demand for labor function derived in part a.

$$L_1 = 2,375,000 - 250,000(3.35)$$

$$= 1,537,500 \text{ worker hours}$$

$$L_2 = 2,375,000 - 250,000(4)$$

$$= 1,375,000 \text{ worker hours}$$

Thus, a \$4 minimum wage would reduce labor demand by:

$$\text{Employment Loss} = L_1 - L_2$$

$$= 1,537,500 - 1,375,000$$

$$= \underline{-162,500} \text{ worker hours}$$

Assuming 2,000 worker hours per year for each employee, this is a reduction of 81.25 jobs (= 162,500/2,000).

c. Insight concerning long-run effects on employment can be gained by analyzing profits for the firm at the optimal output levels associated with the \$3.35 and \$4 wage rates, respectively.

With P_L = \$3.35, labor usage will be 1,537,500 worker hours as determined above. This implies that $Q = L/(L/Q) =$ 1,537/500/100 = 15,375 units of output will be produced. From the profit equation we find:

$$\pi = \$950Q - 100P_LQ - \$0.02Q^2 - \$4,500,000$$

$$= 950(15,375) - 100(3.35)(15,375)$$

$$- 0.02(15,375^2) - 4,500,000$$

$$= \underline{\$227,813}$$

With P_L = \$4 and Q = 13,750,

$$\pi = \$950Q - 100P_LQ - \$0.02Q^2 - \$4,500,000$$

$$= 950(13,750) - 100(4)(13,750)$$

$$- 0.02(13,750^2) - 4,500,000$$

$$= -\$718,750$$

Thus, at the $3.35 wage rate, economic profits are positive and, therefore, the firm will have an incentive to operate and expand in the long-run. Remember that the $4,500,000 fixed cost is the required return on capital. At $P_L = \$4$, however, economic profits are negative, indicating that the required return on capital is not being met. The firm will not be able to attract the capital necessary to continue operating in the long run. This means that the impact of the agricultural minimum wage law could be to eliminate all such jobs at the firm.

12.6

New Castle Iron Products, Inc., produces steel at a New Castle, Pennsylvania, steel mill. With each ton of steel produced, the firm has been dumping particulate matter (smoke and dust) into the local atmosphere. As a concerned citizen, you are appalled at the aesthetic implications of the company's policies, as well as the potential health hazard to the local population.

a. You cite the occurrence of pollution as a negative externality and an example of market failure. What might you cite as reasons why markets fail?

b. In analyzing possible remedies to the current situation, you consider three general types of controls to limit pollution:

1. Regulations: Licenses, permits, compulsory standards, etc.

2. Payments: Various types of government aid to help companies install pollution control equipment. Aid can be the forgiveness of local property taxes, income tax credits, special accelerated depreciation allowances for pollution control equipment, low cost government loans, and so on.

3. Charges: Excise taxes on polluting fuels (coal, oil, etc.), pollution discharge taxes, etc.

Review each of these methods of pollution control and:

(i) Determine the incentive structure for the polluter under each form of control.

258

(ii)   Decide who pays for a clean environment under each form of control. (Note: Each form of control has something definite to say about who owns the property rights to a clean environment.)

(iii)   Defend a particular form of control based on your analysis, including both efficiency and equity considerations.

c.   Suppose that you decide that a pollution tax (alternative 3) constitutes the most desirable form of pollution control. What is the minimum pollution tax which would eliminate pollution completely given the following total cost (TC) and demand functions for steel (X_1) and particulates (X_2)? Assume that each unit of production, X, is composed of one unit of X_1 and one unit of X_2. (Demand for recycled particulates is for use as an input in the steel-making process.)

$$TC = \$10,000 + \$4X + \$4X^2 \quad \text{(Total cost)}$$

$$MC = \$4 + \$8X \quad \text{(Marginal cost)}$$

Steel

$$P_1 = \$2,504 - \$2X_1$$

$$MR_1 = \$2,504 - \$4X_1$$

Particulates

$$P_2 = \$100 - \$0.5X_2$$

$$MR_2 = \$100 - X_2$$

12.6 SOLUTION

a.   Markets can fail due to:

1.   Structural problems: fewness in the number of buyers and/or sellers.

2.   Incentive problems: if some product benefit (cost) is not reflected in firm revenues (costs), then non-optimal production quantities will result due to improper firm incentives.

b.   Methods of pollution control

259

(i)   Incentive structure:

    (a)   Regulation: incentive is to avoid regulation, be made a "special case."

    (b)   Payments: incentive is to reduce pollution in order to earn subsidy.

    (c)   Charges: incentive is to reduce pollution in order to avoid charges.

(ii)   Who pays for a clean environment?

    (a)   Regulation: The company and its customers pay to reduce pollution. The implication is that society has a right to a clean environment.

    (b)   Payments: Society pays to reduce pollution, implying that the firm has a right to pollute.

    (c)   Charges: The company and its customers pay to reduce pollution. Again, society's right to a clean environment is implied.

(iii)   Defense of the alternatives:

Efficiency considerations favor payments and charges as the more efficient methods of pollution control.

Equity considerations are less certain.

    (a)   Regulation: Insures due process, a day in court, for firms.

    (b)   Payments: Avoids penalty to firms with "sunk" investment costs.

    (c)   Charges: Perhaps the polluter should pay full costs of production/consumption.

c.   Set MR = MC to determine the profit maximizing output level, where:

$$MR_1 + MR_2 = MC$$

$$\$2,504 - \$4X + \$100 - X = \$4 + \$8X$$

$$13X = 2,600$$

$$X = \underline{\underline{200}}$$

At X = 200, we note:

$$MR_1 = \$2,504 - \$4X_1 \qquad MR_2 = \$100 - X_2$$

$$= 2,504 - 4(200) \qquad\qquad = 100 - 200$$

$$= \$1,704 \qquad\qquad\qquad = -\$100$$

The above solution is optimal assuming that the firm must sell all units of both X_1 and X_2. If the firm could dispose of the excess units of X_2 (i.e., units beyond $MR_{X_2} = 0$) at a cost less than $100, they would do so. At any disposal or pollution tax below $100, the firm will choose to pollute and pay the tax. With a tax of $100 or more, the firm would maximize profits by refraining from any release of particulates. Thus, $100 constitutes the minimum tax that will prevent pollution.

(Note: profits are falling for X > 200, so X = 200 is a point of maximum profits.)

12.7

Idaho Natural Resources, Inc. processes enriched ore to extract silver and lead. Each ton of processed ore yields one ounce of silver and one pound of lead. Marginal processing costs equal $5 per ton. After insurance, transportation and other marketing costs, the relation describing the net price and marginal revenue of silver received by INR is:

$$P_S = \$10 - \$0.00025Q_S$$

$$MR_S = \$10 - \$0.0005Q_S$$

and for lead are:

$$P_L = \$2 - \$0.0001Q_L$$

$$MR_L = \$2 - \$0.0002Q_L$$

Here, Q_S is ounces of silver, and Q_L is pounds of lead.

a. Calculate INR's optimal sales quantities and prices for silver and lead.

b. Calculate INR's optimal sales quantities and prices in the event of a 5 percent state silver revenue tax.

261

c. Calculate INR's optimal sales quantities and prices in the event of a 5 percent state lead revenue tax.

d. Which state tax is preferable in terms of minimizing short-run employment effects in the mining industry?

12.7 SOLUTION

a. We begin our analysis by examining the optimal activity level for INR assuming the firm processes and sells equal quantities of silver and lead. Since each unit of production generates revenue from both metals, the optimal activity level will be reached when aggregate marginal revenue (silver plus lead) is equated with marginal cost:

$$MR = MR_S + MR_L = MC$$

$$\$10 - \$0.0005Q + \$2 - \$0.0002Q = \$5 \text{ (Since } Q_S = Q_L = Q)$$

$$12 - 0.0007Q = 5$$

$$0.0007Q = 7$$

$$Q = \underline{\underline{10,000}}$$

and

$$P_S = \$10 - \$0.00025(10,000) = \$7.50 \text{ per ounce}$$

$$P_L = \$2 - \$0.0001(10,000) = \$1 \text{ per pound}$$

To be optimal, marginal revenues for each joint output must be greater than or equal to zero. At this activity level:

$$MR_S = \$10 - \$0.0005(10,000) = \$5$$

$$MR_L = \$2 - \$0.0002(10,000) = \$0$$

Therefore, the quantities and prices derived above are optimal. The marginal revenue from silver covers all marginal production costs. The marginal revenue from lead equals zero, which is the marginal production cost of lead given ore processing for silver production.

b.   The effect of a silver revenue tax is to reduce MR_S. Therefore, as in part a, we consider:

$$MR = MR_S + MR_L = MC$$

$$(1 - 0.05)(\$10 - \$0.0005Q) + \$2 - \$0.0002Q = \$5 \text{ (Since } Q_S = Q_L = Q)$$

$$9.50 - 0.000475Q + 2 - 0.0002Q = 5$$

$$11.50 - 0.000675Q = 5$$

$$0.000675Q = 6.50$$

$$Q = \underline{9,630}$$

and

$$P_S = \$10 - \$0.00025(9,630) = \$7.59 \qquad \text{(Price paid by consumers)}$$

$$P_S = (1 - 0.05)\$7.59 = \$7.25 \qquad \text{(Price received by INR)}$$

$$P_L = \$2 - \$0.0001(9,630) = \$1.037$$

Again, in order to be optimal, marginal revenues to INR for each joint output must be nonnegative at this activity level.

$$MR_S = \$9.50 - \$0.000475(9,630) = \$4.93$$

$$MR_L = \$2 - \$0.0002(9,630) = \$0.07$$

Since the marginal revenues from each joint product are positive, each contributes toward covering marginal processing costs of $5, and the prices and quantities derived above are optimal.

c.   The effect of a lead revenue tax is to reduce MR_L. Therefore, as above:

$$MR_S + MR_L = MC$$

$$\$10 - \$0.0005Q + (1 - 0.05)(\$2 - \$0.0002Q) = \$5 \text{ (Since } Q_S = Q_L = Q)$$

$$10 - 0.0005Q + 1.90 - 0.00019Q = 5$$

263

$$11.90 - 0.00069Q = 5$$

$$0.00069Q = 6.90$$

$$Q = \underline{10,000}$$

and

$$P_S = \$7.50 \qquad \text{(As in part a)}$$

$$P_L = \$1 \qquad \text{(Paid by consumers)}$$

$$P_L = (1 - 0.05)\$1 = \$0.95 \quad \text{(Received by INR)}$$

Marginal revenues to INR at this activity level are again nonnegative since:

$$MR_S = \$10 - \$0.0005(10,000) = \$5$$

$$MR_L = \$1.90 - \$0.00019(10,000) = \$0$$

As in part a, the marginal revenue from silver covers all marginal production costs. The marginal revenue from lead again equals zero, which is the marginal production cost of lead given ore processing for silver production. Prices and quantities shown above are optimal.

d. The lead revenue tax will have no short-run effect on output and employment, and is therefore preferable to a silver revenue tax.

In general, a tax on byproduct revenues will affect neither output nor employment in the short-run. Such a tax on primary product revenues will always reduce both. Also note that, unlike a byproduct tax, a primary product revenue tax will always cause consumer prices to rise for each product.

CHAPTER THIRTEEN: DECISION MAKING UNDER UNCERTAINTY

Theme

In order to make optimal decisions, managers must deal effectively with risk or uncertainty. Here, we define risk as the situation where managers know all possible outcomes resulting from a given course of action as well as each outcome's chance of occurring, but ultimate outcomes or results are unknown. Of course, assuming that managers know all possibilities and all probabilities is assuming quite a bit. Most often, managers estimate a range of probability values in order to construct optimistic to pessimistic scenarios. Once this has been done, the risk of a given course of action can be characterized in terms of the distribution of outcome values. These distributions are commonly expressed using the statistical concepts of standard deviation (dispersion) and coefficient of variation (risk-reward ratio). In order to fully incorporate risk into the managerial decision making process, projects involving various levels of measurable risk must be evaluated in light of personal attitudes towards risk. Risk attitudes are usually characterized as risk averse, risk neutral or risk preferring depending on an individual's change in utility or well-being due to a given change in wealth or income. Once risk levels and risk preferences have been evaluated, managers can deal effectively with decisions involving risk by utilizing certainty equivalent adjustment factors, risk-adjusted discount rates, decision tree analyses, and the standard normal concept. Under extreme uncertainty, managers sometimes apply strategies based on game theory concepts.

Outline

I.   Risk in Economic Analysis

   A.   Importance: Since decisions are seldom made under conditions of perfect certainty, risk must be quantified and introduced into the decision process.

   B.   Probability Distributions: There is a given probability of occurrence associated with each possible outcome in a decision problem. The combination of these probability estimates forms a probability distribution.

      1.   Expected Value: Expected value is the mean of a probability distribution. This mean is found as a weighted average of the possible profit outcomes, π_i, for example, where the weights are the probabilities of occurrence, P_i:

$$\text{Expected Profit} = E(\pi) = \sum_{i=1}^{N} \pi_i \times P_i$$

C. Measuring Risk: Risk in managerial decision making is a function of the variability in possible outcomes.

1. Standard Deviation: The most commonly employed measure of dispersion around the expected value of a probability distribution is the standard deviation. The standard deviation is calculated as a function of the weighted average of the deviations of possible outcomes, π_i, from the expected outcome, $E(\pi)$, where the weights are the probabilities of occurrence.

$$\text{Standard Deviation of Profit} = \sigma = \sqrt{\sum_{i=1}^{N} (\pi_i - E(\pi))^2 P_i}$$

2. Coefficient of Variation: The coefficient of variation, a popular measure of relative risk, is often used to compare risk across the various alternatives in a decision problem.

$$\text{Coefficient of Variation} = V = \frac{\sigma}{E(\pi)}$$

II. The Standard Normal Curve

A. The Standard Normal Curve Concept: The standard normal curve can be fruitfully employed in dealing with decision problems where the underlying revenues, costs or profits are normally distributed.

B. Standardized Variable: The standardized variable (or standard normal) is a method of characterizing the location of a point of interest, x, along a normal distribution in terms of the number of standard deviations x is from the mean, where:

$$z = \frac{x - \mu}{\sigma}$$

and z is the standardized variable, x is the point of interest, μ is the mean and σ is the standard deviation.

III. Utility Theory and Risk Analysis

A. Each decision maker's attitude toward risk is determined by his or her utility of income or wealth.

1. A risk-averse decision maker has a diminishing marginal utility of income or wealth. This is a common, but not universal, attitude.

266

2. A risk-indifferent decision maker has a constant marginal utility of income or wealth.

3. A risk-seeking decision maker has an increasing marginal utility of income or wealth.

B. Upshot: Managerial decisions cannot be based solely on expected outcomes, but must incorporate an analysis of risk attitudes as well.

IV. Adjusting the Valuation Model for Risk

A. Certainty Equivalent Adjustments: A first approach of accounting for risk in the valuation model is to convert profits, π_t, the numerator in the model, into risk adjusted certainty equivalent profits. To do so, we use certainty equivalent adjustment factors that vary from project to project. The value, V, of a given investment becomes:

$$V = \sum_{t=1}^{N} \frac{\alpha \pi_t}{(1+i)^t}$$

where i is a riskless rate of return and α is a certainty equivalent adjustment factor found as:

$$\alpha = \frac{\text{Equivalent certain sum}}{\text{Expected risky sum}}$$

1. Certainty equivalent adjustment factors: It is important to remember that the numerator and denominator of the ratio that describes α vary in dollar terms, but are constant in terms of utility. This means that if the appropriate $\alpha = 0.8$, the individual investor in question would be indifferent between a certain $8 and a risky expected return of $10. In this case, each risky dollar of expected return is "worth" only 80¢ in certain dollars.

B. Calculating Certainty Equivalent Adjustment Factors: Historical observations of investment behavior provide one way of gaining insight regarding appropriate α levels.

1. $\alpha < 1$ implies risk aversion (Most common).

2. $\alpha = 1$ implies risk indifference.

3. $\alpha > 1$ implies risk preference.

267

C.   Risk-adjusted Discount Rates: A second approach of accounting for risk in the valuation model is to adjust the capitalization rate, i, the denominator in the model, for risk by adding a risk premium which varies from project to project. The value, V, of a given investment becomes:

$$V = \sum_{t=1}^{N} \frac{\pi_t}{(1+k)^t}$$

where k is a risk-adjusted discount rate representing the riskless rate of return, i, plus a risk premium, r_p. That is,

$$k = i + r_p$$

V.   Further Techniques for Decision Making under Uncertainty

A.   Decision Trees: A decision tree diagram maps out the sequence of all possible outcomes and their associated probabilities, thus providing a convenient means for analyzing alternative courses of action. When various alternatives have both inferior expected returns and inferior risk characteristics, these alternatives are said to be dominated and can be eliminated from consideration.

B.   Simulation: Computer simulation models can be employed in the analysis of decision problems whose complexity precludes the decision tree approach.

C.   Game Theory: Game theory is an extremely useful means for dealing with extreme uncertainty, and with possible outcomes involving disastrous consequences.

1.   Maximin Decision Rule: Choose the decision alternative with the best worst case scenario.

2.   Minimax Regret Decision Rule: Choose the decision alternative with the smallest possible opportunity loss.

3.   An Alternative Use of the Opportunity-Loss Concept: The expected opportunity loss is the cost of uncertainty.

PROBLEMS AND SOLUTIONS

13.1

A-OK Motors, Inc., estimates that seven out of every fifty individuals who take demonstration test drives actually purchase a car. If the firm's gross profit margin is $200 and a test ride costs $10, what is the expected profit of each test ride given?

13.1 SOLUTION

The probability of an individual who takes a test ride actually purchasing a car is 7/50 = 0.14. Since A-OK's gross profit margin is $200, the expected gross profit margin will be

$$\text{Expected Profit} = (\text{Purchase probability})(\text{Gross margin}) - \text{Test ride cost}$$

$$= (0.14)(\$200) - \$10$$

$$= \underline{\underline{\$18}}$$

13.2

Gamma Computer Corporation (GCC) has just completed development work on a new line of personal computers. Preliminary market research indicates two feasible marketing strategies: (a) concentration on developing general consumer acceptance by advertising through newspapers, television, and other media; or (b) concentration on distributor acceptance of the computer system through intensive sales calls by company representatives, extensive development of software support (user programs), and so forth. Ray Carlos, GCC's marketing manager, has developed sales estimates under each alternative plan, and has arranged rough payoff matrices according to his assessment of likely product acceptance under each plan. These matrices are illustrated below:

Strategy 1: Consumer-Oriented Promotion

Probability	Sales Outcome
0.1	$ 500,000
0.4	1,500,000
0.4	2,500,000
0.1	3,500,000

Strategy 2: Distributor-Oriented Promotion

Probability	Sales Outcome
0.3	$1,000,000
0.4	1,500,000
0.3	2,000,000

a. Assume that the company has a 50 percent profit margin on sales. Calculate the expected profits for each plan.

b. Construct a simple bar graph of the possible profit outcomes for each plan. On the basis of the appearance of the two graphs, which plan appears to be more risky?

c. Calculate the standard deviation and coefficient of variation associated with the profit distribution of each plan.

d. Assume that the management of GCC has a utility function like the one illustrated below. Which marketing strategy should Carlos recommend?

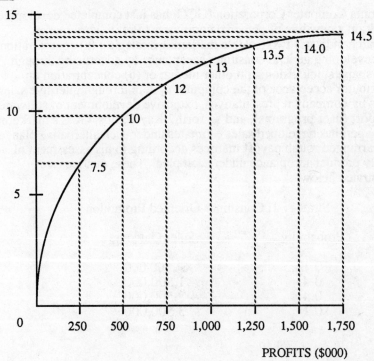

13.2 SOLUTION

a. Strategy 1: Consumer-Oriented Promotion

Probability	Sales Outcomes	Profit	Expected Profit
(1)	(2)	(3) = (2) × 0.5	(4) = (3) × (1)
0.1	$ 500,000	$ 250,000	$ 25,000
0.4	1,500,000	750,000	300,000
0.4	2,500,000	1,250,000	500,000
0.1	3,500,000	1,750,000	175,000
		$E(\pi_1)$	= $1,000,000

Strategy 2: Distributor-Oriented Promotion

Probability	Outcomes (Sales)	Profit	Expected Profit
(1)	(2)	(3) = (2) × 0.5	(4) = (3) × (1)
0.3	$1,000,000	$ 500,000	$150,000
0.4	1,500,000	750,000	300,000
0.3	2,000,000	1,000,000	300,000
		$E(\pi_2)$ =	$750,000

b.

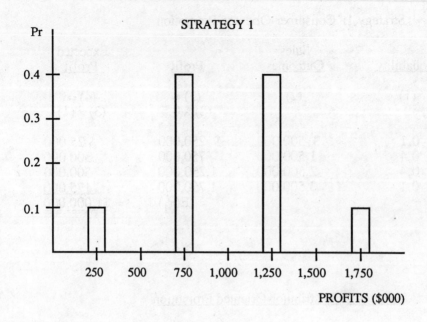

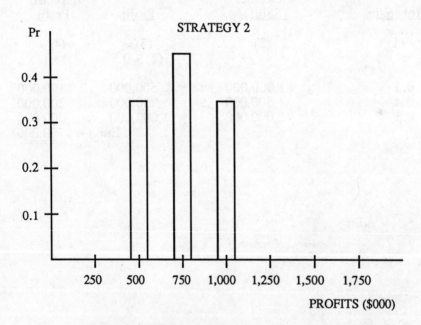

Strategy 1 appears to be more risky than Strategy 2 due to the greater variability of outcomes.

c.   Strategy 1:

Probability (1)	Deviations (2)	(Deviations)^2 (3)	(1) × (3) = (4)
0.1	-750,000	5.625×10^{11}	5.625×10^{10}
0.4	-250,000	6.250×10^{10}	2.5×10^{10}
0.4	250,000	6.250×10^{10}	2.5×10^{10}
0.1	750,000	5.625×10^{11}	$\underline{5.625 \times 10^{10}}$

$$\sigma_1^2 = 16.25 \times 10^{10}$$

$$\sigma_1 = \sqrt{16.25 \times 10^{10}} = 4.0311 \times 10^5 = \underline{\underline{\$403,110}}$$

$$V_1 = \frac{\$403,110}{\$1,000,000} = \underline{\underline{0.403}}$$

Strategy 2:

Probability (1)	Deviations (2)	(Deviations)^2 (3)	(1) × (3) = (4)
0.3	-250,000	6.25×10^{10}	1.875×10^{10}
0.4	0	0	0
0.3	250,000	6.25×10^{10}	$\underline{1.875 \times 10^{10}}$

$$\sigma^2 = 3.75 \times 0^{10}$$

$$\sigma_2 = \sqrt{3.75 \times 10^{10}} = 1.9365 \times 10^5 = \underline{\underline{\$193,650}}$$

$$V_2 = \frac{\$193,650}{\$750,000} = \underline{\underline{0.258}}$$

These calculations make more precise the conclusion reached in part b that Strategy 1 is the more risky marketing approach.

d.   Strategy 1:

Probability (1)	Profits (2)	Utils (3)	Expected Utility (4) = (3) × (1)
0.1	$ 250,000	7.50	0.75
0.4	750,000	12.00	4.80
0.4	1,250,000	13.50	5.40
0.1	1,750,000	14.50	1.45
			$E(U_1)$ = 12.40 utils

Strategy 2:

Probability (1)	Profits (2)	Utils (3)	Expected Utility (4) = (3) × (1)
0.3	$ 500,000	10	3.0
0.4	750,000	12	4.8
0.3	1,000,000	13	3.9
			$E(U_2)$ = 11.7 utils

The marketing manager should recommend Strategy 1 because of its higher expected utility. In this case, the higher expected profit of Strategy 1 more than offsets its greater riskiness.

13.3

Wayne Paterson is considering two alternative investments, each costing $7,000. Present values of possible outcomes and their probabilities of occurrence are:

Investment A

	Outcome		
	1	2	3
Present value	$6,000	$8,000	$10,000
Probability of occurrence	0.25	0.50	0.25

Investment B

	Outcome		
	1	2	3
Present value	$5,000	$9,000	$10,000
Probability of occurrence	0.30	0.50	0.20

a. Calculate the expected present values of the two investments.

b. Calculate the standard deviation for each investment. Which alternative is riskier?

c. If Paterson has a constant marginal utility of income as indicated by the utility function $U = 30 + 2X$, where X is thousands of dollars of present value, which investment should he choose? Why?

d. If Paterson's utility of income is given by the function $U = 30X - X2$, which investment should he select? Why?

13.3 SOLUTION

a.

INVESTMENT A

Present Value (1)	Probability (2)	Expected Present Value (3) = (1) × (2)
$6,000	0.25	$1,500
8,000	0.50	4,000
10,000	0.25	2,500
		$E(PV_A) = \$8,000$

275

Present Value	Probability	Expected Present Value
(1)	(2)	(3) = (1) × (2)
$ 5,000	0.3	$1,500
9,000	0.5	4,500
10,000	0.2	2,000
		$E(PV_B) = \$8,000$

b. $\sigma_A = \sqrt{0.25(\$6,000 - \$8,000)^2 + 0.50(\$8,000 - \$8,000)^2}$

$\overline{+\ 0.25(\$10,000 - \$8,000)^2}$

$= \sqrt{2,000,000}$

$= \$1,414.21$

$\sigma_B = \sqrt{0.3(\$5,000 - \$8,000)^2 + 0.5(\$9,000 - \$8,000)^2}$

$\overline{+\ 0.2(\$10,000 - \$8,000)^2}$

$= \sqrt{4,000,000}$

$= \$2,000$

Investment B is more risky than investment A.

c. When $U = 30 + 2X$, we find:

INVESTMENT A

Probability (1)	PV (2)	X (3)	Utility (U = 30 + 2X) (4)	Expected Utility (5) = (4) × (1)
0.25	$ 6,000	6	42	10.5
0.50	8,000	8	46	23.0
0.25	10,000	10	50	12.5
				$E(U_A) = 46$ utils

INVESTMENT B

Probability (1)	PV (2)	X (3)	Expected Utility (4)	Utility (5) = (4) × (1)
0.3	$ 5,000	5	40	12
0.5	9,000	9	48	24
0.2	10,000	10	50	10
				$E(U_B) = \underline{46}$ utils

With a linear utility function (constant marginal utility), Dick would be <u>indifferent</u> between the two investments. That is, so long as the alternatives have equal expected dollar returns, they must provide the same expected utility to an individual exhibiting an indifference to risk.

d.   When utility $U = 30X - X^2$, we find:

INVESTMENT A

Probability (1)	PV (2)	X (3)	Utility (4)	Expected Utility (5) = (4) × (1)
0.25	$ 6,000	6	144	36
0.50	8,000	8	176	88
0.25	10,000	10	200	50
				$E(U_A) = \underline{174}$ utils

INVESTMENT B

Probability (1)	PV (2)	X (3)	Expected Utility (4)	Utility (5) = (4) × (1)
0.3	$ 5,000	5	125	37.5
0.5	9,000	9	189	94.5
0.2	10,000	10	200	40.0
				$E(U_B) = \underline{172}$ utils

<u>Investment A</u> should be selected because of its higher expected utility. In this case, Dick Badger exhibits risk aversion (diminishing marginal utility), and, hence, with equal expected dollar returns, he prefers the alternative with less risk. We know Dick has a diminishing marginal utility of income since MU = dU/dX = 30 - 2X, and marginal utility will fall as income grows.

13.4

Blue Chip Investors, Ltd. offers limited partnership investments to individual investors. A current $1.5 million offering consists of 25 equal shares priced at $60,000 each. Proceeds from the offering will be used to purchase and renovate a local apartment complex. BCI projects a total investment return for the project of $4 million, or $160,000 per unit, to be paid in one lump sum at the end of 7 years.

a. Using a 6 percent risk-free rate of return, calculate the discounted present value of projected returns for a single unit.

b. Calculate and interpret the minimum certainty equivalent adjustment factor α necessary to justify investment in the project.

13.4 SOLUTION

a. PV of future returns $=$ Projected returns $\times$ (PVIF, N = 7, i = 6%)

$$= \$160,000(0.6651)$$

$$= \underline{\underline{\$106,416}}$$

b. From the certainty equivalent adjustment factor formula, we note:

$$\alpha = \frac{\text{Certain Sum}}{\text{Expected Risky Return}}$$

$$= \frac{\$60,000}{\$106,416}$$

$$= \underline{\underline{0.56}}$$

Therefore, in order for investors to justify investment in the project, each dollar of expected risky return must be worth at least 56¢ in certain dollars.

13.5

Taco Bravo, Inc., is considering opening a new restaurant offering Mexican specialties in Evanston, Illinois. Projecting net profits for such an outlet is quite subjective, but Taco Bravo's marketing director estimates:

Probability	Annual Net Profits
0.3	$100,000
0.4	200,000
0.3	300,000

During the past year, Taco Bravo's management approved opening new restaurants in four different markets. In analyzing these investment decisions, you discover the following:

Market	Certainty Equivalent	Coefficient of Variation
A	0.80	0.35
B	0.75	0.39
C	0.70	0.43
D	0.60	0.50

a. Calculate the expected return, standard deviation and coefficient of variation of annual net profits for the Evanston restaurant.

b. Given Taco Bravo's historical management decisions, calculate the range for the maximum acceptable investment requirement for the Evanston restaurant given an anticipated ten-year project life, and a 14 percent risk-free rate of return.

13.5 SOLUTION

a. $$E(R) = \$100,000(0.3) + \$200,000(0.4)$$

$$+ \$300,000(0.3) = \underline{\underline{\$200,000}}$$

$$\sigma = \sqrt{(\$100,000 - \$200,000)^2(0.3)}$$

$$\overline{+ (\$200,000 - \$200,000)^2(0.4)}$$

$$\overline{+ (\$300,000 - \$200,000)^2(0.3)}$$

$$= \sqrt{3 \times 10^9 + 3 \times 10^9}$$

$$= \underline{\underline{\$77,460}}$$

$$V = \frac{\sigma}{E(R)} = \frac{\$77,460}{\$200,000} = \underline{\underline{0.387}}$$

b. By definition,

$$\alpha = \frac{\text{Certain sum}}{\text{Expected risky return}}$$

$$= \frac{\text{Investment requirement}}{E(R)}$$

Therefore, it is obvious that an acceptable investment requirement for an investment with a one year life would be:

$$\text{Investment Requirement} = \alpha \times E(R)$$

For the Evanston restaurant, which has a life span of more than one year, we can calculate the range within which an acceptable investment requirement will be found using the relation:

$$\text{Investment Requirement} = \sum_{t=1}^{N} \frac{\alpha \times E(R)}{(1+i)^t}$$

The Evanston restaurant has a $V = 0.387$, which is between $V_A = 0.35$ and $V_B = 0.39$. This implies that an acceptable certainty equivalent lies between $\alpha_A = 0.80$ and $\alpha_B = 0.75$.

In this instance, an acceptable investment requirement is found within the range:

$$\text{"High" Investment Limit} = \sum_{t=1}^{N} \frac{\alpha_A \times E(R)}{(1+i)^t}$$

$$= \sum_{t=1}^{10} \frac{0.80(\$200,000)}{(1.14)^{10}}$$

$$= (\text{PVIFA}, N = 10, i = 14\%)(0.80)\ (\$200,000)$$

$$= (5.216)(0.80)(200,000)$$

$$= \$834,560$$

$$\text{"Low" Investment Limit} = \sum_{t=1}^{N} \frac{\alpha_B \times E(R)}{(1+i)^t}$$

$$= \sum_{t=1}^{10} \frac{0.75(\$200,000)}{(1.14)^{10}}$$

$$= \text{(PVIFA, N = 10, i = 14\%)(0.75) (\$200,000)}$$

$$= (5.216)(0.75)(200,000)$$

$$= \underline{\$782,400}$$

Thus, the maximum acceptable investment requirement which would be consistent with Taco Bravo's past management decisions will be found within the range $782,400 to $834,560.

13.6

Epsilon Racquets, Ltd. is currently engaged in the production of racquetball rackets. An obsolete assembly machine is to be replaced by one of two innovative pieces of equipment. The following cost savings (cash flows) will be generated over the four-year useful lives of the new machines.

	Probability	Cash Flow
Alternative 1	0.3	$ 2,900
	0.5	3,500
	0.2	4,100
Alternative 2	0.3	$ 0
	0.5	4,000
	0.2	8,000

Whichever piece of equipment is chosen, the total investment cost will be the same, $4,000.

Given that Epsilon uses a discount rate of 12 percent for cash flows with a high degree of dispersion and a 10 percent rate for less risky cash values, which machine has the highest expected net present value?

281

13.6   SOLUTION

The expected values of cash flows for each alternative are:

Alternative 1

Proba- bility	Cash Flow	Expected Cash Flow (1) × (2)
0.3	$2,900	$ 870
0.5	3,500	1,750
0.2	4,100	820
		$E(CF_1) = \$3,440$

Alternative 2

Proba- bility	Cash Flow	Expected Cash Flow (1) × (2)
0.3	$ 0	$ 0
0.5	4,000	2,000
0.2	8,000	1,600
		$E(CF_2) = \$3,600$

Alternative 2 is riskier because it has the greater variability in its cash flows. This is obvious from an inspection of the distributions of possible returns and could be verified by calculating the standard deviations of each alternative.

Alternative 1

$$\sigma_1 = \sqrt{(\$2,900 - \$3,440)^2(0.3) + (\$3,500 - \$3,440)^2(0.5)}$$

$$\overline{+ (\$4,100 - \$3,440)^2(0.2)}$$

$$= \underline{\$420}$$

$$V_1 = \frac{\sigma_1}{E(R_1)} = \frac{\$420}{\$3,440} = \underline{0.122}$$

Alternative 2

$$\sigma_2 = \sqrt{(\$0 - \$3,600)^2(0.3) + (\$4,000 - \$3,600)^2(0.5)}$$

$$\overline{+ (\$8{,}000 - \$3{,}600)^2 (0.2)}$$

$$= \$2{,}800$$

$$V_2 = \frac{\sigma_2}{E(R_2)} = \frac{2{,}800}{3{,}600} = 0.778$$

Obviously, Alternative 2 is to be evaluated at the 12 percent cost of capital, while Alternative 1 requires only a 10 percent cost of capital.

$$NPV_1 = \sum_{t=1}^{4} \frac{\$3{,}440}{(1.10)^t} - \$4{,}000$$

$$= \$3{,}440(PVIFA, N = 4, i = 10\%) - \$4{,}000$$

$$= 3{,}440(3.170) - 4{,}000$$

$$= \$6{,}905$$

$$NPV_2 = \sum_{t=1}^{4} \frac{\$3{,}600}{(1.12)^t} - \$4{,}000$$

$$= \$3{,}600(PVIFA, N = 4, i = 12\%) - \$4{,}000$$

$$= 3{,}600(3.037) - 4{,}000$$

$$= \$6{,}933$$

Since Alternative 2 has the higher risk adjusted net present value, it is the appropriate investment for Epsilon.

13.7

Bill's Copy Shop is considering a boost in advertising in order to increase sales. The firm's management plans to make its media decision using the following data on the expected success of television versus newspaper promotions:

283

	Market Response	Net Probability	Revenues
Newspaper	Poor	0.2	$ 5,000
	Good	0.6	6,000
	Very good	0.2	7,000
Television	Poor	0.2	6,000
	Good	0.6	8,000
	Very good	0.2	10,000

Assume that the returns from each promotion are normally distributed, and that net revenues are before advertising expenses.

a. Calculate the expected return, standard deviation, and coefficient of variation for each promotion.

b. Which promotion is most risky? Why?

c. If the newspaper promotion costs $5,178 while the television promotion costs $5,344, what is the probability each will generate a profit?

d. Which promotion should be chosen?

13.7 SOLUTION

a. Newspaper Promotion

$$E(R_N) = \$5,000(0.2) + \$6,000(0.6) + \$7,000(0.2)$$

$$= \underline{\$6,000}$$

$$\sigma_N = \sqrt{(\$5,000 - \$6,000)^2(0.2) + (\$6,000 - \$6,000)^2(0.6)}$$

$$\overline{+ (\$7,000 - \$6,000)^2(0.2)}$$

$$= \underline{\$632.46}$$

$$V_N = \frac{\sigma_N}{E(R_N)} = \frac{\$632.46}{\$6,000} = \underline{0.105}$$

Television Promotion

$$E(R_{TV}) = \$6,000(0.2) + \$8,000(0.6) + \$10,000(0.2)$$

$$= \underline{\underline{\$8,000}}$$

$$\sigma_{TV} = \sqrt{(\$6,000 - \$8,000)^2(0.2) + (\$8,000 - \$8,000)^2(0.6)}$$

$$\overline{+ (\$10,000 - \$8,000)^2(0.2)}$$

$$= \underline{\underline{\$1,264.91}}$$

$$V_{TV} = \frac{\sigma_{TV}}{E(R_{TV})} = \frac{\$1,264.91}{\$8,000} = \underline{\underline{0.158}}$$

b. The television promotion has a higher standard deviation and coefficient of variation than does the newspaper promotion, and is thus the more risky of the two promotion alternatives.

c. In order to calculate the probability that each promotion will generate a profit we must consider the normal curve and relevant values of the standard normal. In graphic terms, we must calculate the share of the total area under the normal curve which is to the right of each breakeven point, our relevant point of interest.

Return Distribution

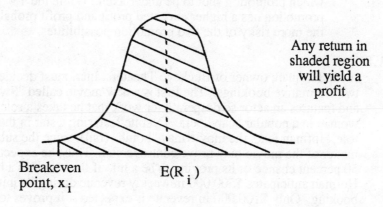

Any return in shaded region will yield a profit

Breakeven point, x_i

$E(R_i)$

Newspaper Promotion Profit Probability

$$z = \frac{x_N - E(R_N)}{\sigma_N}$$

$$= \frac{\$5,178 - \$6,000}{\$632.46}$$

$$= -1.3$$

The standard normal distribution function value for $z = -1.3$ is 0.4032. This means that 0.4032 or 40.32 percent of the total area under the normal curve lies between x_N and $E(R_N)$, and implies a profit probability for the newspaper promotion of $0.4032 + 0.5 = 0.9032$ or <u>90.32 percent</u>.

<u>Television Promotion Profit Probability</u>

$$z = \frac{x_{TV} - E(R_{TV})}{\sigma_{TV}}$$

$$= \frac{\$5,344 - \$8,000}{\$1,264.91}$$

$$= -2.1$$

The standard normal distribution function value for $z = -2.1$ is 0.4821. This means that 0.4821 or 48.21 percent of the total area under the normal curve lies between x_{TV} and $E(R_{TV})$, and implies a profit probability for the television promotion of $0.4821 + 0.5 = 0.9821$ or <u>98.21 percent</u>.

d.   Without firm evidence on the firm's risk attitudes, we can't say which promotion should be undertaken. While the TV promotion has a higher expected profit and profit probability, it is the more risky of the two promotion possibilities.

13.8

Justin Hofman, owner of Buckeye Theaters, Inc., must decide between two alternative bookings. The first is a new movie called "Sweetie," and features an actor so desperate for work that he takes a role as a woman in a popular soap opera. Despite featuring a star in the leading role, Hofman fears the movie may "bomb" (fail), since the subject matter of the movie may prove controversial. Thus, he expects only a 50 percent chance of its proving to be a hit. If the movie is a hit, Hofman anticipates $500,000 in weekly revenue during its initial booking. Only $100,000 in revenue is expected if it proves to be a bomb.

As an alternative to booking "Sweetie," Hofman can rebook a second run of an action packed thriller called "Raiders." Since "Sweetie" will be featured by other theaters in the Buckeye market area, Hofman projects revenue for "Raiders" of $50,000 if "Sweetie" is a hit, and $75,000 if "Sweetie" bombs. Both movies would be rented by

Buckeye from regional distributors on a fixed fee basis of $200,000 per week for "Sweetie", and $40,000 for "Raiders."

a. Construct a net profit (revenues minus fixed fee) payoff matrix for the two alternatives. Which would be chosen using the maximin criterion?

b. Construct a net profit regret or opportunity loss matrix for the two alternatives. Which would be chosen using the minimax regret criterion?

c. Which alternative would be chosen if Buckeye solely wished to maximize its expected net profit?

d. Calculate the cost of uncertainty in this problem.

e. Briefly describe when the choices made in parts a, b and c would be appropriate.

13.8 SOLUTION

Payoff Matrix

a.

States of Nature

Decision Alternatives	1. "Sweetie" is a hit	2. "Sweetie" bombs
A. Book "Sweetie"	$300,000 (= $500,000 - $200,000)	-$100,000 (= $100,000 - $200,000)
B. Book "Raiders"	$ 10,000 (= $50,000 - $40,000)	$ 35,000 (= $75,000 - $40,000)

Booking "Sweetie" exposes Hofman to the possibility of a $100,000 loss which would be incurred if the movie bombs. This worst payoff outcome can be avoided by choosing to book "Raiders" instead. Thus, Decision B is the maximin strategy, and will result in only the best worst outcome being possible.

b.   Regret Matrix

Decision Alternatives	1. "Sweetie" is a hit	2. "Sweetie" bombs
A. Book "Sweetie"	$0 (= $300,000 - $300,000)	$135,000 (= $35,000 - (- $100,000))
B. Book "Raiders"	$290,000 (= $300,000 - $10,000)	$0 (= $35,000 - $35,000)

Booking "Raiders" exposes Hofman to the possibility of a $290,000 opportunity loss in the event "Sweetie" proves to be a hit. This worst opportunity loss outcome can be avoided by booking "Sweetie" instead. Thus, Decision A is the minimax strategy, and will result in only the smallest maximum opportunity loss being possible.

c.   Using an expected profit criterion, we find:

$E(\pi_A) = \$300,000(0.5) + (-\$100,000)(0.5) = \$100,000$

$E(\pi_B) = \$10,000(0.5) + \$35,000(0.5) = \$22,500$

Thus, Decision A is the preferred alternative based upon a criterion of simply choosing the alternative with the highest expected net profit.

d.   The expected opportunity loss under each alternative is:

$E(Loss_A) = \$0(0.5) + \$135,000(0.5) = \$67,500$

$E(Loss_B) = \$290,000(0.5) + \$0(0.5) = \$145,000$

The cost of uncertainty is the minimum or unavoidable expected opportunity loss of $67,500.

e.   If Hofman is extremely risk averse, as would be true if a $100,000 loss would be a disasterous outcome for Buckeye, then the maximin strategy B would be most appropriate.

A less risk averse decision maker would choose A, the minimax strategy.

288

Decision making based on an expected profit criterion, part c, is most appropriate in the case of risk neutral decision makers.

13.9

Ginseng Exports, Ltd., is faced with a very uncertain market for next summer's ginseng root harvest. Ginseng has the opportunity to contract now for purchase of 1,000 pounds of ginseng root at $80 per pound. Alternatively, they can wait until summer and pay the current market rate at that time. With a good harvest, ginseng will sell for $70 per pound. With a poor harvest, ginseng will sell for $100 per pound.

a. Assuming risk indifference, at what probability of a good harvest would the firm contract now for 1,000 pounds of ginseng root?

b. If there is a 90 percent probability of a good harvest, what would the firm pay for an option to purchase 1,000 pounds at $80?

13.9 SOLUTION

a. Let X equal the probability of a good harvest needed to induce the firm to contract now. For indifference, the expected cost of waiting to purchase must be equal to the $80,000 (= $80 × 1,000) cost if the ginseng root purchase is contracted for immediately.

$$
\begin{array}{rcl}
\text{Expected Cost of Waiting} & = & \text{Expected Cost of Current Purchase} \\
\end{array}
$$

$$X(\$70,000) + (1 - X)(\$100,000) = \$80,000$$

$$70,000X + 100,000 - 100,000X = 80,000$$

$$30,000X = 20,000$$

$$X = \underline{\underline{0.67}} \text{ or 67 percent}$$

b. The option described would allow the firm to wait until all uncertainty had been resolved before making its purchase decision. Assuming risk indifference, the cost of uncertainty measures the maximum amount the manager would pay for such an option.

The cost of uncertainty is measured as the minimum expected opportunity loss associated with the two alternatives.

289

$$E(\text{Loss}_{\text{Current purchase}}) = \$0(0.1) + \$10,000(0.9)$$

$$= \$9,000$$

$$E(\text{Loss}_{\text{Wait to purchase}}) = \$20,000(0.1) + \$0(0.9)$$

$$= \$2,000$$

Therefore, the firm should be willing to pay up to $2,000 for the option.

13.10

The Scribe Pen Company has just designed a new fiber tip pen. It has priced the pen to sell for 50¢ each to retail outlets. The firm is trying to decide whether to use Method A or Method B for producing the pen. Under Method A, the fixed costs of producing the pen are $1,000 and variable costs are 30¢ per unit. With Method B, fixed costs are $3,000, and unit costs are 20¢. The firm has approached you and requested information that will aid in making the decision. You have examined the market for the pen and estimate the probability distribution of sales volume to be:

Unit Sales	Probability
5,000	0.25
30,000	0.50
50,000	0.25

a. Construct the payoff matrix for this problem.

b. Calculate the expected payoff for each alternative.

c. Calculate the expected opportunity loss for each alternative.

d. What is the cost of uncertainty in this problem?

e. Should Scribe be willing to spend an amount equal to the cost of uncertainty to remove all uncertainty in this case? Why or why not?

13.10   SOLUTION

a. Profits using Method A are given by the equation:

$$\pi_A = PQ - TC_A$$

$$= \$0.50Q - \$1,000 - \$0.30Q$$

$$= \$0.20Q - \$1,000$$

Profits under the three possible states of nature will be:

$$\pi_{A1} = 0.2(5,000) - 1,000 = \$0$$

$$\pi_{A2} = 0.2(30,000) - 1,000 = \$5,000$$

$$\pi_{A3} = 0.2(50,000) - 1,000 = \$9,000$$

Profits using Method B are:

$$\pi_B = PQ - TC_B$$

$$= \$0.50Q - \$3,000 - \$0.20Q$$

$$= \$0.30Q - \$3,000$$

Profits under the three states of nature will be:

$$\pi_{B1} = 0.3(5,000) - 3,000 = -\$1,500$$

$$\pi_{B2} = 0.3(30,000) - 3,000 = \$6,000$$

$$\pi_{B3} = 0.3(50,000) - 3,000 = \$12,000$$

The payoff matrix for the problem is:

Payoff Matrix

Decision Alternatives	States of Nature		
	$Q = 5,000$	$Q = 30,000$	$Q = 50,000$
Method A	$0	$5,000	$ 9,000
Method B	-$1,500	$6,000	$12,000

b. The expected payoff for Method A is:

$$E(\pi_A) = \$0(0.25) + \$5,000(0.50) + \$9,000(0.25)$$

$$= \underline{\underline{\$4,750}}$$

The expected payoff for Method B is:

$$E(\pi_B) = (-\$1,500)(0.25) + \$6,000(0.5) + \$12,000(0.25)$$

291

$$= \underline{\underline{\$5,625}}$$

c.   The opportunity loss or regret matrix for the problem is:

Regret Matrix

States of Nature

Decision Alternatives	Q = 5,000	Q = 30,000	Q = 50,000
Method A	$0	$1,000	$3,000
Method B	$1,500	$0	$0

The expected opportunity loss for each alternative is:

$$E(Loss_A) = \$0(0.25) + \$1,000(0.5) + \$3,000(0.25)$$

$$= \underline{\underline{\$1,250}}$$

$$E(Loss_B) = \$1,500(0.25) + \$0(0.5) + \$0(0.25)$$

$$= \underline{\underline{\$375}}$$

d.   The cost of uncertainty is equal to the minimum expected opportunity loss of $375, which is the expected opportunity loss associated with production Method B.

e.   The cost of uncertainty is the expected gain associated with making the right decision after the fact. A firm attempting to maximize expected profits without regard to riskiness should be willing to spend precisely that amount to remove all uncertainty. A risk-averse individual would spend at least that amount, and possibly significantly more, to remove the potential variation in profits.

13.11

Freight Forwarders, Inc. is preparing to ship valuable medical equipment from a warehouse in Portland, Oregon to a hospital in San Diego, California. The hospital has offered $5,000 for delivery by noon tomorrow. The equipment can be shipped by air freight at a cost of $4,000, or by truck at a cost of $2,000. If shipped by air freight, there is an 90 percent probability of arrival prior to noon tomorrow, while the probability of meeting the deadline is only one in five with truck transportation.

292

A late shipment will not be accepted by the hospital, and Freight Forwarders will be forced to absorb out-of-pocket freight costs.

a. Diagram a decision tree that completely lays out Freight Forwarders' profit possibilities.

b. Calculate the expected return for each alternative.

c. Which alternative is the more risky? Why?

d. The probability of on-time arrival by truck is highly subjective. Assuming Freight Forwarders' management attempts to maximize expected profits, what probability of noon arrival by truck would lead to indifference between shipping modes?

13.11 SOLUTION

a., b.

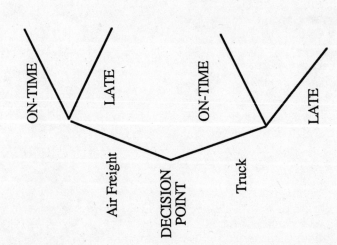

	Revenue (1)	Profit (2)	Pr (3)	Expected Profit (4) = (2) x (3)
Air Freight				
ON-TIME	$5,000	$1,000	0.9	$900
LATE	$ 0	-$4,000	0.1	-$400
				$E(\pi_A) = \underline{\underline{\$500}}$
Truck				
ON-TIME	$5,000	$3,000	0.2	$600
LATE	$ 0	-$2,000	0.8	-$1,600
				$E(\pi_T) = \underline{\underline{-\$1,000}}$

c.   The profit risk accompanying air freight shipment is:

$$\sigma_A = \sqrt{0.9(\$1{,}000 - \$500)^2 + 0.1(-\$4{,}000 - \$500)^2}$$

$$= \underline{\$1{,}500}$$

$$V_A = \frac{\sigma_A}{E(\pi_A)} = \frac{\$1{,}500}{\$500} = \underline{3}$$

The profit risk accompanying truck shipment is:

$$\sigma_T = \sqrt{0.2(\$3{,}000 - (-\$1{,}000))^2 + 0.8(-\$2{,}000 - (-\$1{,}000))^2}$$

$$= \underline{\$2{,}000}$$

$$V_T = \frac{\sigma_T}{E(\pi_T)} = \frac{\$2{,}000}{(-\$1{,}000)} = -2$$

Since the coefficient of variation for shipment by air freight is larger, this is the more risky alternative.

d.   Let X be the probability of on-time arrival by truck. The value of X which provides an indifference as to the mode of shipment will be that value which results in the expected profit for shipment by truck being equal to the value for shipment by air freight.

$$\text{Expected profit by truck} = \text{Expected profit by air freight}$$

$$(X)(\$3{,}000) + (1 - X)(-\$2{,}000) = \$500$$

$$5{,}000X = 2{,}500$$

$$X = \underline{0.5} \text{ or } 50 \text{ percent}$$

Thus, a probability of on-time arrival of 0.5 or 50 percent would make Freight Forwarders indifferent between the two shipment alternatives.

13.12
ZetaPhysics, Inc., produces electronic equipment which readily lends itself to various design alternatives. The company is considering two experimental changes in the design of one of its products. However, both success and failure are possible. The design changes under

consideration would have an effect on both the expected demand and costs of the product. ZetaPhysics' managers expect a major reaction from competitors during the first year if any design innovations are successful, but none thereafter. If the design changes are undertaken, the firm has estimated the following relevant data for the next two years (the firm's planning horizon):

		YEAR 1		
			Total	Total Incre-
		Competitor	Incremental	mental
Design	Success	Reaction	Revenue	Cost
A	Yes (0.85)	Yes (0.75)	$50,000	$40,000
	No (0.15)	No (0.85)	20,000	30,000
	Yes (0.85)	No (0.25)	55,000	42,000
	No (0.15)	Yes (0.15)	17,000	29,000
B	Yes (0.75)	Yes (0.55)	60,000	48,000
	No (0.25)	No (0.80)	18,000	30,000
	Yes (0.75)	No (0.45)	65,000	50,000
	No (0.25)	Yes (0.20)	15,000	28,000

		YEAR 2	
		Total	Total
Design	Probability	Inc. Rev.	Inc. Cost
A	0.65 given "successful" 1st year	$70,000	$55,000
	0.35 given "successful" 1st year	10,000	25,000
	1.0 given "failure" in 1st year	0	0
B	0.70 given "successful" 1st year	$80,000	$60,000
	0.30 given "successful" 1st year	5,000	20,000
	1.0 given "failure" in 1st year	0	0

a. Construct a decision tree for the problem.

b. Assuming incremental revenues come in at the end of the year costs are incurred at the beginning of the year, and a 12 percent discount rate, compute the NPV of each alternative at each of the final branch terminals.

c.   Which is the more risky alternative in terms of potential variation in total return?

d.   Which design should ZetaPhysics select?

13.12 SOLUTION

a. Design A graph.

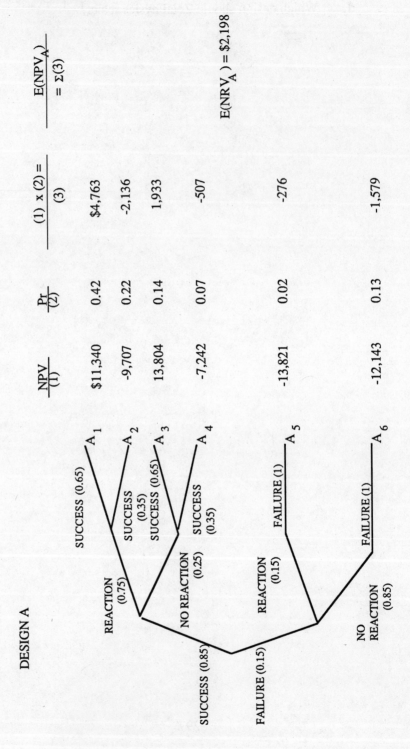

DESIGN A

	NPV (1)	Pr (2)	(1) x (2) = (3)	E(NPV$_A$) = Σ(3)
A_1	$11,340	0.42	$4,763	
A_2	-9,707	0.22	-2,136	
A_3	13,804	0.14	1,933	
A_4	-7,242	0.07	-507	
A_5	-13,821	0.02	-276	E(NRV$_A$) = $2,198
A_6	-12,143	0.13	-1,579	

SUCCESS (0.65)
SUCCESS (0.35)
SUCCESS (0.65)
SUCCESS (0.35)
FAILURE (1)
FAILURE (1)
REACTION (0.75)
NO REACTION (0.25)
REACTION (0.15)
NO REACTION (0.85)
SUCCESS (0.85)
FAILURE (0.15)

Design B graph.

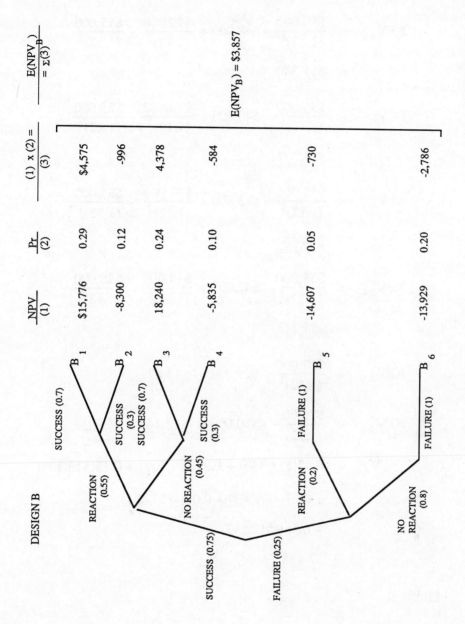

	NPV (1)	Pr (2)	(1) x (2) = (3)	E(NPV) = Σ(3)B
B 1	$15,776	0.29	$4,575	
B 2	-8,300	0.12	-996	
B 3	18,240	0.24	4,378	
B 4	-5,835	0.10	-584	
B 5	-14,607	0.05	-730	
B 6	-13,929	0.20	-2,786	

E(NPV_B) = $3,857

( ) indicates probability.

b. Net Present Value calculations:

<u>Project A</u>

$$NPV_{A1} = \frac{\$50,000}{(1.12)^1} - \$40,000 + \frac{\$70,000}{(1.12)^2} - \frac{\$55,000}{(1.12)^1}$$

$$= \$11,340$$

$$NPV_{A2} = \frac{\$50,000}{(1.12)^1} - \$40,000 + \frac{\$10,000}{(1.12)^2} - \frac{\$25,000}{(1.12)^1}$$

$$= -\$9,707$$

$$NPV_{A3} = \frac{\$55,000}{(1.12)^1} - \$42,000 + \frac{\$70,000}{(1.12)^2} - \frac{\$55,000}{(1.12)^1}$$

$$= \$13,804$$

$$NPV_{A4} = \frac{\$55,000}{(1.12)^1} - \$42,000 + \frac{\$10,000}{(1.12)^2} - \frac{\$25,000}{(1.12)^1}$$

$$= -\$7,242$$

$$NPV_{A5} = \frac{\$17,000}{(1.12)^1} - \$29,000 = -\$13,821$$

$$NPV_{A6} = \frac{\$20,000}{(1.12)^1} - \$30,000 = -\$12,143$$

$$E(NPV_A) = 0.42(\$11,340) + 0.22(-\$9,707) + 0.14(\$13,804)$$

$$+ 0.07(-\$7,242) + 0.02(-\$13,821)$$

$$+ 0.13(-\$12,143)$$

$$= \$2,198$$

<u>Project B</u>

$$NPV_{B1} = \frac{\$60,000}{(1.12)^1} - \$48,000 + \frac{\$80,000}{(1.12)^2} - \frac{\$60,000}{(1.12)^1}$$

300

$$= \underline{\$15{,}776}$$

$$NPV_{B2} = \frac{\$60{,}000}{(1.12)^1} - \$48{,}000 + \frac{\$5{,}000}{(1.12)^2} - \frac{\$20{,}000}{(1.12)^1}$$

$$= -\underline{\$8{,}300}$$

$$NPV_{B3} = \frac{\$65{,}000}{(1.12)^1} - \$50{,}000 + \frac{\$80{,}000}{(1.12)^2} - \frac{\$60{,}000}{(1.12)^1}$$

$$= \underline{\$18{,}240}$$

$$NPV_{B4} = \frac{\$65{,}000}{(1.12)^1} - \$50{,}000 + \frac{\$5{,}000}{(1.12)^2} - \frac{\$20{,}000}{(1.12)^1}$$

$$= -\underline{\$5{,}835}$$

$$NPV_{B5} = \frac{\$15{,}000}{(1.12)^1} - \$28{,}000 = -\underline{\$14{,}607}$$

$$NPV_{B6} = \frac{\$18{,}000}{(1.12)^1} - \$30{,}000 = -\underline{\$13{,}929}$$

$$E(NPV_B) = 0.29(\$15{,}776) + 0.12(-\$8{,}300)$$

$$+ 0.24(\$18{,}240) + 0.10(-\$5{,}835)$$

$$+ 0.05(-\$14{,}607) + 0.20(-\$13{,}929)$$

$$= \underline{\$3{,}857}$$

c.   The risk of these two alternatives can be examined by calculating the coefficient of variation for each.

Project A

Outcome (1)	Deviation from mean (2)	$(\text{Deviation})^2$ (3)	Probability (4)	$(3) \times (4) =$ (5)
$11,340	$ 9,142	$ 83,576,164	0.42	$35,101,989
-9,707	-11,905	141,729,030	0.22	31,180,386
13,804	11,606	134,699,240	0.14	18,857,893
-7,242	-9,440	89,113,600	0.07	6,237,952
-13,821	-16,019	256,608,360	0.02	5,132,167
-12,143	-14,341	205,664,280	0.13	26,736,357

$$\sigma_A^2 = \$123,246,740$$

$$\sigma_A = \sqrt{\$123,246,740} = \underline{\underline{\$11,102}}$$

$$V_A = \frac{\sigma_A}{E(NPV_A)} = \frac{\$11,102}{\$2,198} = \underline{\underline{5.051}}$$

Project B

Outcome (1)	Deviation from mean (2)	$(\text{Deviation})^2$ (3)	Probability (4)	$(3) \times (4) =$ (5)
$15,776	$11,919	$142,062,560	0.29	41,198,143
-8,300	-12,157	147,792,650	0.12	17,735,118
18,240	14,383	206,870,690	0.24	49,648,965
-5,835	-9,692	93,934,864	0.10	9,393,486
-14,607	-18,464	340,919,300	0.05	17,045,965
-13,929	-17,786	316,341,800	0.20	63,268,359

$$\sigma_B^2 = \$198,290,040$$

$$\sigma_B = \sqrt{\$198,290,040} = \underline{\underline{\$14,082}}$$

$$V_B = \frac{\sigma_B}{E(NPV_B)} = \frac{\$14,082}{\$3,857} = \underline{\underline{3.651}}$$

Project B's coefficient of variation is approximately 28 percent smaller than that of Project A, indicating that it is a considerably less risky alternative.

d. Typically, it is difficult to determine what choice a decision maker should make between risky alternatives without explicit information concerning their risk aversion or utility function.

302

expected return and a lower risk, we can say it dominates Design A and would be chosen regardless of the decision maker's degree of risk aversion. Note, however, that this does not preclude the possibility that a very risk averse individual might decline both projects, since they are quite risky. Design B, although superior to Design A, still entails a good deal of risk relative to the expected return. We cannot say for sure that ZetaPhysics would choose to go ahead with Design B without more knowledge about the risk-return tradeoff function used in such decision problems.

Theme

The process by which firms make long-run investment decisions is called capital budgeting. By definition, long-run investment decisions are decisions involving cash inflows and/or cash outflows which are expected to extend beyond one year. Optimal capital budgeting decisions can be made by equating the marginal return on investment with the marginal cost of capital. This approach is completely analogous to decision making for short-run operating problems where marginal revenues are equated to marginal costs in order to maximize profits. A highly useful methodology for comparing marginal returns on investment and marginal costs of capital is provided by net present value analysis. Basically, the net present value of a given investment project is the discounted present value of all project revenues, less the discounted present value of all project costs. The value of the firm will be maximized when all projects with a positive net present value are accepted. In instances where capital is scarce, capital can be rationed among available investment projects through use of mathematical programming approaches to project evaluation.

Outline

I. **The Capital Budgeting Process**

A. Definition: Capital budgeting is the process by which firms make investment decisions involving projects whose cash inflows and cash outflows are expected to extend beyond one year.

B. Profit Maximization Rule: Analogous to the case of short-term investment decisions, profit maximization requires an equating of the marginal revenues of long-term investment projects with the marginal cost of capital.

C. Investment Proposals: Capital budgeting starts with the generation of a large number of potential investment alternatives.

D. Project Classification: Often, firms establish a number of broad classifications as a first step in characterizing the risk and return of various investment alternatives. Common project classifications are:

1. Replacement - maintenance of business.

2. Replacement - cost reduction.

3. Expansion of existing products or market lines.

4. Expansion into new product lines.

5. Safety and/or environmental.

6. Other (exploration, research and development, etc.).

E. Estimating Cash Flows: A crucially important aspect of any capital budgeting decision is cash flow estimation. Like any forecasting problem, this estimation is more difficult the less familiar is the project to be undertaken, and the more distant in the future are expected costs and revenues. In many instances, these problems can be minimized if multiple forecasts can be constructed to illustrate the range of possibilities from optimistic to pessimistic scenarios.

II. Net Present Value Analysis

A. The NPV Technique: To find the net present value (NPV) of a project, subtract the estimated cost of the project from the present value of expected receipts:

$$NPV = \sum_{t=1}^{N} \frac{R_t}{(1 + k)^t} - C$$

where R_t = expected net cash flows of the project to the Nth year, k = risk adjusted discount rate, and C = project's cost (initial investment required).

1. Decision rule: Projects should be accepted only if NPV > 0.

B. NPV as an Application of Marginal Analysis: The NPV technique essentially involves a comparison of the marginal return on investment with the marginal cost of capital. The marginal return on investment is typically measured by the internal rate of return (IRR), or the discount rate which equates the present value of project inflows and outflows. If the NPV of a project is positive, this implies that the marginal return on capital (the IRR) is greater than the marginal cost of capital (k).

III. Other Issues in Project Evaluation

A. Capital Rationing: Often, insufficient capital is available to undertake all available investment opportunities with projected positive net present values. In such instances, mathematical programs can be created to ration capital with specific recognition

305

of the important interrelations among timing of cash flows, payback period, project size, and so on.

B.   Profitability Index or Benefit-Cost Ratio Analysis: The profitability Index (PI) of a project shows the return per dollar of cost, where both are expressed in present value terms:

$$PI = \frac{PV\ of\ Cash\ Flows}{Cost}$$

1.   Decision Rule: Projects should be accepted only if PI > 1.

IV.   Steps in the Capital Budgeting Process

A.   Demand Forecasts: Revenues are often estimated as an important first step in the capital budgeting process. Since revenue forecasts are typically highly variable, using a variety of assumptions to construct a range of forecasts is usually prudent.

B.   Cost Forecasts: While investment costs are often easier to forecast than revenues, unanticipated equipment costs, maintenance expenses and tax law changes can all cause substantial forecast error. As before, constructing multiple forecasts can be useful in illuminating the range of possible future cost experience.

C.   Cash Flow Forecasts: Cash flow forecasts are at the heart of capital budgeting analysis. Typically, cash flow forecasts can be derived from revenue and cost forecasts by simply adjusting cost forecasts for noncash expenditures.

D.   Cost of Capital: The firm's cost of capital, k, is properly calculated as the weighted average cost of the various sources of funds. The set of weights to be used is determined by the optimal financial structure of the firm (i.e., the financial structure that minimizes k).

1.   The Cost of Debt: The interest rate investors require on debt issues, adjusted for the tax deductibility of interest payments by the firm, provides the appropriate measure of a firm's debt cost.

a.   After-tax cost of debt = (Interest rate)
$\times$ (1.0 - Tax rate).

2. Cost of Equity: The rate of return shareholders require on the common stock of a firm can be analyzed in either one of two equivalent approaches:

   a. Cost of equity = Riskless rate of return
   + Required risk premium

   b. Cost of equity = $\dfrac{\text{Dividend}}{\text{Price}} + \dfrac{\text{Expected}}{\text{Growth}}$

3. Weighted Cost of Capital: The relevant weights accorded to debt and equity in calculating the firm's weighted cost of capital are based upon the firm's optimal capital structure.

E. The Post Audit: An important final aspect of the capital budgeting process is the post audit. Here, predicted and actual results are compared so that future operating results and forecasts can be improved.

PROBLEMS AND SOLUTIONS

14.1

Indicate whether each of the following statements is true or false. Explain why.

a. By accepting all projects with NPV > 0, the value of the firm will be maximized.

b. The IRR of a project equals the cost of capital when PI = 1.

c. Under capital rationing, the NPV approach can be preferred to the PI for ranking project attractiveness.

d. Holding all else equal, doubling the size of project revenues and costs will leave the IRR unaffected.

e. When NPV > 0, the IRR is below the cost of capital.

14.1 SOLUTION

a. <u>True</u>. By definition, value maximization requires undertaking all NPV > 0 projects.

b. <u>True</u>. When the IRR equals the cost of capital, the PV of cash flows equals the cost of the project, and PI = 1.

c. <u>False</u>. With capital rationing, use of the PI criterion ensures that projects with the highest return per dollar of investment will be adopted.

d. <u>True</u>. Holding all else equal, changes in the size of projects leave the IRR unaffected.

e. <u>False</u>. When the IRR is below the cost of capital, NPV < 0.

14.2

The Metro Communications Company is considering two mutually exclusive capital budgeting projects. These projects have equal lives of 2 years, and similar costs of $8,000. Relevant cash flow data for the two projects are as follows:

Project 1

	Year 1			Year 2
Pr	Cash Flow		Pr	Cash Flow
0.35	$4,000		0.25	$5,000
0.40	5,000		0.50	6,000
0.25	6,000		0.25	7,000

Project 2

	Year 1			Year 2
Pr	Cash Flow		Pr	Cash Flow
0.20	$(200)		0.10	$1,000
0.30	4,000		0.30	4,500
0.30	5,000		0.35	6,500
0.20	7,000		0.25	8,000

a.   What is the expected value of the annual cash flows from each project?

b.   Using 10 percent for the more risky project and 8 percent for the other, and using variability of cash flows as an indicator of risk, what is the risk-adjusted NPV of each project?

c.   Which project should MCC accept?

14.2 SOLUTION

a.

Project 1

Year 1:

$$0.35(4,000) = \$1,400$$
$$0.40(5,000) = 2,000$$
$$0.25(6,000) = \underline{1,500}$$
$$E(CF_{11}) = \$4,900$$

Year 2:

$$0.25(5,000) = \$1,250$$
$$0.50(6,000) = 3,000$$
$$0.25(7,000) = \underline{1,750}$$
$$E(CF_{12}) = \$6,000$$

Project 2

Year 1:

$$0.20(-200) = \$ -40$$
$$0.30(4,000) = 1,200$$
$$0.30(5,000) = 1,500$$
$$0.20(7,000) = \underline{1,400}$$

Year 2:

$$0.10(1,000) = \$ 100$$
$$0.30(4,500) = 1,350$$
$$0.35(6,500) = 2,275$$
$$0.25(8,000) = \underline{2,000}$$

309

$$E(CF_{21}) = \underline{\underline{\$4,060}} \qquad\qquad E(CF_{22}) = \underline{\underline{\$5,725}}$$

b. Project 2 appears to be more risky since, by inspection, the variability of cash flows is obviously higher. Thus, Project 1 will be discounted at 8 percent and Project 2 will be discounted at 10 percent.

Project 1

$$
\begin{aligned}
NPV_1 \; &= \; E(CF_{11}) \times (PVIF, N = 1, i = 8\%) \\
&\quad + E(CF_{12}) \times (PVIF, N = 2, i = 8\%) - Cost \\
&= \; \$4,900(0.926) + \$6,000(0.857) - \$8,000 \\
&= \; \underline{\underline{\$1,679.40}}
\end{aligned}
$$

Project 2

$$
\begin{aligned}
NPV_2 \; &= \; E(CF_{21}) \times (PVIF, N=1, i=10\%) \\
&\quad + E(CF_{22}) \times (PVIF, N=2, i=10\%) - Cost \\
&= \; \$4,060(0.909) + \$5,725(0.826) - \$8,000 \\
&= \; \underline{\underline{\$419.39}}
\end{aligned}
$$

c. Project 1 should be chosen since it has the higher risk-adjusted NPV.

14.3

Venture Corporation is considering investing \$50,000 in production facilities in order to produce a new product. The product is sold in an essentially competitive market at a price of \$390 per unit. Assume that the facility will have fixed costs of \$5,000 annually (plus depreciation on the facility which is computed in a straight-line manner) and variable costs given by the equation:

$$\text{Total Variable Costs} = -\$10Q + \$2Q^2$$

If the facility is expected to have an economic life of ten years, should the firm make the investment if its after-tax cost of capital is 12 percent? (Assume a 50 percent state plus federal income tax rate, and a salvage value of \$0).

14.3 SOLUTION

This problem is solved using a net present value approach. It would also be possible to solve it using the internal rate of return method.

Annual cash flows from the project can be determined as follows:

$$\text{Cash Flow} = (TR - TC) \times (1 - \text{Tax Rate}) + \text{Depreciation}$$

$$= (\$390Q - (\$10,000 - \$10Q + \$2Q^2))(0.5) + \$5,000$$

$$= (400Q - 10,000 - 2Q^2)(0.5) + 5,000$$

$$= 200Q - 5,000 - Q^2 + 5,000$$

$$= \$200Q - Q^2$$

Set $dCF/dQ = 0$ to find cash flow maximizing output level:

$$dCF/dQ = 200 - 2Q = 0$$

$$2Q = 200$$

$$Q = \underline{\underline{100}}$$

(Note: $d^2CF/dQ^2 = -2$, so $Q = 100$ is a point of cash flow maximization).

And the maximum cash flow is:

$$CF = \$200(100) - \$100^2$$

$$= 20,000 - 10,000$$

$$= \underline{\underline{\$10,000}}$$

The net present value of the project is:

$$NPV = \sum_{t=1}^{10} \frac{\$10,000}{(1.12)^t} - \$50,000$$

$$= \$10,000 \times (\text{PVIFA}, N = 10, i = 12\%) - \$50,000$$

$$= \$10,000(5.650) - \$50,000$$

$$= \underline{\underline{\$6,500}}$$

Thus, Venture should undertake the investment.

14.4

Jersey Tool & Die, Inc. must choose between two mutually exclusive investment projects. Each project costs $6,000 and has an expected life of four years. Annual net cash flows from each project begin one year after the initial investment is made and have the following characteristics:

	Probability	Annual Net Cash Flow
Project A	0.05	$2,200
	0.40	3,300
	0.25	3,800
	0.30	3,600
Project B	0.15	$300
	0.35	3,700
	0.22	6,900
	0.28	6,200

Jersey has decided to evaluate the riskier project at a 14 percent cost of capital and the less risky project at 12 percent.

a.   What is the expected value of the annual net cash flows from each project?

b.   What is the risk-adjusted NPV of each project?

14.4 SOLUTION

a. $E(CF_A) = \$2,200(0.05) + \$3,300(0.40) + \$3,800(0.25)$

$$+ \$3,600(0.30)$$

$$= \underline{\underline{\$3,460}}$$

$E(CF_B) = \$300(0.15) + \$3,700(0.35) + \$6,900(0.22)$

$$+ \$6,200(0.28)$$

$$= \underline{\$4,594}$$

b. Project B is the riskier project because it has the greater
variability in its expected cash flows. Accordingly, Project B is
evaluated at a 14 percent cost of capital versus 12 percent for
Project A. The net present values for each project are:

$$NPV_A = \$3,460(PVIFA, N = 4, i = 12\%) - \$6,000$$

$$= \$3,460(3.037) - \$6,000$$

$$= \underline{\$4,508}$$

$$NPV_B = \$4,594(PVIFA, N = 4, i = 14\%) - \$6,000$$

$$= \$4,594(2.914) - \$6,000$$

$$= \underline{\$7,387}$$

The above calculations indicate that Jersey should accept Project
B despite its higher risk.

14.5

The ASU Co-op, a nonprofit student organization, runs a laundromat
located in the main dormitory complex at a large southwestern
university. The latest monthly operating statement for the laundromat is
presented below.

Revenues		
5,000 loads at 50¢ per load		$2,500
Costs:		
Rent	$300	
Maintenance	200	
Depreciation	250	
Electricity	950	
Water	500	
Miscellaneous Expenses	100	$2,300
Profit		$ 200

The month represented by this statement is typical of the average month
over the entire year, although there is considerable variation from
month to month. Of the expenses incurred in the operation of the
laundromat, only electricity, water, and the miscellaneous expenses are

313

directly related to the level of output. (Note: Maintenance is done under a service contract for a fixed fee).

Currently, the Co-op is considering the purchase of dry-cleaning equipment for the laundromat. The dry-cleaning equipment costs $15,000 and has an expected life of three years with a zero salvage value. At a price of $1 per load, it is estimated that 2,000 loads of dry-cleaning per month will be the average use factor for the equipment. Cleaning fluid and electricity costs per load are 50¢ and 20¢, respectively. Additional annual maintenance costs of $150 are also expected. And finally, it is expected that by installing dry-cleaning equipment overall usage of laundry equipment will fall by 1,000 loads per month.

a. Develop the relevant cash flows for an analysis of this decision.

b. Assume the Co-op has the capital necessary to purchase the dry-cleaning equipment and that it places a 6 percent opportunity cost on those funds. Should the equipment be purchased? Why or why not?

14.5 SOLUTION

a. <u>Initial Investment</u>:   <u>$15,000</u>

   <u>Incremental Annual Revenues</u>:
     (2,000 loads/mo. × 12 × $1) $24,000
   <u>Incremental Annual Costs</u>:
     Cleaning Fluid: (2,000 loads/mo.
       × 12 × $0.50)   12,000
     Electricity (20,000 loads/mo.
       × 12 × $0.20)   4,800
     Maintenance   150
     Loss of profit contribution from
     laundry (1,000 loads/mo. × 12
       × $0.19)   2,280
                                                         <u>$19,230</u>
   <u>Incremental Annual Cash Flows</u>:   <u>$ 4,770</u>

b. $$NPV = \sum_{t=1}^{3} \frac{\text{Incremental Annual Cash Flows}}{(1.06)^t} - \text{Initial investment}$$

$$= \sum_{t=1}^{3} \frac{\$4,770}{(1.06)^t} - \$15,000$$

314

$$= \$4,770(\text{PVIFA}, N = 3, i = 6\%) - \$15,000$$

$$= \$4,770(2.673) - \$15,000$$

$$= -\$2,250$$

The dry-cleaning equipment has a negative net present value and, therefore, should not be purchased.

14.6

Dr. Anthony Jaspers is considering three investment alternatives for expanding his dental practice. Project A involves extending his current hours until 9:00 PM three days per week. Project B involves the purchase of new equipment, thereby allowing him to handle patients faster. Project C involves opening a new office in a suburban mall location. Expected net cash flows (before investment costs) over the next five years and investment requirements for each project are given below:

	Project		
	A	B	C
Annual Net Cash Flows	$ 3,000	$ 7,500	$14,000
Investment Cost	10,000	25,000	50,000

a. Rank each project according to the NPV criterion using an 8 percent cost of capital.

b. Using the same cost of capital, rank each project according to the PI criterion.

c. Rank each project according to the IRR criterion.

14.6 SOLUTION

a. In the NPV approach, NPV = PV cash flows - Cost. Therefore,

$$\text{NPV}_A = \$3,000(\text{PVIFA}, N = 5, i = 8\%) - \$10,000$$

$$= \$3,000(3.9927) - \$10,000$$

$$= \$1,978.10$$

$$\text{NPV}_B = \$7,500(\text{PVIFA}, N = 5, i = 8\%) - \$25,000$$

$$= \$7,500(3.9927) - \$25,000$$

$$= \$4,945.25$$

$$NPV_C = \$14,000(PVIFA, N = 5, i = 8\%) - \$50,000$$

$$= \$14,000(3.9927) - \$50,000$$

$$= \$5,897.80$$

Since $NPV_C > NPV_B > NPV_A$, a project rank ordering using the NPV criterion is $\underline{C > B > A}$.

b.   In the PI approach, PI = PV cash flows/Cost. Therefore,

$$PI_A = \$3,000(3.9927)/\$10,000$$

$$= 1.198$$

$$PI_B = \$7,500(3.9927)/\$25,000$$

$$= 1.198$$

$$PI_C = \$14,000(3.9927)/\$50,000$$

$$= 1.118$$

Since $PI_A = PI_B > PI_C$, a project rank ordering using the PI criterion is $\underline{A = B > C}$.

It is interesting to note how Project B, which is simply 2.5 times larger than Project A, is preferred to Project A using the NPV criterion despite their equivalence using the PI approach. Moreover, note how the relatively large size of Project C causes it to be preferred using the NPV approach despite the fact that it is the least attractive project on a PI basis.

c.   The IRR is the interest rate which equates the PV of cash flows and investment costs. Thus,

$$PV \text{ cash flows} = Cost$$

$$CF(PVIFA, N = 5, i = IRR) = Cost$$

316

$$(\text{PVIFA}, N = 5, i = \text{IRR}) = \frac{\text{Cost}}{\text{CF}}$$

$$\text{For Project A:} \quad (\text{PVIFA}, N = 5, i = \text{IRR}) = \frac{\$10,000}{\$3,000}$$

$$= 3.3333$$

From the present value tables, we see that this interest factor falls between 15 and 16 percent. Interpolating, we find,

i	PVIFA(N = 5)
15%	3.3522
15 + ?	3.3333
16	3.2743

since this factor covers 0.24 of the distance between 15 and 16 percent, the relevant $\text{IRR}_A = 0.1524$, or 15.24 percent.

The IRR for Project B is the same as above since:

$$\text{For Project B:} \quad (\text{PVIFA}, N = 5, i = \text{IRR}) = \frac{\$25,000}{\$7,500}$$

$$= 3.333$$

And finally,

$$\text{For Project C:} \quad (\text{PVIFA}, N = 5, i = \text{IRR}) = \frac{\$50,000}{\$14,000}$$

$$= 3.5714$$

From the present value tables, we see that this interest factor falls between 12 and 14 percent. Interpolating, we find,

i	PVIFA(N = 5)
12%	3.6048
12 + ?	3.5714
14	3.4331

since this factor covers 0.19 of the distance between 12 and 14 percent, the relevant $\text{IRR}_C = 0.1219$, or 12.19 percent.

Therefore, since $\text{IRR}_A = \text{IRR}_B > \text{IRR}_C$, a project rank ordering using the IRR criterion is $\underline{A = B > C}$.

317

14.7

Clemens, Ryan & Viola, Inc., a leading distributor of heat dispensers, is considering two mutually exclusive capital budgeting projects. These projects have equal lives of two years and identical costs of $8,000. Relevant cash flow data for the two projects is as follows:

Project A

Year 1		Year 2	
Pr.	Cash Flow	Pr.	Cash Flow
0.35	$4,500	0.25	$5,000
0.40	5,000	0.50	6,000
0.25	6,000	0.25	7,000

Project B

Year 1		Year 2	
Pr.	Cash Flow	Pr.	Cash Flow
0.20	-$200	0.10	$1,000
0.30	4,000	0.30	4,500
0.30	5,000	0.35	6,500
0.20	7,200	0.25	8,000

a. Calculate the expected value of the annual cash flows from each project.

b. Calculate the risk-adjusted NPV of each project, using a 14 percent cost of capital for the more risky project, and 12 percent for the less risky one. Use variability of cash flows as an indicator of risk.

c. Calculate the PI for each project.

d. Calculate the IRR of each project.

e. Rank order the projects, using the NPV, PI, and IRR criteria.

14.7 Solution

a. The expected annual cash flow from each project can be calculated as:

Project A

	Year 1 Cash			Year 2 Cash	
Pr. (1)	Flow (2)	$(1) \times (2) = (3)$	Pr. (1)	Flow (2)	$(1) \times (2) = (3)$
0.35 ×	\$4,500	= \$1,575	0.25 ×	\$5,000	= \$1,250
0.40 ×	5,000	= 2,000	0.50 ×	6,000	= 3,000
0.25 ×	6,000	= 1,500	0.25 ×	7,000	= 1,750
		$E(CF_{A1}) = \$5,075$			$E(CF_{A2}) = \$6,000$

Project B

	Year 1 Cash			Year 2 Cash	
Pr. (1)	Flow (2)	$(1) \times (2) = (3)$	Pr. (1)	Flow (2)	$(1) \times (2) = (3)$
0.20 ×	\$ -200	= \$ -40	0.10 ×	\$1,000	= \$ 100
0.30 ×	4,000	= 1,200	0.30 ×	4,500	= 1,350
0.30 ×	5,000	= 1,500	0.35 ×	6,500	= 2,275
0.20 ×	7,200	= 1,440	0.25 ×	8,000	= 2,000
		$E(CF_{B1}) = \$4,100$			$E(CF_{B2}) = \$5,725$

b. Project B appears to be the more risky since it has a higher variability of cash flows. Project B will thus be discounted at 14 percent. Project A will be evaluated by using a 12 percent cost of capital.

$NPV_A = \$5,075(PVIF, N = 1, i = 12\%)$

$+ \$6,000(PVIF, N = 2, i = 12\%) - \$8,000$

$= \$5,075(0.8929) + \$6,000(0.7972) - \$8,000$

$= \$9,314.67 - \$8,000$

$= \underline{\$1,314.67}$

$NPV_B = \$4,100(PVIF, N = 1, i = 14\%)$

$+ \$5,725(PVIF, N = 2, i = 14\%) - \$8,000$

$= \$4,100(0.8772) + \$5,725(0.7695) - \$8,000$

$= \$8,001.91 - \$8,000$

319

$$= \underline{\underline{\$1.91}}$$

c. The profitability index for each project is:

$$PI_A = \frac{PV \text{ of Cash Flows}}{Cost}$$

$$= \frac{\$9,314.67}{\$8,000.00}$$

$$= \underline{\underline{1.164}}$$

$$PI_B = \frac{PV \text{ of Cash Flows}}{Cost}$$

$$= \frac{\$8,001.91}{\$8,000.00}$$

$$= \underline{\underline{1.000}}$$

d. The IRR is the interest rate that produces an NPV equal to zero. For Project A, set:

$$NPV_A = \$5,075(PVIF, N = 1, i = X\%)$$

$$+ \$6,000(PVIF, N = 2, i = X\%) - \$8,000 = 0$$

The IRR can be easily calculated by many types of hand-held calculators, or by trial and error with various interest rates in the preceding equation.

Interest Rate	NPV
20%	$395.40
24%	-4.61
28%	-372.50

The IRR for Project A is just under <u>24 percent</u>.

For Project B set:

$$NPV_B = \$4,100(PVIF, N = 1, i = X\%)$$

$$+ \$5,725(PVIF, N = 2, i = X\%) - \$8,000 = 0$$

320

Using trial and error with various interest rates in the above equation, we find:

Interest Rate	NPV
12%	$224.86
14%	1.91
16%	-210.57

The IRR for Project B is slightly more than <u>14 percent</u>.

e. The rank order of the two investment alternatives is:

$$NPV: NPV_A > NPV_B \rightarrow A,B$$

$$PI: PI_A > PI_B \rightarrow A,B$$

$$IRR: IRR_A > IRR_B \rightarrow A,B$$

Therefore, irrespective of which criterion is adopted, Project A is preferred to Project B.

14.8

Nirvana Products, Inc. is considering a range of capital budgeting projects. In order to decide on whether or not to accept specific investment proposals, the firm needs to determine its opportunity cost of capital. Nirvana has learned that new 13 percent bonds can be sold at par, and new common stock can be sold for $30. Earnings per share have been growing at 10 percent, and this growth rate is expected to continue. Dividends per share next year are estimated to be $1.50, and the firm faces a 50 percent federal plus state corporate income tax rate.

a. What are the values of the component costs that are needed for a cost of capital calculation?

b. Assuming equal weights for the cost of capital components, calculate the weighted average cost of capital.

14.8   Solution

a.

$$\text{Cost of Debt} = i(1 - t) = 0.13(1 - 0.5) = \underline{\underline{0.065}}$$

$$\text{Cost of Equity} = k_e = \frac{D}{P} + g = \frac{1.50}{30} + 0.10 = \underline{\underline{0.15}}$$

b. The weighted average cost of capital, using equal weights for debt and equity, is:

$$K = \text{(Debt Weight)(Debt Cost)}$$

$$+ \text{(Equity Weight)(Equity Cost)}$$

$$= (0.5)(0.065) + (0.5)(0.15)$$

$$= \underline{\underline{0.1075}}, \text{ or } 10.75 \text{ Percent}$$